RESEARCH DESIGN
in URBAN PLANNING

SAGE was founded in 1965 by Sara Miller McCune to support the dissemination of usable knowledge by publishing innovative and high-quality research and teaching content. Today, we publish over 900 journals, including those of more than 400 learned societies, more than 800 new books per year, and a growing range of library products including archives, data, case studies, reports, and video. SAGE remains majority-owned by our founder, and after Sara's lifetime will become owned by a charitable trust that secures our continued independence.

Los Angeles | London | New Delhi | Singapore | Washington DC

RESEARCH DESIGN in URBAN PLANNING

A Student's Guide

Stuart Farthing

$SAGE

Los Angeles | London | New Delhi
Singapore | Washington DC

SAGE

Los Angeles | London | New Delhi
Singapore | Washington DC

SAGE Publications Ltd
1 Oliver's Yard
55 City Road
London EC1Y 1SP

SAGE Publications Inc.
2455 Teller Road
Thousand Oaks, California 91320

SAGE Publications India Pvt Ltd
B 1/I 1 Mohan Cooperative Industrial Area
Mathura Road
New Delhi 110 044

SAGE Publications Asia-Pacific Pte Ltd
3 Church Street
#10-04 Samsung Hub
Singapore 049483

Editor: Robert Rojek
Editorial assistant: Matt Oldfield
Production editor: Katherine Haw
Copyeditor: Catja Pafort
Proofreader: Bryan Campbell
Indexer: Martin Hargreaves
Marketing manager: Michael Ainsley
Cover design: Francis Kenney
Typeset by: C&M Digitals (P) Ltd, Chennai, India
Printed and bound by CPI Group (UK) Ltd,
  Croydon, CR0 4YY

© Stuart Farthing 2016

First published 2016

Apart from any fair dealing for the purposes of research or private study, or criticism or review, as permitted under the Copyright, Designs and Patents Act, 1988, this publication may be reproduced, stored or transmitted in any form, or by any means, only with the prior permission in writing of the publishers, or in the case of reprographic reproduction, in accordance with the terms of licences issued by the Copyright Licensing Agency. Enquiries concerning reproduction outside those terms should be sent to the publishers.

Library of Congress Control Number: 2015939445

British Library Cataloguing in Publication data

A catalogue record for this book is available from the British Library

ISBN 978-1-4462-9444-4
ISBN 978-1-4462-9445-1 (pbk)

At SAGE we take sustainability seriously. Most of our products are printed in the UK using FSC papers and boards. When we print overseas we ensure sustainable papers are used as measured by the PREPS grading system. We undertake an annual audit to monitor our sustainability.

CONTENTS

List of figures and tables — x
About the author — xii
Preface — xiii
Acknowledgements — xv

1 THE DESIGN OF PLANNING RESEARCH — 1

Key questions — 1
Key concepts — 1
Overview — 1
Research design — 2
Types of research design — 3
Structure of the book — 5
Summary/key lessons — 9
Exercise — 10
Further reading — 11
References — 11

2 POST-POSITIVISM AND PLANNING RESEARCH — 13

Key questions — 13
Key concepts — 13
Overview — 13
A popular conception of science — 15
Post-positivism — 16
Box 2.1 Values and the research process — 16
Hidden assumptions in research: The iceberg model — 23
Conclusions — 32
Summary/key lessons — 33
Exercise — 34
Further reading — 34
References — 34

3 POLICY ISSUES AND RESEARCH QUESTIONS   37

Key questions   37
Key concepts   37
Overview   37
What sort of discipline is planning?   38
What arguments are used in planning policy debates?   39
Box 3.1 Types of research question   43
Research questions   43
Generating research questions: reviewing the literature   46
How to recognise research questions in published research   47
Research questions, hypotheses and theories   50
Creating helpful research questions from initial ideas   51
Conclusion   56
Summary/key lessons   57
Exercise   58
Further reading   58
References   59

4 A JUSTIFICATION FOR YOUR RESEARCH QUESTION   61

Key questions   61
Key concepts   61
Overview   61
Practical justifications for further research: Two examples   62
Reviews of literature: Justifying research in academic terms   64
Box 4.1 Arguments typically developed by researchers to justify further research   66
The structure of a literature review   68
Box 4.2 Example of a short literature review   69
Summary/key lessons   71
Exercise   71
Further reading   73
References   73

5 DESCRIPTIVE QUESTIONS: SCOPE, CLAIMS AND SAMPLING   75

Key questions   75
Key concepts   75
Overview   75

Scoping research questions	76
Box 5.1 Scoping your research questions	77
Sampling: data sources and methods	79
Sampling and the selection of cases to study	80
Sampling methods	84
Box 5.2 Example – Quota sampling as used by Burgess et al. (1988)	89
Summary/key lessons	92
Exercise	92
Further reading	93
References	93

6 EXPLANATORY QUESTIONS: STARTING POINTS, CLAIMS AND SAMPLING — 95

Key questions	95
Key concepts	95
Overview	95
Starting points	96
Causal explanation or understanding?	98
Box 6.1 Criteria for assessing the existence of a causal relationship	101
Sampling and the selection of cases to study	107
Box 6.2 Example – Theoretical sampling in a study	113
Case studies	116
Summary/key lessons	116
Exercise	118
Further reading	119
References	120

7 METHODS OF DATA GENERATION IN RESEARCH — 123

Key questions	123
Key concepts	123
Overview	123
Key issues in the choice of methods	124
Interviews and questionnaires	127
Ethnography and observation	131
Documents	136
Official Statistics	140
Summary/key lessons	144

Exercise	144
Further reading	145
References	146

8 DATA ANALYSIS — 149

Key questions	149
Key concepts	149
Overview	149
Qualitative and quantitative data	151
Quantitative analysis of survey data	152
Box 8.1 Statistical significance of Table 8.3 from Atkinson and Kintrea (2001)	160
Qualitative analysis	163
Box 8.2 Example of discourse analysis	171
Summary/key lessons	174
Exercise	174
Further reading	175
References	176

9 ETHICS OF RESEARCH — 178

Key questions	178
Key concepts	178
Overview	178
The framing of research	179
How close should the relationship between academic researchers and practice be?	180
The generation and analysis of data	187
Summary/key lessons	188
Exercise	189
Further reading	190
References	190

10 CROSS-NATIONAL COMPARATIVE RESEARCH IN URBAN PLANNING — 192

Key questions	192
Key concepts	192
Overview	192
What is cross-national comparative research in planning?	193

Research purposes and research questions 195
A justification of the question 198
An appropriate logic for answering the question 198
Methods of data generation 201
Analysis 204
Ethics 206
Summary/key lessons 206
Further reading 207
References 208

11 CONCLUSION 211

Index 215

LIST OF FIGURES AND TABLES

Figures

1.1	The cycle of research design	5
2.1	Hidden assumptions in research: the iceberg model	24
2.2	A simplified diagram of possible casual influences on the life chances and opportunities of residents of a neighbourhood in a city	27
3.1	Knowledge claims in planning debates	40
4.1	Classifying the documents from a literature search	65
5.1	Types of probabilistic sampling	85
5.2	Types of non-probabilistic sampling	87
6.1	Inductive approach to explanation and the development of theory	97
6.2	Deductive approach to explanation and the development of theory	97
6.3	The importance of time order in casual analysis: alternative explanations for an association between the type of people living in an area and an area's reputation	103
6.4	Development application approval rate vs. appeal rate	111
7.1	Influences on the choice of methods of data generation	125
8.1	Relationship between the population, the sample frame, the random sample and the achieved sample used for analysis	153
8.2	Some possible reason for finding an association in a study	162

Tables

3.1	Knowledge claims in urban planning	41
5.1	Framework for quota sampling in Greenwich neighbourhoods	90
5.2	Framework for purposive case selection: Styles of planning in Great Britain	91
8.1	Types of conflict experienced	154
8.2	Efforts to prevent political conflict by successful avoidance	155
8.3	Cross-tabulation of employment by tenure	157
8.4	A typology of neighbourhood communities	169

ABOUT THE AUTHOR

Stuart Farthing was Principal Lecturer in Urban Planning in the Department of Planning and Architecture at the University of the West of England, Bristol until his retirement in July 2011. He was the programme leader for the MA, Applied Social Research from 1997 until 2011, the (then) ESRC-recognised cross-disciplinary doctoral training programme at UWE, and leader of the specialist 'Environmental planning' pathway in that degree. Much of his career was spent in Bristol but he also taught at the Universities of Reading and Cardiff in the 1980s and early 1990s as a specialist in planning methods. Under Erasmus exchange programmes he taught at the Universities of Hannover and Tours and was a British Council visiting researcher in the Department of Planning at the University of Melbourne, Australia. He was Visiting Professor in the Département Aménagement et Environnement de l'École Polytechnique of the University of Tours, France for a number of years. His teaching interests were in urban planning research, social research methods, and research methodology. His research interests have been in planning for housing, and, more recently, comparative planning and city-region planning. He can be contacted at: Stuart.Farthing@yahoo.com.

PREFACE

Students on planning courses are usually expected to conduct a small-scale research project, and to write up the results of this project in a dissertation. But there are few texts which deal with the issue of how to conduct research for those students and researchers working in the discipline of planning and a lack of books on research design, though there are some aimed at the social sciences more generally. The starting point for this book is that this neglect of the question of research design in urban planning has been an unfortunate one, which has resulted in the production of dissertations which have been less worthwhile than they should have been, given the time that students have spent on them.

Research design is about thinking through the key decisions which have to be made in advance of the stage where you set about collecting or generating the data and before you have to face the practical problems of conducting your research.

When starting work on a dissertation it may not be immediately obvious how important thinking about research design is, and many students recognising the tight deadlines involved in producing a dissertation, are sensibly quite anxious to 'get on with it'. But getting the design decisions 'right' will have a major impact on the claims that you can make on the basis of your research and, in turn, will have a major impact on how well your dissertation is received. For you as students, the critical audience for a dissertation is primarily composed of those who will be assessing the research you conducted as part of the dissertation and the justification you give for it. Parsons and Knight (2005: 45) say that one of the examiner's favourite questions for a viva is 'Could you explain the logic of your research design?' So one reason for bothering with research design is that it maximises the chances of producing evidence that will convince your examiners, given the limitations of time and other practicalities involved.

Academics are not the only possible audience for your dissertation. If you are a planning student who is sponsored by a planning authority or consultancy to obtain a planning qualification, and if your sponsor sees your dissertation as a way of understanding and responding to a problematic issue, then they too will be concerned about the trustworthiness of the claims that you make.

A second reason for thinking about research design, and why you might find reading this book useful, is that increasing attention is being paid to the ethics of research in urban planning (discussed in Chapter 9), and to the need to get ethical approval for proposed student projects. You therefore may be asked to produce a research proposal as a formal part of the dissertation or thesis process. Requirements for the format of a research proposal vary but the issues considered in this book will help you to complete a proposal effectively, whatever the precise format.

Finally I want to suggest that you should spend a considerable part of the time available for the dissertation in thinking about research design. Most of you will be faced with the challenge of writing a dissertation in no more than a year, often less. And of course the time available will be restricted by the need to engage in other academic work and courses which have deadlines of their own, apart from the dissertation. If, as a rule of thumb, we might say that a third of the time available should be used for planning and developing the research design, a third of the time to conducting the research and a third of the time to analysis and writing, then, you can see that research design is a very significant part of the research process.

The book, then, is intended to be of assistance to planning students, both undergraduate and postgraduate, who are at the initial stages of work on their dissertations and to be a useful reference source for supervisors or tutors who help guide students through the process. Many planning degrees include taught courses on research methods alongside a dissertation module but these do not always consider design explicitly, so this book can fill that gap and be used to complement such courses.

The book is structured in terms of the key decisions which have to be made in research design, and the chapters have been written on the assumption that they will be read in order. Hence there are discussions and activities in chapters which are intended to be of help when you are making decisions about the design of your own projects. But I recognise that students' needs vary and you can sample chapters selectively depending on your own requirements (Not everyone, for example, will be contemplating undertaking comparative research in planning (Chapter 10)).

Reference

Parsons, T. and Knight, P.G. (2005) *How to Do Your Dissertation in Geography and Related Disciplines*. London: Routledge.

ACKNOWLEDGEMENTS

The author and publisher are grateful to Liverpool University Press for permission to use copyright material from: Wood, R. (2000) 'Using appeal data to characterise local planning authorities', *Town Planning Review*, 71: 97–107.

I was fortunate whilst at UWE Bristol, to have worked over an extended period with colleagues in the Department of Planning and Architecture (and its previous incarnations) who taught me a lot about planning and planning research. Students and colleagues, too, particularly those on the Masters in Applied Social Research coming from departments across UWE challenged my thinking about social research and helped me to formulate the ideas underpinning this text. I would like to thank Professor David James for the idea of the iceberg model. Of course, I absolve all of the above of responsibility for any of my misunderstandings or any errors to be found in the text. Particular thanks go to Paul Revell who produced the diagrams, and to my wife, Ann, who encouraged me to finish the book, whilst she, almost unaided, redecorated the house.

1

THE DESIGN OF PLANNING RESEARCH

Key questions

What is research design?

Why is there an interest in research design? And why bother with it?

How many types of research designs are there? How does research design differ from questions about research strategies and methodologies?

What is well-designed research?

Key concepts 🔑

Research design, strategy, methodology

Overview

The starting point for this book, as explained in the Preface, is that when undertaking research for a dissertation it is essential to spend time planning how the research will be conducted – that is, working on a research design – in advance of implementing those decisions. Time spent on research design will have a significant potential payoff in terms of the quality of your final written dissertation or thesis. This chapter addresses a number of introductory issues connected with research design. The first section looks at the concept of research design: What is a research design? Next I explore the reasons for an interest in research design. Turning to the types of research design, I ask whether there are a limited number of research designs, and, if so, what are these types? What are the differences between research designs, research strategies and research methodologies? Finally, I set out the approach to research design taken in this book and briefly introduce the contents of the remaining chapters in the book

Research design

A research design is generally understood in the literature to be produced in *advance* of the stage when you get down to conducting the research, and it is about planning how the research will be conducted.

Because a design is thought about in advance of the conduct of the research, it sets out provisional decisions on how the research is to be conducted. Such provisional decisions may be recorded in a research proposal which also may be submitted for approval by tutors or supervisors. Blaikie (2000) makes a distinction between a research proposal and a research design with the emphasis on the audience for the documents, with the former being restricted to those documents which are public and which are needed either to gain approval for a project or to obtain funds for a project, the latter being more private documents, restricted perhaps to the researcher and their supervisors or tutors. In both cases, however, the same type of forward planning needs to be undertaken to produce them.

Yin (1989: 28) argued that a research design is about getting from 'here' to 'there' – from a set of research questions at or near the beginning of the research process to 'there' – the end of the process and an answer to those research questions. Now much attention in textbooks on research is given to the different methods of data generation, the choice of structured versus unstructured interviewing, for example, but research design is concerned with much more than the selection of appropriate methods of generation and analysis, important though these decisions are. As Hakim (2000: 2) suggests, it is concerned with 'when and why a particular type of study should be chosen'.

The reason for the interest in research design is essentially that it underpins the trustworthiness of the claims that a researcher makes in a particular study. For example, planning researchers may make claims or come to conclusions about the nature of planning and its practice, or of its social, economic or environmental impacts. A critical evaluation of these claims involves asking about the evidence that has been produced to support them.

There has been much discussion in recent years of the importance of justifying public policies by the evidence (Alasuutari et al., 2008). Gorard (2013) similarly justifies the importance of research design in terms of the practical or policy decisions which might be made on the basis of research, and the unnecessary harm that might be done if research findings are not well-founded. This notion of evidence-based policy has been discussed in the planning literature by Krizek et al. (2009). A number of writers in the policy and planning literature (for example, Fischer 2003; Healey 2007) emphasise the collective judgement which is made by the community of researchers about the plausibility of knowledge claims, though they seek to widen the scope of those who participate in such judgements where evidence is used to inform policy.

Given the importance of the decisions which have to be made, and their implications for the quality of the dissertation you will write, I argue that you should aim to spend something like a third of the time you have available for completing the dissertation to the research design stage.

Types of research design

Some writers on research design take the view that there are only a few standard research designs from which the researcher must choose (Cresswell, 2003; Hakim, 2000; de Vaus, 2001). The approach taken in this book rejects that view. This follows from the fact that in any project a number of design decisions have to be taken, and since these decisions can vary, the consequence is that there could be a large number of possible research designs for any project. However, certain decisions are more important than others. Here I would cite as crucial the decision on the research question to be answered. Research can be seen as a process of asking questions, and trying to answer them. Research questions have, perhaps, not been given the attention they deserve by planning students thinking about small-scale research. Research questions are important because they provide a focus and a direction to research, influencing the other design decisions which you make, from identifying the type of data you need to answer your question to the best way of going about getting it. It follows that one of the most important stages in research design is moving from the initial ideas you have about the topic and the issue you want to investigate to an appropriate research question.

Another key consideration in research design is the assumption that you make about the nature of the social world you are interested in investigating. Planning researchers start their research with different conceptions of what the social world is like. One way of characterising these differing assumptions is whether in designing the study, you are interested in trying to find 'causes and effects' or put more emphasis on exploring 'interpretations and meanings' (see Gomm, 2004). This, together with your view on the nature of research itself, will have consequences for the way that your research will be designed, and the justifications which you use to support those decisions. What is not helpful in this context is to pose research design decisions in terms of a choice between qualitative and quantitative approaches to research, though this is commonly done in the literature (see, for example, Cresswell, 2003).

What are the differences between research designs, research strategies and research methodologies? Here, there is an almost bewildering array of usages to be found in the literature on research. Research design, as discussed above, is about the provisional decisions taken about research at the initial stages of developing the project. The terms research strategy and methodology, are sometimes used as synonyms for research design, as in 'describe your research strategy or methodology'. But methodology, as used in this book, is about the criteria one should use in making these decisions, and thus the justifications for the decisions and choices made in designing a project. Methodology draws on debates about the nature of the social world and the appropriate ways of finding out about it.

What is 'well-designed' research? The answer is, first, that the key decisions which shape the subsequent conduct of the research have been thought about in advance, and the justifications are clear (even though not everyone will necessarily agree with them). This therefore excludes approaches to urban planning research which involve setting out without an initial plan, an approach sometimes associated with the work of qualitative researchers. These key decisions are:

- What research questions to pose?
- What justification is there for the research question to be studied?
- What is the logic of the approach I will use to answer my research question?
- What methods will I use to generate the data?
- How will I analyse the data?
- Have I thought about the ethics of what I am proposing to study? Will the project get ethical approval?

These decisions are shown in Figure 1.1 as a cycle of decisions. This is to suggest that in any research design exercise you may, and probably will, need to reconsider earlier decisions in the light of considerations raised by reflection on subsequent stages of the process. Design is an iterative process.

Second, the test of a design is whether, taking into account what is known about the strengths and weaknesses of different ways of conducting research, and the resources available to conduct the research, the provisional decisions which have been made 'ensure that the evidence obtained enables us to answer the initial question as unambiguously as possible' (de Vaus 2001: 9). Of course, unforeseen things may happen which impact on the feasibility of particular designs, which may require a re-think during the process. Flexibility in research in this sense is therefore essential.

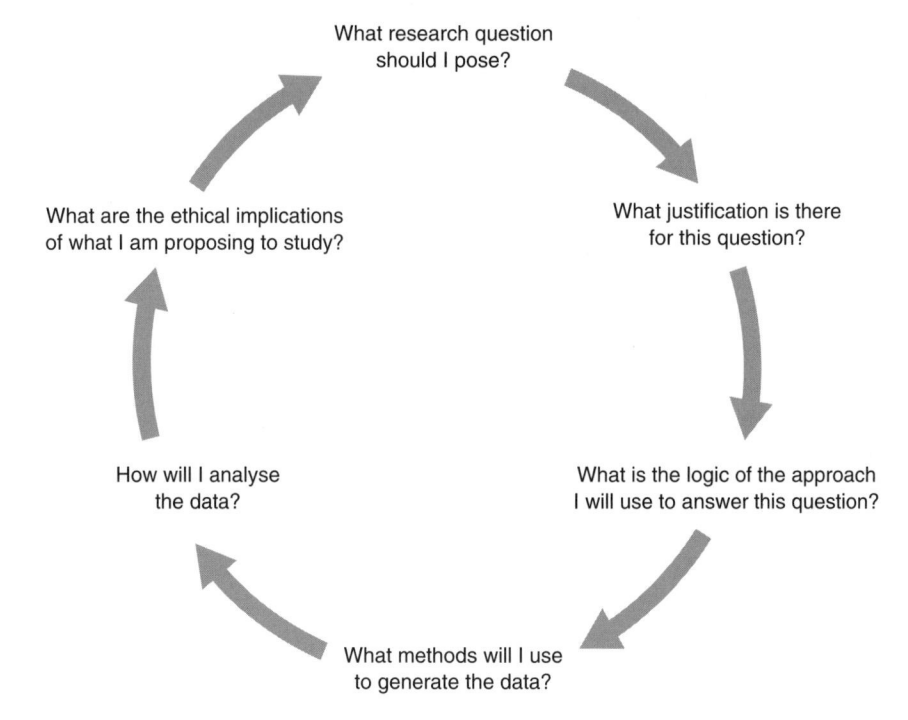

Figure 1.1 The Cycle of Research Design

Structure of the book

The next chapter of the book examines some of the key issues raised in the debate about whether urban planning research should be based on a scientific model derived from an interpretation of research in the natural sciences. It highlights the critique of this model and a consequent shift to 'post-positivist' thinking in the planning theory literature: the recognition that values help shape the research process; that knowledge is socially constructed rather than given by the facts of observation; that planning is political and that planning research, too, is political in the sense that there are different ways of framing or conceptualising any piece of research; that research findings are 'at best' provisional and that there is scepticism about the validity of expert knowledge. If there ever was a consensus that planning research should be scientific, that is no longer the case. The final section explores the different assumptions that underpin the practice of urban planning research, assumptions which are often hidden, but which have important consequences for research design. The chapter concludes by arguing that whilst research cannot deliver certainty of knowledge, nevertheless there is still a role for research findings to contribute to policy debate, though not to determine the outcome of such debates.

Chapter 3 examines the relationship between policy issues and research questions. Academic planning research, including student dissertations, tends to be driven by the changing political agendas in planning. The starting point for an interest in conducting some research may be a current policy issue. But policy issues tend to be complex and contested and accordingly planning problems can be defined in different ways, using different discourses and frames of reference (Fischer, 2003). For those undertaking research the difficulty is distilling answerable questions which can form the basis of a dissertation or thesis from broader policy debates. Achieving this objective constitutes the first condition for developing a proposal which is well-designed. This chapter explores the differences between policy issues and research questions, highlighting the importance of asking the right questions, 'researchable questions', as a necessary (but not sufficient) basis for designing a piece of research.

A second condition for a well-designed piece of research is that the research question which you pose should be justified. Not all research questions are appropriate. Planning researchers usually give some justification for their research in the introductory sections of their published research reports or papers drawing on and reviewing the literature. Chapter 4 explores the nature of the justifications to be found in literature reviews. It is sometimes said that to undertake research and to publish is to engage in an on-going 'conversation' within the field of study. There may of course be endless conversations within any field of study, and any piece of research is unlikely to contribute to more than one of these. The argument of this chapter is that an effective literature review develops an academic argument about why further research is needed on a particular topic or issue. Here, further research will (it should be argued in the literature review) contribute to one of these conversations. A second justification often to be found in published work is that the knowledge produced by the research will have some practical benefit.

The third condition for a well-designed piece of research is some logic to, reasoning behind, or convincing way of, answering your research question. As suggested above all the decisions in research design are essentially concerned with this issue. But the nature of the answer you are seeking, and the claim that you would make at the end of the research, depends on the type of research question you have developed. Some research questions require a descriptive answer; others require an explanatory answer. The next two chapters deal with the initial work that needs to be done here, including both the scoping of research questions and thinking about the selection of cases for study (sampling). Chapter 5 examines descriptive research questions. Particular attention here is given to how to focus your research questions, how you might identify potential data sources from which (or from whom) you might generate data, and the sampling strategies that are available. Here the question of the relationship between the sample you study and some wider population of cases that might exist is raised. This is one sense in which researchers talk about generalising their findings (empirical generalisation).

Chapter 6 deals with explanatory research questions, and how they can be answered. Simplifying some often complex philosophical issues about the logic of research, this chapter looks at the starting point for addressing this question, and the nature of the answer that you might give. It can be helpful to think of two different starting points for a piece of research which aims to answer a 'why' (explanatory) question. Your literature review covering the work of previous researchers may give you some quite precise ideas about why something has happened. You might be interested in the issue of 'planning gain' negotiations, negotiations between planners and developers about the contributions expected from developers towards the costs of public infrastructure associated with new development. Why, for example, might two planning authorities take a different approach to negotiations with developers over planning gain? Here you may have found Bunnell's (1995) study in your review. Bunnell's claim in the cases he investigated was that the explanation for different approaches was to be found in the attitudes of chief planning officers. Here you can start your own research with the hypothesis that the attitudes of chief planning officers will also apply to the cases you are interested in, hypotheses which can be tested against the evidence of your own research. This starting point is often described as taking a deductive approach to research. But in the absence of much previous research you might start with more of an open-ended question, giving your project an inductive orientation. Planning researchers adopting this approach may want to keep a rather open mind about why something has happened, and reserve their conclusions until their research is completed. Whatever starting point you adopt, the nature of the answer you might give to a 'why' question may either refer to 'causes' and 'causal relationships' or to the 'understanding' which comes from finding out what was in the minds of the actors involved in the situations you have studied.

The focus of Chapter 7 on a fourth condition for having a well-designed research proposal is that appropriate methods of data generation are proposed. The term data 'generation' rather than 'collection' is used to emphasise the point made by Mason (1996) that data is not lying around waiting to be collected by a neutral researcher but that the data is constructed by the decisions which are made about how to 'frame' a project (see Chapter 2), what concepts are used, and how they are defined, about the cases to be sampled and the methods used. This chapter describes the options for data generation available under the heading of interviews and questionnaires; ethnography and observation; and documents.

Well-designed research involves thinking about both the generation of data and how data will be analysed to produce research findings. The consideration of analysis cannot be left until a later stage of research, after the data has been generated. Analysis is a key decision in research design, and the type of analysis to be undertaken needs to be seen in the light of its role in helping you answer your research question. Chapter 8 explores some of the different approaches that planning researchers have taken to the analysis of qualitative and quantitative data based on an examination of some examples from published research, introduced in earlier chapters. The aim is to alert you to the issues involved in analysis, rather than to provide a detailed guidance on how to use particular techniques.

The focus of Chapter 9 is the need for an appropriate approach to ethical issues. A key concern for some researchers is the values that shape the choice of questions for research. Whose interests inform the nature of the identified problem? Some researchers are interested in highlighting the voices and perspectives of, and in some way speaking for, those who are commonly ignored in policy discussion: women, the poor, the disabled, ethnic minorities. The conventional approach is to accept that values are important in defining the topic of study and the precise aspect of that topic to be investigated (a position called value-neutrality), but that in the conduct of the research the only concern of the researcher should be to reveal the truth about the topic investigated. But what about the interests of planning practitioners? Should their concerns be the ones that guide planning research so that research is 'relevant'? Some argue for a close relationship with practice, others wish to keep their distance in order to insulate themselves from what are often contested political issues and, in turn, to protect politics from research. Beyond the framing of the research, a second way in which students have to confront ethical issues is the common requirement to get ethical approval for their projects. Here the ethical issues relating to research in planning are little different from those in social science more generally and there are ethical codes of practice which are often used for these purposes.

The final chapter looks at cross-national comparative research in urban planning. There has been a growing interest in comparative planning research in recent years by students. Part of this can be explained by the development of the EU, and the opportunities it has opened up for exchanges between planning academics and students across Europe, and the funding of cross-national planning studies under the Interreg and ESPON programmes in Europe. Moreover, there have been international conferences where planning researchers from Europe, the US and Asia have met to exchange experiences of planning in different states and cultures. Some of the interest in comparative planning also comes from the interest in the scope for policy learning, and policy transfer between countries. Chapter 10 discusses some of the purposes underlying cross-national comparative studies in planning, and emphasises some of the challenges involved in studying planning within the 'institutional context' of a different country, and the practical difficulties that might be faced in designing and conducting a successful study.

Summary/Key lessons

1. The main lesson of this chapter, and of the book as a whole, is that it is important when working on a dissertation to plan your research: that is to think about the design of your research in advance of launching into conducting it.

2. You should spend around a third of the time available to complete your dissertation working on research design.

3. Well-planned or designed research requires that:

- key decisions which shape the subsequent conduct of the research have been thought about in advance

- these decisions are taken in the light of the time you have to complete the project and write the dissertation

- that the justifications for these decisions are clear (even though not everyone will necessarily agree with them, because there are different views on how research should be conducted).

(Continued)

(Continued)

4. These key decision areas are highlighted by the following questions:

- What research questions should I pose?
- What justification is there for the research question to be studied?
- What type of approach will I use to answer my research question – descriptive or explanatory?
- What methods will I use to generate the data?
- How will I analyse the data?
- Have I thought about the ethics of what I am proposing to study? Will the project get ethical approval?

If you come up with satisfactory answers to all these questions you will have produced a well-designed project.

Exercise: A topic for your dissertation

You can't start thinking about research and research design without some initial idea about the topic which you wish to investigate, so it is important to start thinking about this as early as possible. Ideas for dissertations can come from many sources. You might look at previous dissertations in your department, to find out the sorts of topic, often policy issues, that have interested previous generations of students. You might do this to come up with some topic which is new or original. But there can be benefits from building on previous studies too. You might try to think of a different angle on a topic that has been investigated before, or see the scope for investigating it in a different way.

You could think imaginatively about the kinds of economic, social or political changes that are taking place in different places and about the kinds of issues or debates that are going on in planning at the moment. Potential sources of ideas are planning literature, local or national newspapers (these tend to be critical of planning (see Clifford, 2006)), projects that you have been involved in during your course, or lectures or seminars where 'interesting' planning issues have been discussed. You need a topic which is going to be sufficiently interesting to motivate you to keep working on it for the usually extended period over which you are expected to work on it.

It is really important to start writing, as well as thinking, about your dissertation so even if you spend only half an hour thinking about this:

1. Write down the topic you think you will investigate. (100 words)

2. Write a short explanation for your personal motivation in looking at this topic. (50 words)

3. Send these to your tutor and arrange a date when you can talk to them about this.

Further Reading

A number of texts cover the issue of research design, taking somewhat different approaches to the concept from the one taken here. Blaikie (2000), for example, has a chapter which distinguishes between research proposals and research designs.

Blaikie, N. (2000) *Designing Social Research*. Cambridge: Polity Press.

Blaxter, L., Hughes, C. and Tight, M. (2010) *How to Research*. Maidenhead: Open University Press/McGraw Hill Education.

de Vaus, D. (2001) *Research Design in Social Research*. London: Sage.

Gorard, S. (2013) *Research Design: Creating Robust Approaches for the Social Sciences*. London: Sage.

Greener, I. (2011) *Designing Social Research*. London: Sage.

Hakim, C. (2000) *Research Design: Successful Designs for Social and Economic Research*. London: Routledge.

Hunt, A. (2005) *Your Research Project*. Abingdon: Routledge.

References

Alasuutari, P., Bickman, L. and Brannen, J. (2008) 'Social Research in Changing Social Conditions', in P. Alasuutari, L. Bickman and J. Brannen (eds), *The Sage Handbook of Social Research Methods*. London: Sage. pp. 1–8.

Blaikie, N. (2000) *Designing Social Research*. Cambridge: Polity.

Bunnell, G. (1995) 'Planning Gain in Theory and Practice: Negotiation or Agreements in Cambridgeshire', *Progress in Planning*, 44: 1–113.

Cresswell, J. W. (2003) *Research Design: Qualitative, Quantitative and Mixed Methods*. London: Sage.

de Vaus, D. (2001) *Research Design in Social Research*. London: Sage.
Fischer, F. (2003) *Reframing Public Policy: Discursive Politics and Deliberative Practices*. Oxford: Oxford University Press.
Gomm, R. (2004) *Social Research Methodology*. Basingstoke: Palgrave Macmillan.
Gorard, S. (2013) *Research Design: Creating Robust Approaches for the Social Sciences*. London: Sage.
Hakim, C. (2000) *Research Design: Successful Designs for Social and Economic Research*. London: Routledge.
Healey, P. (2007) *Urban Complexity and Spatial Strategy*. London: Routledge.
Krizek, K. Forsyth, A. and Slotterback, C. S. (2009) 'Is There a Role for Evidence-Based Practice in Urban Planning and Policy?', *Planning Theory & Practice*, 10 (4): 459–78.
Mason, J. (1996) *Qualitative Researching*. London: Sage.
Yin, R.(1989) *Case Study Research: Design and Methods*. London: Sage.

2

POST-POSITIVISM AND PLANNING RESEARCH

Key questions

What sort of view of the nature of science, as practiced in the natural sciences, is commonly held?

What contribution did planning theorists think research on this model could contribute to the justification of planning policies?

What criticisms have subsequently been made of this view?

What alternative assumptions about research do we find amongst planning researchers today?

Key concepts

Positivism, post-positivism, value neutrality, framing, social construction, interpretivism, expert knowledge, paradigms, ontology, epistemology, methodology, methods, control, naturalism, ecological validity, realism, naïve realism

Overview

This chapter starts with a discussion of a widely held view of science, a view which underpins positivism and which has also influenced thinking about the nature of social research, the type of research that planners and planning academics conduct. Next, I outline some of the main criticisms that have been levelled at this view of research. It is now recognised that before you can begin to 'do research' or make observations of the social world, you need to make assumptions about what the social world is like, that is, what it is composed of (ontology), what one can know about the world (epistemology) and how to go about investigating it (methodology). The final section looks at some examples of planning research, and the pre-suppositions which underpin these investigations

Modern urban planning had its roots in a critique of the industrial city of the nineteenth century, and was based on the assumption that the city could be consciously re-designed to produce, if not the ideal city, at least a better place to live and work. In the post-war period, thinking about planning as an activity in the Anglo-American world changed from seeing the city as an object which could be re-designed, to seeing planning as a generic process, of which urban planning was just one type. 'Planning is a much more general, a commoner activity than planners have considered it to be: common to all human beings, common to all scientific investigation; planning is a general method, quite independent of the field in which it is practiced.' (Chadwick, 1971: xi).

In this view, knowledge – and particularly scientific theory and knowledge – became important to planners and to planning academics. This way of thinking about planning as a scientific activity, based on the model of the natural sciences, is one which Sandercock (1998) claims is rooted in a modernist conception of society, a conception which is itself a 'child of the Enlightenment'. In Britain, where increased numbers of geographers entered the field both as practitioners and as planning academics, planning was influenced by ideas from social science and research came to be seen as an essential activity (Healey, 1991).

If this foundation of urban planning research in science was ever widely believed, that is no longer the case. For the period covering the end of the twentieth century, and the beginning of the twenty-first, planning theorists have been influenced by significant changes in philosophical views about the nature of science, and by the subsequent challenge to positivism (seen as the dominant view of Western science) as an account of how social research should be conducted. These changes led to what was called the 'paradigm wars' in the social sciences more generally, which were portrayed as a fight between positivism, the discredited view of social research, and the rival paradigms which sought to replace it. This was reflected in the planning theory literature in a somewhat altered form (see Farthing, 2000), but anyone looking at the academic literature on urban planning today will find a wide range of approaches to the conduct of research.

A popular conception of science

There has been some debate amongst philosophers and social scientists about what exactly the scientific model of the natural sciences is, and how scientists should go about acquiring knowledge (epistemology). But we will begin with a view which has influenced planning thinkers. This is a popular view of science which emphasises the foundation of science in facts. Chalmers puts it like this:

> Science is to be based on what we can see, hear and touch rather than on personal opinions or speculative imaginings. If observation of the world is carried out in a careful, unprejudiced way then the facts established in this way will constitute a secure, objective basis for science. If, further, the reasoning that takes us from the factual basis to the laws and theories that constitute scientific knowledge is sound, then the resulting knowledge can itself be taken to be securely established and objective. (1999: 1)

This view has been identified, in recent planning theory literature, with positivism, a twentieth century philosophy of science, and whilst there is some variation in the characterisation of positivism in the literature, this view of science has been a prominent target and feature of debate. Three of the key ideas outlined in this quotation can be emphasised here. First, that the world that science describes is directly observable by scientists. Second, the basis of science – the facts – are not established by reference to the personal opinions of the scientist but through unprejudiced observation. So the values held by the scientist do not, or should not enter into the process of observation. Scientists, therefore, separate their values from their observations and science is said to be value-free or value-neutral and the knowledge obtained is accordingly seen as being objective. Science has no comment to make about values, about what the world ought to be like, or on prescriptive matters. A third important aspect of this account of science is that decisions on what counts as knowledge, what is true, the laws and theories and explanations given by scientists for the behaviour of natural phenomena are arrived at by a process of reason or logic in relation to the evidence that has been obtained through observation of the world (or 'empirical inquiry' as it is often called).

These ideas about science, with the further concept that any attempt to gain knowledge of the world, whatever the subject matter, should be based on the logic of science, have been applied, therefore, to research in planning.

Now some have argued that planners have not in practice spent a lot of time conducting research into the impact of their policies (Reade, 1987; Preece, 1990; Fainstein, 2005) or using research-based evidence to develop or justify their policies, though they ought to do so. Schon (1983) and others have argued that the kind of knowledge that is produced by research in universities does not match the needs of the professionals, and even if it does, there is more to professional practice then the straightforward application of scientific results.

However, in recent years there have been a range of writers in planning who have questioned, the central place of research-based knowledge in planning in a more fundamental way. Goldstein and Carmin (2006) have suggested that planning as a discipline is a technological rather than a scientific one, so that planning scholarship is focussed on achieving certain environmental and social goals rather than on research and theory building per se. Others have developed a critique of the philosophy behind the 'dominant tradition in Western science', positivism. We are now in a post-positivist (Allmendinger, 2002) or post-empiricist phase of planning's history where we find a rather sceptical attitude to claims to knowledge by researchers, and challenges which would seem to undermine the value of conducting research at all. In this chapter I will set out these philosophical challenges and respond to them.

Post-positivism

The critique of positivism that is to be found in the planning theory literature challenges the key ideas of the popular, or taken-for-granted view of research.

BOX 2.1

VALUES AND THE RESEARCH PROCESS

1. Interests leading to the research
2. Aims, objectives and design of research project
3. Data collection process
4. Interpretation of the data
5. The use made of research findings

Source: May (2001)

---

1. Values, far from being excluded from research, help shape the research process

Much of this criticism stems from the notion that theoretical knowledge based on research has been presented, as we saw above, as being 'objective' in the sense that a dispassionate approach to the facts of the case can be adopted by researchers. The response to this view is that one cannot observe the world without some prior assumptions about what you are looking for, with assumptions about what reality is composed of. These are called ontological assumptions. It follows that descriptions of the world, whether the world is studied by natural or social scientists, are based on some presuppositions rather than on 'brute' observation. But when a planning researcher is studying the world, it is argued, the views of the researcher on the desirability of certain situations, such as the use of environmental resources, the issue of climate change or social inequality, are bound to colour their research. A second critique therefore concerns the place of values in the conduct and the results of research. According to widely held views about the nature of science, the researcher's values do not, and should not, enter into the process of conducting research and research is therefore value-neutral or value-free. Allmendinger on the contrary claims that 'All theory is to greater or lesser degrees normative, i.e., suffused with values and embedded within a social and historical context' (2002: 89), hence all research includes a subjective element.

What is the relation between the values that a researcher might espouse, and the research that is conducted? May (2001) argues that values enter the research process at five stages (see Box 2.1). If one adopted the popular conception of research, which emphasises that scientists should start with an open mind about the conduct of a piece of research, then, a moment's thought would show that if one had no pre-conceptions about what should be observed then it would be impossible to know what to look for, or where to start, and the number of possible things to observe would be infinite. As Nagel (1961: 486) acknowledges – writing some considerable time ago – it is almost a truism to say that all research has to be selective.

The broad topic and the more precise 'problem' that are identified for research at the first stage of the process arise from the interests of the researcher or, in the case of some funded research, from the interests of those funding the research, such as governments at different levels (national, regional, local) or private bodies. Researchers find different aspects of a discipline more or less appealing as inspiration for research topics. Some of the appeal may lie in the perceived importance of the topic. For example, some researchers may be concerned about environmental issues, and be struck by the importance of 'saving the planet' from further environmental damage. Others might be concerned about the plight of the poor and disadvantaged in society. Their values therefore lead them to focus their research on such issues or problems. Of course, these concerns are not shared by all and are based on values which not all groups in society may accept. This selectivity of perspective and observation, and the role of values in the process is, of course, a direct challenge to the widely held view of research outlined above, and to simple notions of value-free research. But this leads to the next debate about the influence of values on planning research.

2. Planning research is political in the sense that there are different ways of framing or conceptualising any piece of research

Beyond having broad concerns or interests which influence researchers to conduct research on some topics rather than others, there is the matter of defining in more detail the precise aspect of the topic which will be investigated. This is essentially what 'framing the research' means in this context. Schon and Rein (1994) introduced this notion into the study of policy problems.

Framing is necessarily a selective process. A researcher cannot study every aspect of a problem so, once again, there has to be some selection of those aspects to focus on. Stretton (1978) uses the issue of urban land ownership to illustrate this point, an example which I draw on here, and a subject which has historically been of considerable political concern in relation to planning at least in Britain. Different investigators might want to know what the structure of land ownership is in a particular city or country, and why that structure exists. But the precise aspect that the researchers will investigate might vary. Some researchers might look at those who are currently active in the land market, at the thinking that motivated them to buy land, at the purposes they had in doing so, and what they wanted to do with the land. Why are some landowners 'active' in trying to develop their land, and others not? Another researcher might focus on the way that the legal conditions shape the pattern of use and ownership of land, conditions governing the rights of owners when they own land, the way that the transfer of ownership takes place, the taxes that owners have to pay on land they own, and the regulation of the use of land through the planning system. A third might look at historical change and the impact of technology and economic organisation on patterns and use of land and a fourth, influenced by neo-Marxism perhaps might want to know 'how half the people got possession of all the private land, and how they enforce the perpetual flow of rent, from poorer to richer which follows from that capital inequality' (Stretton, 1978: 13).

The focus on these different aspects of the situation – which help explain the current structure of land ownership – might be prompted because the researchers involved want to change the situation, and thus have political views not just on the ends but also on the means that might be pursued to achieve those ends. And certainly at the end of the research process, after publication of the results (stage 5 of the research process), those with political aims may well see the conclusions of the research about why a particular structure of land ownership exists as being helpful for deciding on what political action to take so that once the results of a piece of research are published, politicians may seize on the results to support their views about policy. Those opposed to such views may seek to discredit the way that the research was conducted or quote selectively from any report to bolster their political stance (see Sabatier and Jenkins-Smith, 1999). One concern amongst planning academics has been that the powerful can set the terms of the political debate in which issues about, for example, urban development are discussed, as well as how the research is framed and subsequently designed. The recent attention to discourse in planning (and in communicative planning theory) is based on this view and underpinned by the idea that 'people went along with courses of action, contrary to their own best interests because of the distorting effect of communication' (Fainstein, 2005: 124–5). In this way too, the framing of research could be called 'political'.

3. Knowledge is socially constructed rather than given by the facts of observation

One conclusion that some planning academics, and those who study policy have come to as a result of these considerations is that the knowledge which is produced by research – far from being the result of dispassionate observation of the natural or social world, as suggested by a popular conception of science – is 'socially constructed'. This is a central insight of a perspective on social research known as interpretivism. Fischer spells out this view highlighting the difference between the human and natural worlds discussed above: 'Whereas physical objects have no intrinsic meaning structures, human actors actively construct their social world. They do so by assigning meaning to events and actions, both physical and social. Human experience, as such, is enveloped in a non-material social, cultural and personal realm of thought and meaning'. And 'Most basically it is an inquiry into the way objects are seen through different mental structures or worldviews, how they are interpreted in different social circumstances and understood.'(2003b: 48)

Up to this point I have suggested that the critique of positivism has focussed on the selectivity of the topics or aspects of the topics under investigation, that the values of researchers or those of the bodies who sponsor research shape which aspects of reality are investigated. Thus, the starting point for any investigation is influenced by cultural values and interests. The questions which social researchers choose to investigate, the social reality they wish to understand, and the resulting knowledge which they claim as a result of their research is shaped to some extent by the socio-historical context in which it is conducted. Hence, for example, the issue of urban land ownership in Britain has sometimes been more prominent in the agenda of planning researchers and commentators than at other times. Moreover, the detailed design of research is organised in terms of concepts, perhaps deriving from particular theoretical writing or mental frameworks which direct the researcher's attention to specific things to observe during the course of the research in order to understand or explain what is going on.

The argument of the interpretivist perspective goes further and has led some to argue that the starting point for any piece of research has to be the social meanings or interpretations that the actors have of the situation they were in, and of the actions they took. Fischer says that 'to accurately explain social phenomena, the investigator must first attempt to understand the meaning of the social phenomenon from the actor's perspective.' (2003b: 50). In other words, we need to know what people think they are doing before we can explain or understand their actions.

A more fundamental critique of positivism, tied to the idea of social construction, aims to undermine the idea that there is one reality to be investigated. Instead it posits that people live in multiple social realities. So truth is always relative to a particular way of seeing or interpreting the social world and there are, accordingly, multiple truths. The conclusion of this line of argument is the sceptical one, that the findings of an inquiry 'are not a report of that which is "out there" but part of the process that creates that particular version of reality.' (Fischer 2003b: 124). This argument – as a number of writers have pointed out – undermines not just positivism but any research, since research pre-supposes that there is a reality which can be investigated to produce truth.

4. Distrust of expert knowledge

One ground for questioning the trust to be put in the findings of the research conducted on urban issues could, therefore, stem from the realisation that any piece of social research is necessarily partial and value-structured. Those who commission research on such issues shape the nature of the research subsequently conducted. Further, a community of experts, such as planning practitioners in a country, might be considered to constitute a 'policy community' or an 'epistemic community', following the terminology of Haas (1992). As an 'epistemic community' there will be some consensus among members about the knowledge which defines problems and appropriate solutions, and therefore a consensus about the sort of research to conduct, or invoke in any situation. This perspective may not be in accord with the values of other interested parties in discussion over planning and development. This is the primary concern of writers like Fischer and Healey. Some argue that the role of planning researchers should therefore be a partisan one: to recognise the diversity of perspectives, and to conduct research which 'gives voice' to those whose views have been marginalised in policy debates.

A further reason for distrust of expert knowledge may relate to the possible influence of values on the conduct of research, that is, the collection of data and its interpretation (or analysis) (stages 3 and 4 of the process above). May (2001) suggests that there may be grounds for this distrust. For example, he cites the pressure on researchers whose research has been sponsored to produce results which are in accord with the sponsor's view of the world and with their interests. One example from my own research arose when a study of the land developed by housing associations (providers of social housing in Britain) revealed that in England the land on which housing associations were building in the 1990s was more expensive on average than the land used by private sector builders building housing for owner-occupiers. The explanation for this was that housing associations were generally building in urban areas where housing need was most acute but where land values were higher, whilst private builders were more likely to be building in suburban areas. This, however, caused consternation within the Housing Corporation, the sponsors of the research, because the politics of public expenditure was such that it would be seen to be very wasteful of public money to build social housing on expensive land, especially as it might be claimed that people who are struggling to buy their own housing would be likely to be subsidising the tenants of social housing through the tax system. Not only were the results questioned but publication of the report was delayed until a less politically sensitive period had arrived.

Sponsors may not be the only source of pressure on researchers. One might also add that researchers themselves have their own pet theories, which they might be resistant to give up, whatever the research findings. This is very far from saying that researchers would deliberately distort or make up the evidence to support their theories or those of their sponsors, but it would be wrong to deny that researchers may be influenced by their values or those of other people when conducting research.

5. Scepticism about the certainty of research findings

The third feature of the positivist view of knowledge highlighted above is that conclusions about what is to count as established knowledge is ascertained by a logical process of reasoning given the facts produced by research. One approach to this reasoning known as 'inductivism' argues that the more evidence we have, the more studies there have been which support our claims, the more certain we can be that our knowledge is secure and reliable. An alternative view, 'falsificationism', argues that however much evidence we have, we can never be certain that our belief about the world is true since scientific theories make universal claims but one piece of evidence can show that a belief is false. In reviewing these positions Chalmers argues that 'a strong case can be made for the claim that scientific knowledge can neither be conclusively proved nor conclusively disproved by reference to the facts' (1999: xxi). The results of research are therefore always fallible and subject to future revision. Studies of how scientists actually work have also shown that factual claims or observations are themselves subject to criticism and debate. For one thing, a piece of research might not be well-designed – it might be flawed – so that the facts which have been ascertained may be questionable. But for another, the argument is that any decision about whether to accept any new set of facts is a matter of judgement made by a group of scientists on the basis of what is 'known' already, and there is an element, perhaps a very large element, of agreement within any group of scientists at any one time about what is accepted as true. The work of Thomas Kuhn has been influential here (Kuhn, 1970). Thus knowledge is based on a set of assumptions which are accepted within the group. Any new set of facts is assessed against that background. In practice, scientists are loath to question these assumptions about the world and instead tend to stick with established ideas rather than give them up in the face of new facts. They try to reject the new facts or accommodate them within their existing belief structures (or 'paradigms' as they are called by Kuhn).

In the next section of the chapter we will see something about the nature of the assumptions that are made by social researchers.

Hidden assumptions in research: The iceberg model

Academic papers often describe the methods writers have used in the course of their research to collect or generate data, but typically spend little time on why the research was conducted in the way it was. The decisions on which methods to use are just part of the set of decisions which are needed in research design, as discussed in Chapter 1. I want to suggest such decisions can be seen as representing just the 'tip of the iceberg' (see Figure 2.1). A number of assumptions underpin the research and are, as it were, hidden under the water line and rarely discussed explicitly in research papers. They are based on philosophical arguments about the nature of what sorts of things are thought to exist (ontology) and what we can know about these things (epistemology). I draw on Blaikie (2000) to explore these concepts in a little more detail.

Ontological claims are 'the claims or assumptions that are made about the nature of social reality, claims about what exists, what it looks like, what units make it up and how these units interact with each other. In short, ontological assumptions are concerned with what we believe constitutes social reality.' (Blaikie, 2000: 8). For example, Healey talks about the institutionalist approach that she has adopted in studying change in urban regions. Her approach

> rejects the notion that the social world is constituted of autonomous individuals, each pursuing their own preferences in order to obtain material satisfaction – the utilities of neoclassical economic theory. It is based instead on the conception of individual identities, as socially constructed. Ways of seeing and knowing the world, and ways of acting in it, are understood as constituted in social relations with others, and, through these relations, as embedded in particular social contexts. Through the particular geographies and histories of these contexts, attitudes and values are framed. It is in these relational contexts that frames of reference and systems of meaning are evolved.' (1997: 55–6).

Here she is contrasting two sets of ontological assumptions. One involves the existence of 'autonomous individuals' and 'preferences', which she rejects. Her assumed social world is different, it still contains individuals but they do not have 'preferences' they have 'ways of seeing and knowing the world' and they develop 'attitudes and values' which are produced by 'social relations with others' in particular social contexts.

Ontological assumptions are at the base of the iceberg, well below the water line. Above them are assumptions about epistemology. Epistemology, as presented by Blaikie 'refers to the claims or assumptions made about possible ways of gaining knowledge of social reality, whatever it is understood to be.' (2000: 8). One epistemological perspective sees no distinctive difference between the ways of studying the natural and social worlds so that a scientific approach is equally applicable to both. This view is seen as constituting one of the underpinnings of positivism (Halfpenny, 2001). In turn, it is also assumed by a number of writers on planning (Moore-Milroy, 1991; Allmendinger 2002; Fischer 2003a; Healey 2007) that this means that scientific research is based on a search for cause-and-effect relationships in the social world. A contrasting epistemological position is that there is something distinctive about the social world, that people possess consciousness and can reflect on their situation, indeed they make sense of the world they live in, so that social research needs to pay particular attention to the way that people understand and give meaning to their actions, rather than make assumptions about these interpretations. This position is commonly labelled as interpretivism, introduced above.

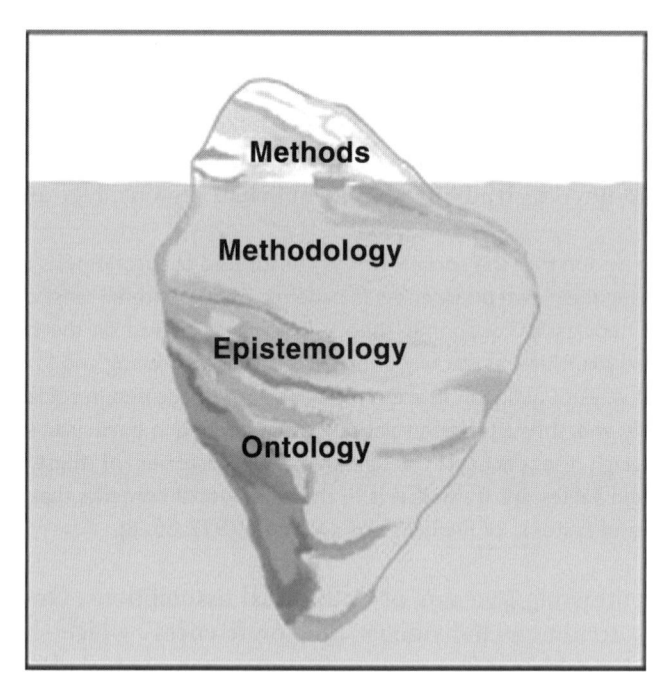

Figure 2.1 Hidden Assumptions in Research: The Iceberg Model

Although Healey sees the social world with which planning deals as a world composed of individuals and groups who construct different interpretations or perspectives on the nature of reality, it seems to me that she does not apply this perspective to her own research practice. The research which she has conducted on spatial strategies in city regions (Healey, 2007), for example, is based on the ontological assumption of realism. She is attempting to represent the reality of the episodes of spatial strategy-making which she investigated, although this is necessarily a selective view of reality, influenced by her 'institutionalist' approach. Nor does she reject the applicability of cause-and-effect relationships to the investigation of the social world, since she makes causal statements about the influences of agency and structure in the evolution of governance phenomena.

Methodology, the third layer in the iceberg, is a 'theory and analysis of how research should proceed' (Harding, 1987: 2, quoted in Carter and Little, 2007). It refers to discussions of how research is done, or should be done, and to the critical analysis of methods of research. It also deals with

> logics of enquiry, of how new knowledge is generated and justified. This includes a consideration of how theories are generated and tested – what kinds of logic should be used, what theory looks like, what criteria a theory has to satisfy, how it relates to a particular research problem, and how it can be tested. (Blaikie, 2000: 8).

One set of these methodological preoccupations can be summarised by contrasting those researchers who are concerned with 'control' and those concerned with 'naturalism' in social research. Control is important if cause-and-effect relationships are to be assessed, because in any situation there are many possible causes of any effect a researcher is interested in studying. Usually researchers are interested in isolating the impact of one particular cause amongst the many that might exist. It is very useful when designing research to see how previous researchers have written about their research process and goals.

ACTIVITY 2.1

The idea of 'control' in research design

Please read the following extract and note how the idea of control is interpreted in the design of this study.

3. Approaching the Area Effects Debate: The Research Design

Our approach to researching the existence and importance of area effects in the British context is to compare residents' experiences of living in two pairs of deprived and socially mixed neighbourhoods through a household survey. Our reasoning for this approach is that it addresses head-on the central question of whether it is worse to be poor in a poor area than one

(Continued)

(Continued)

> which is socially mixed. By selecting paired neighbourhoods located close together in the same city, we are able to hold constant many of the contextual factors shown in Figure 2. Of further relevance is the contrasting economic positions of Glasgow, still struggling to recover from industrial decline, and Edinburgh with its successful service-led economy and higher employment rates (Bailey et al., 1999). In each city, an extensively deprived and a 'typically' integrated neighbourhood were selected using the revised Scottish deprivation index (Gibb et al., 1998), census indicators and area classifications. The deprived neighbourhoods were both council estates ranked in the worst 5 per cent of deprived areas in Scotland and both had been subject to a range of area-based initiatives over the past decade: currently both are Social Inclusion Partnerships, Scotland's principal area-based initiative programme. The mixed neighbourhoods were selected as pairings for the deprived areas with the rationale being that they contained a wider social and tenurial base. The more mixed social areas were also selected because they represent potential templates or forecasted visions for the deprived neighbourhoods; the policies that are being applied to the deprived areas are striving to achieve levels of social integration more often found in the mixed areas. Finally, the comparison of relatively mixed and deprived areas allows us to tease out which are place-based effects and which might be more strongly related to key explanatory positions such as membership of a particular social or tenurial group.

Source: Atkinson and Kintrea (2001: 2280–82)

Activity 2.1 asks you to read part of a paper where the discussion of the design of the research suggests that the researchers are interested in identifying causes and are concerned with the issue of control. The paper is by Atkinson and Kintrea (2001). It deals with 'area effects'. Urban planners have been interested not only in the physical characteristics of parts of cities but also in their social characteristics. There have been various arguments in favour of supporting social mix within local areas or neighbourhoods but the interest in this paper is mainly about whether the concentration of poor or deprived people in an area has adverse effects on the lives of the people living there, over and above the effect of their being poor. Atkinson and Kintrea (2001: 2278) define area effects as 'The search for area effects is the attempt to consider the outcome in life-chances and opportunities that might vary if one lived or grew up in different types of area. We define area effects as the net change in the contribution to life-chances made by living in one area rather than another.' Figure 2.2 shows a highly simplified diagram of the factors which might affect the lives of people living in a given neighbourhood of a city, where social mix is just one of a number factors which might impinge on their lives. In this diagram, the boxes refer to factors which are thought to affect the life chances and opportunities of residents, and the arrows represent the direction of the relationship between the factors. For example, the tenure of housing in the neighbourhood affects the social groups to be found living in the neighbourhood, on the theory that access to different tenures (owner-occupation in comparison with social housing) depends on income and the ability to pay for housing, with poorer people being found particularly in social housing. Life chances and opportunities will vary between these two groups because of the differences in income. The mix of tenures in a neighbourhood will also thus affect the social mix in the neighbourhood which is thought to have an independent effect on life chances.

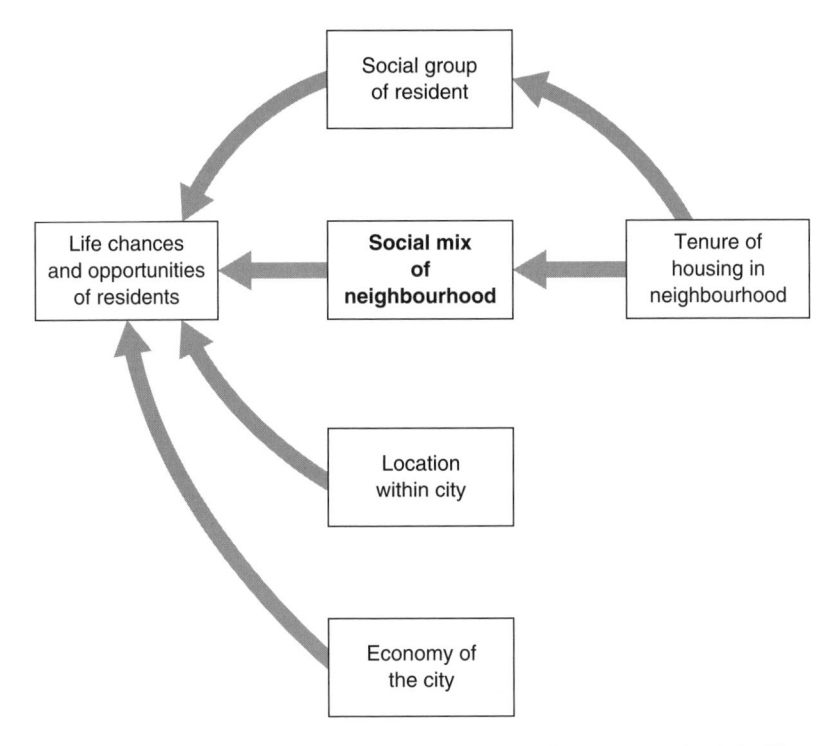

Figure 2.2 A Simplified Diagram of Possible Casual Influences on the Life Chances and Opportunities of Residents of a Neighbourhood in a City

The authors' concern with control in research design is manifested in the way that they write about 'holding constant many of the contextual factors' which affect the neighbourhoods. It is also clear in their discussion of the comparison of relatively mixed and deprived areas which allows them to 'tease out' the effect of living in a particular place (in comparison to the effect of being part of a given social or tenurial group). The language here very much relates to the language used by those discussing experimental methods.

'Naturalism' in social research means

> the view that the aim of social research is to capture the character of naturally occurring human behaviour, and that this can only be achieved by first-hand contact with it, not by inferences from what people do in artificial settings like experiments or from what they say in interviews about what they do elsewhere.' (Hammersley, 1990: 7).

Those influenced by 'naturalism' are concerned by what is sometimes called 'reactivity' – the reaction of those researched to the researcher and to the research techniques used. If there is a strong reaction there can be questions about the quality of the data that is produced. Naturalism is the methodological theory that social research should be conducted in situations which are as normal or natural as possible, so that people are acting and talking in a manner that is normal or habitual in the context of their daily lives, and the views that they are expressing are typical of what is in their minds in these situations. If research allows this to happen then it has what is sometimes called 'ecological validity'. In this view, research approaches which attempt to control the situation too closely run the risk of distorting behaviour and the expression of peoples' views and so will lack ecological validity. In some situations the research process has no impact on behaviour. One could secretly observe what is going on (though this would raise ethical concerns), or use documents or existing records about behaviour and events (sometimes called 'unobtrusive methods').

One example of this methodological position can be found in the work of Underwood (1980). She was interested in the ideas that planners in a London Borough (Haringey) had about their role, and how these 'ideas, concepts, theories and ideologies' were put into practice in their day-to-day work. The best way of conducting such research, she argued was 'to be with people as ideas are being formulated and used. There is also the possibility for the researcher to check on the meaning ascribed to observed events by actively seeking out accounts of those involved.' (1980: 195). Describing this approach to research as participant observation, she argues that its value 'lies in its interpretive stance which emphasises the "language" of the subjects being studied and of understanding the world seen through their eyes.' (1980: 196). She goes on to argue that 'By focussing on the way in which individuals account for events and issues, the researcher can discover the normative rules which give shared understandings and can build up a picture of "reality" that is socially constructed.' (1980: 198). In this way she would avoid imposing her own ideas about planning on the situation which might 'miss the very concepts sought' (1980: 195).

Conscious of the potential impact of her presence in this situation and the way that this might influence what people said and how they acted, Underwood aimed at the start of the field work to play the role of a new entrant in the department, one who wanted to find out about the working relationships of the department so that she could potentially operate as a planner there. This also involved going to coffee and lunch with a variety of people in order to enter the 'gossip grapevine'. In this way she hoped to be sufficiently 'part of the furniture' to participate in meetings and discussions without influencing what was being said and done, though she acknowledged that some people still found her presence difficult, and that as time went on she too found it difficult to maintain an uninvolved stance in discussions since she was expected 'to offer something in return for confidences' (1980: 200).

A different methodological theory informed the design of the research carried out by Burgess et al. (1988). Activity 2.2 invites you to read a section of their paper which discusses their approach to the conduct of in-depth discussion groups. Their paper is concerned with a topic, the importance of open green space in cities, a preoccupation of urban planners for some considerable time, and its contribution to the quality of life of those living in cities, and how such open spaces should be managed. Its more specific concern lies with the attitudes and values that people have for open space. They argued that they were interested in a way of conducting research which was 'sensitive to the language, concepts and beliefs of people whose views are rarely heard.' (Burgess et al., 1988: 456). The project had three stages. The first was four 'in-depth discussion groups' with residents in different localities in the London Borough of Greenwich. The neighbourhoods had different socio-economic and ethnic characteristics, housing-types and open space supplies. The second stage was a 'neighbourhood-based social survey' which was 'designed to explore some of the issues raised by the groups amongst a wider community'. The final stage involved interviews with planners and with professionals in the leisure services department of the local authority.

ACTIVITY 2.2

The Greenwich Open-Space Project

Read the extract below. What is the main claim that the researchers make for this method?

"a) The Groups. We adopted the principles and practices of Group-Analytic Psychotherapy (Foulkes, 1964; 1975; Whitaker, 1985) to conduct four in-depth discussion groups which focused on the significance of open spaces in people's daily lives. Members were recruited from different neighbourhoods in Greenwich borough.....

(Continued)

(Continued)

The decision to explore environmental values through the use of small, in-depth discussion groups was based on a fundamental dissatisfaction with existing methods on the one hand, and on the other, a much more positive evaluation of the kind of research results which might be obtained from group analysis, based on our personal participation in both counselling and work groups led by trained group analysts. Burgess also had experience of conducting such groups with student members. Group Analysis is particularly valuable because it is based on an understanding of both individual and collective psychoanalytic processes (see Pines, 1983) and creates a setting within which people are able to talk frankly and openly about their feelings. To summarise: of the central principles of Group Analysis, three especially can be considered to be important. First, over time, the group develops a *group matrix* of shared experiences which acts as a common memory and binds people together. Second, people bring their own preoccupations to the discussions and through a process of *free association*, begin to get in touch with their deeper feelings and concerns. Third, the communications between the group members convey both *manifest and latent meanings*:, i.e., the specific details of the topic under discussion as well as the unconscious projections and transferences of the group members (see Burgess et al., 1988b for a group-analytic interpretation of the life of the Eltham group).

The mode of conducting the groups is crucial to their success. The conductor facilitates a secure, unthreatening and supportive structure for the members who are thus enabled to explore, share and negotiate their unique experiences and feelings. In the context of social research rather than psychotherapy, it is essential that members understand that they are engaged in a *work* group with a clear task and that therapeutic demands and needs do not become an overt focus for the group. The conductor must play an active role, monitoring the contributions of the individual members and the group as a whole, but not continually intervening in discussions by asking direct questions or directing the flow of conversation. In the open-space project, each group met for an evening meeting of one and a half hours over a period of six weeks. The groups were led by Burgess with Limb acting as a participant-observer. To establish the work-orientation of the groups, members were asked to think about the topic for the following week at the end of each session. This provided a means of breaking the ice initially and also enabled the conductor to bring the group back if discussion had strayed too far or if the group were stuck. The six themes were as follows: Week one was taken up within introductions of the members and initial discussion of open space in the borough. Weeks two and three were devoted to discussions of 'places I like' and 'places I dislike'. Week four, at a time when members were very comfortable with one another and able to share more intimate feelings, was devoted to memories of childhood places. In week five, recognising that the group would soon be ending, the group focused on a much more 'public' topic and talked about the management of open space.

> In the final session, members were encouraged to review their experiences in the group and say goodbye to one another. With the permission of the group members, all the sessions were tape-recorded and then transcribed by Limb and Burgess. The ground rules used to interpret the transcripts of the recorded discussions included a collective responsibility for interpretation and constant cross-referencing at all stages of the work: in the preparation of the transcripts; the construction of indices; the interpretation of themes that are selectively or commonly-held among the group members; and in the production of reports and papers (see, for example, Harrison et al., 1986; 1987).
>
> *Source*: Edited extract from Burgess et al. (1988: 456–8).

My interest here lies in the justification they have used for the in-depth discussion groups. The researchers adopted Group Analytic theory as their methodological guide in their use of in-depth discussion groups, and in their interpretation of the results of such work. This stemmed from fundamental dissatisfaction with existing methods and 'a much more positive evaluation of the kind of research results which can be obtained from group analysis' (1988: 459). The main claim here would seem to be that the extended process of interaction (Six evening sessions of one and a half hours discussion) creates a setting in which 'people are able to talk frankly and openly about their feelings' which would not be the case in answer to an interview survey, for example, where questions would have to be answered quite quickly and where people might be guarded about discussing their deeper feelings. It also provides a contrast to the view that research needs to be conducted in settings which are as normal and natural as possible to get at people's feelings and concerns. The groups are by no means seen to be naturally existing or part of normal or everyday life, unlike the working groups of planners that Underwood was observing. The groups were set up by the researchers, though some participants might have known each other in advance of the meetings through the way that the groups were recruited. Interestingly they recognise that not all researchers on open space accept their methodological views. They quote Goldsmith in Burgess et al. (1990) dismissing group interviews as being 'irrelevant, unrepresentative of environmental values and not susceptible to rigorous analysis.'

The final layer of the iceberg is the top layer, the methods of research. These are the tools and techniques used in gathering the data that is analysed to produce evidence and claims to knowledge that researchers make.

These are usually the most 'visible' part of any paper written on urban planning, and the ones with which most students will be familiar. Researchers may go into some detail on these methods. In the papers we have looked at, Atkinson and Kintrea (2001) used a household survey with householders and/or their partners. Underwood (1980) used observations of what planners were doing in their daily work, what was being said in meetings by planners and conducted formal and informal interviews with members of the planning department. Finally, Burgess et al. (1988) used in-depth discussion groups, which were led and facilitated by the researchers.

Conclusions

Nowadays there is something of a disenchantment amongst many planning academics about the role of research in supporting policy development. The hoped-for certainty of knowledge that underpinned the rational model of planning has been replaced by considerable uncertainty about the value of research findings. One response has been to turn away from expert research and to encourage dialogue amongst groups with different perspectives on policy (the communicative theory of planning) to create a shared social construction of the world. Another response has been to argue that since we have no way of independently assessing what the nature of reality is, all we can do is little more than provide our own descriptions and accounts without any claims about the relationship of these to reality.

Few planning academics are happy to be called positivists these days, but many continue to believe in the importance of research and to conduct research. This is my own position. In particular, just because we accept that in important ways the social reality in which people live is socially constructed, it does not follow that there is no independent reality. Fischer, who was quoted earlier in this chapter as supporting the idea of the social construction of knowledge, goes on to assert that this is 'not to argue that there are no real and separate objects of inquiry independent of the investigators' (Fischer 2003a: 217). Indeed he 'accepts that something called 'reality' exists' (Fischer 2003b: 121, footnote 2) but a reality that can never be fully understood or explained. This view about the nature of reality is a key ontological assumption. Whilst positivism is associated with the view that there is a reality to which we can have direct access by careful observation and measurement of the world, a view labelled as naïve realism by Hammersley (1990), Fischer's view is a more subtle version of realism.

According to this view there is a reality which exists independently of any attempt to find out about it (ontological realism) but that our accounts of reality are necessarily filtered through our mental frameworks and through the concepts we use to describe and explain the world (epistemological relativism). The findings of our research are therefore tentatively proposed as being claims to knowledge about the social world. Any piece of research is a contribution to a debate about policy but founded on both value and factual assumptions that are open to question. But this does not mean that all the knowledge (research evidence) that is used by groups to support their arguments is equally acceptable, and that we should accept 'multiple epistemologies' (Sandercock, 1998) uncritically.

Summary/Key lessons

The growing importance of philosophical concerns and arguments in social research and urban planning has led to a diversity of views amongst researchers about certain fundamental assumptions underpinning research. The main lessons for anyone undertaking research for a dissertation in urban planning are that:

1. To conduct research you have to start with the assumption that there is a 'real' reality which can be investigated.

2. Your interest in the subject is likely to derive from your values, which make you think that the topic is important and relates to some problematic situation which ought to be addressed.

3. Any research that you undertake has to be selective in those phenomena that you aim to investigate so all research is necessarily partial in this sense. The way you think about the social world and describe it will be influenced either explicitly or implicitly by certain ideas, categories, concepts or theories which tell you what the social world is composed of (individuals, classes, practices, feelings, normative rules, discourses, institutions and so on).

4. You will have to decide whether it is sensible to investigate cause and effect relationships in the subject that you are interested in or whether there is something distinctive about the social world that means that a different approach might be needed, one which gives attention to social meanings and interpretations of the world.

5. You will have to decide how to go about conducting your research (methodology). These different methodological theories (sometimes called data theories) have important consequences for research design, and for the interpretation of the results you derive from the use of specific methods of research.

> **Exercise: Key concepts in research**
>
> - A helpful discussion of ontology, epistemology and methodology, and the link between them, is to be found in Grix, J. (2002) 'Introducing Students to the Generic Terminology of Social Research', *Politics* 22 (3): 175–86.
> - Read the paper by Grix (2002) which gives some examples of the different ontological positions (labelled 'objectivism' and 'constructivism') and epistemological positions (labelled 'positivism' and 'interpretivism') that are found amongst social researchers.
> - Which of these positions do you find most convincing when thinking about your own research?

Further Reading

Changing views of the nature of planning, including consideration of the rational planning model are to be found in: Taylor, N. (1998) *Urban Planning Theory Since 1945*. London: Sage.

Chalmers, A. (1999) *What is This Thing Called Science?* Buckingham: Open University Press is a good introduction to the philosophy of science.

On positivist interpretations of natural science methods and their application to the social sciences see Halfpenny, P. (2001) 'Positivism in the Twentieth Century' in G. Ritter and B. Smart (eds) *Handbook of Social Theory*. London: Sage. pp. 371–85.

On the role of values in social research and value neutrality, see Hammersley, M. (1995) *The Politics of Social Research*. London: Sage and May, T. (2001) *Social Research*. Third Edition. Buckingham: Open University Press.

The idea of framing of research is discussed in Schon, D. and Rein, M. (1994) *Frame Reflection: Towards the Resolution of Intractable Policy Controversies*. New York: Basic Books.

A book which sets out to show how different ontological, epistemological and methodological positions might combine with the sorts of questions you might pose and the methods you might use is Greener, I. (2011) *Designing Social Research*. London: Sage.

References

Allmendinger, P. (2002) 'Towards a Post-Positivist Typology of Planning Theory' *Planning Theory* 1 (1): 77–99.

Atkinson, R. and Kintrea, K. (2001) 'Disentangling Area Effects: Evidence from Deprived and non-deprived Neighbourhoods', *Urban Studies* 38 (12): 2277–98.

Blaikie, N. (2000) *Designing Social Research*. Cambridge: Polity Press.

Burgess, J., Harrison, C.M. and Limb, M. (1988) 'People, Parks and the Urban Green: A Study of Popular Meanings and Values for Open Spaces in the City', *Urban Studies* 25: 455–73.

Burgess, J., Goldsmith, B. and Harrison, C. (1990) 'Pale Shadows for Policy: Reflections on the Greenwich Open Space Project', *Studies in Qualitative Methodology* 2: 141–67.

Carter, S.M. and Little, M. (2007) 'Justifying Knowledge, Justifying Method, Taking Action: Epistemologies, Methodologies, and Methods in Qualitative Research', *Qualitative Health Research* 17 (10): 1316–28.

Chadwick, G. (1971) *A Systems View of Planning*. Oxford: Pergamon.

Chalmers, A. (1999) *What is This Thing Called Science?* Buckingham: Open University Press.

Fainstein, S. S., (2005) 'Planning Theory and the City', *Journal of Planning Education and Research* 25: 121–30.

Farthing, S.M. (2000) 'Town planning theory and the 'paradigm wars' in the social sciences' paper presented at the Planning Research Conference at the London School of Economics, London.

Fischer, F. (2003a) 'Beyond Empiricism: Policy Analysis as Deliberative Practice', in M.A. Hajer and H. Wagenaar (eds) *Deliberative Policy Analysis*. Cambridge: Cambridge University Press. pp. 209–27.

Fischer, F. (2003b) *Reframing Public Policy: Discursive Politics and Deliberative Practices*. Oxford: Oxford University Press.

Goldstein, H.A. and Carmin J. (2006) 'Compact, Diffuse, or Would-be Discipline? Assessing Cohesion in Planning Scholarship, 1963–2002', *Journal of Planning Education and Research* 26: 66–79.

Haas, P.M. (1992) 'Introduction: Epistemic Communities and International Policy Coordination' *International Organization* 46: 1–35.

Halfpenny, P. (2001) 'Positivism in the Twentieth Century', in G. Ritter and B. Smart (eds), *Handbook of Social Theory*. London: Sage. pp. 371–85.

Hammersley, M. (1990) *Reading Ethnographic Research: A Critical Guide*. London: Longman.

Harding, S. (1987) 'Introduction: Is there a Feminist Method?' In S. Harding (ed.) *Feminism and Methodology: Social Science Issues*. Bloomington: University of Indiana Press.

Healey, P. (1991) 'Researching Planning Practice', *Town Planning Review*, 62 (4): 447–59.

Healey, P. (1997) *Collaborative Planning*. London: Macmillan.

Healey, P. (2007) *Urban Complexity and Spatial Strategy*. London: Routledge.

Kuhn, T.S. (1970) *The Structure of Scientific Revolutions*. Chicago: University of Chicago Press.

May, T. (2001) *Social Research*. Buckingham: Open University Press.

Moore-Milroy, B. (1991) 'Into Postmodern Weightlessness', *Journal of Planning Education and Research* 10 (3): 181–7.

Nagel, E. (1961) *The Structure of Science*. London: Routledge and Kegan Paul.

Preece, R. (1990) 'Development Control Studies: Scientific Method and Policy Analysis', *Town Planning Review* 61: 59–74.

Reade, E. (1987) *British Town and Country Planning*. Milton Keynes: Open University Press.

Sabatier, P.A. and Jenkins-Smith, H.C. (1999) 'The Advocacy Coalition Framework: An Assessment' in P.A. Sabatier (ed.) *Theories of the Policy Process*. Oxford: Westview Press. pp. 117–66.

Sandercock, L. (1998) *Towards Cosmopolis: Planning for Multicultural Cities*. Chichester: Wiley.

Schon, D.A. (1983) *The Reflective Practitioner: How Professionals Think in Action*. New York: Basic Books.

Schon, D. and Rein, M. (1994) *Frame Reflection: Towards the Resolution of Intractable Policy Controversies*. New York: Basic Books.

Stretton, H. (1978) *Urban Planning in Rich and Poor Countries*. Cambridge: Cambridge University Press.

Underwood, J. (1980) 'Town Planners in Search of a Role: a Participant Observation Study of Local Planners in a London Borough', *School for Advanced Urban Studies, Bristol: Occasional paper No. 6*.

3

POLICY ISSUES AND RESEARCH QUESTIONS

Key questions

What type of discipline is planning?

What types of knowledge claims are found in planning policy debates?

What are research questions and how do they relate to knowledge claims?

How can I recognise research questions in published research?

How can I create helpful questions from my initial ideas?

Key concepts

Descriptions, explanations, understanding, predictions, evaluations, prescriptions, hypotheses, theories

Overview

My argument in this chapter is that the first condition for having a project which is likely to produce results which will be worthwhile is to have a 'researchable' question to answer. This is absolutely indispensable because research design, by definition, is intended to give the best possible answer to the research question which has been posed, within the limits of the resources available to do any project. So you have to have a research question in order to design and conduct some research. But many of you, when working on your dissertations, might start with some current policy issue in mind, rather than with a question, and might wish to conduct some research which will lead to some change or improvement in policy. This starting point, I think, is quite understandable because of the nature of planning as a discipline and its professional practice orientation, but it is necessary to deconstruct planning policy debates to carve out a researchable question. To this end in this chapter I look at the arguments and types of knowledge claims which are embedded in these policy debates. These knowledge claims are important because they can be seen as answers to two types of research questions: descriptive questions (What is happening?) and explanatory questions (Why is it happening?). So, if the broad topic for your dissertation is a policy issue, you need to identify one of these types of question to help guide your research. I suggest that there is a logic to the order in which they should be answered. You need to know what is happening before you can understand why it is happening. Any proposals for change in policy should be based on an understanding both of what is happening (what the problem is) and why it occurs, and what therefore might be likely to help resolve the problem. This is one of the main reasons why in deciding on a research question, you also need to think about the existing literature on the topic. What research questions have been addressed before? Is further research required? This is the subject of Chapter 4.

If research questions are so central to the whole research enterprise, it is reasonable to ask of any piece of published research 'to what research question is this research an answer?' and subsequently to go on to evaluate it. For this reason, it is important to be able to spot research questions in other people's work, and to be able to classify them into 'what' and 'why' questions. I also look at the relationship between research questions, hypotheses and theories. Finally, I take some examples of ideas that students might suggest for a dissertation and see how these could be turned into answerable research questions.

What sort of discipline is planning?

We introduced a brief discussion of the nature of planning as a discipline in Chapter 2. Here we look in a little more depth at this issue as a way of looking at the influences on the topics and questions which planning researchers address in their research. Becher and Trowler (2001) undertook a study of a range of academic disciplines. They used the metaphor of 'academic tribes' and their 'territories'. They suggest that territories are constituted by 'bodies of knowledge', 'fields' or 'academic disciplines'. The distinction between pure and applied that they used is well-known, with pure disciplines being concerned to develop 'pure' theory, whilst applied disciplines are devoted to the application of knowledge to problems in policy and practice settings. Though urban planning as an academic discipline was not the subject of their research, it could be categorised as applied in these terms. Goldstein and Carmin (2006) make a rather similar distinction between scientific and technical disciplines. Scientific disciplines, they say, are concerned with explanations of the world, that is theory, but planning is a technical discipline, and its goals tend to be practical and its outputs are 'designs, recipes, techniques, instruments, procedures, institutions and policies' so that explanatory research is only sometimes required. My view is that this understates the importance of theory or explanatory research in planning (as we will see in the rest of this chapter), but it is true that many planning academics have a significant concern with policy and practice and its improvement and many studies are prompted by aspects of planning policy and changes to these policies. The starting point for many dissertations, too, is often a policy issue or policy question. A policy question is a broad area of policy interest, in which the main interest is a normative one: what should be done? Some planning academics are happy to 'nail their colours to the mast' and take up explicit value positions on current debates, arguing explicitly what values should be endorsed and how planning policy should achieve objectives consistent with those values. Here I adopt a neo-Weberian position in which I suggest planning researchers should not try through their research to convince people about the rightness of their values, though they can contribute to the debate about the means by which objectives, enshrining certain values, could be achieved. This is discussed further in Chapter 9.

What arguments are used in planning policy debates?

A plan, a planning report or a policy document typically aims to convince those reading it and examining its content that the policies that are being proposed are appropriate for the situation it deals with. It therefore develops an argument about why some change is necessary. What sorts of knowledge claims are made in these documents and in the debates surrounding the policies?

A useful way of thinking about this question is to adapt a typology presented by Rydin (2007) but using as an example the report by the Urban Task Force (1999). The report describes what Rydin calls the 'current state' in England at the end of the twentieth century and in doing so makes a large number of claims. Here I focus only on one of the main claims. It claims that people have been leaving or 'escaping' the cities and that this has resulted in the loss of rural land and that the 'qualities which we all associate with the countryside – wildlife, tranquillity and beauty – are becoming seriously eroded' (Urban Task Force, 1999: 36). Why is this happening? Partly, the report claims, this escape from the city reflects an attitude to the city which differs from that in other European countries, which in turn stems from the history of industrialisation and urbanisation in Britain, processes which were associated with the creation of pollution and poor housing conditions for urban residents. Partly, too, it relates to the current unattractiveness of cities as places to live, citing examples such as the 'worst of our social housing estates' and 'the swathes of industrial dereliction' (1999: 27).

In terms of knowledge claims, the current situation contains a mix of **descriptions** and **explanations**. There are descriptive claims, such as 'people have been leaving the city' and an explanatory claim of why that is happening. The explanation refers to two immediate factors concerning the effect of attitudes to the city and of the unattractiveness of cities, and a more distant cause affecting current attitudes – the history of urban development in Britain.

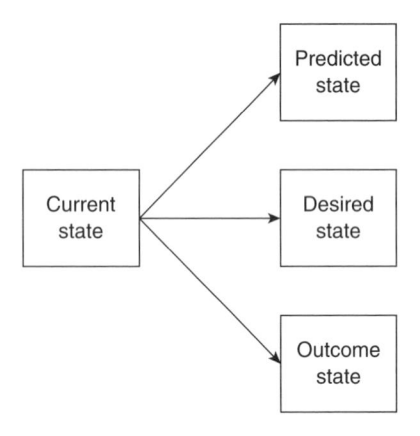

Figure 3.1 Knowledge Claims in Planning Debates (*Source*: based on Rydin, 2007)

The report also makes **predictions** about the future – **the predicted state** – what the future will be like if nothing is done about the problem. It uses a prediction about the future number of households that will exist in 2021, a prediction that suggests that there will be an additional 3.8 million households who will need to be housed by that date. It goes on to claim that 'If we were to build 3.8 million new dwellings at prevailing average density levels for new development, they would cover an area greater than the size of Greater London'. But the problem goes beyond just the loss of land to new housing. 'The implications of non-sustainable forms of development go much wider. It means more traffic on overcrowded roads, more energy use, further depletion of natural resources, fewer tranquil areas, loss of biodiversity, increased air pollution and intensified social polarisation.' (Urban Task Force, 1999: 46). Here we have two main predictive claims: that the number of households will increase and that substantial land will be needed for new housing if present trends continue. The final sentence above contains the word 'implications', which is being used in this context as synonymous with predictions. There are seven predictions about 'non-sustainable' forms of development (that is, in this context, building new housing outside cities). If explanations try to make some current or recent situation, event or trend less puzzling and therefore intelligible, predictions take a current or future situation and make claims about the consequences or future effects of that situation. The report makes this prediction on the basis of the claim that the recent loss of wildlife, tranquillity and beauty has been caused by building outside cities and hence if we continue building in this way, we expect the continuation of these effects. If an explanation works back as it were from an effect to discover a cause, predictions work from causes to effects.

In describing the current situation and the predicted future state, the authors refer to the loss of wildlife, tranquillity and beauty 'as qualities we all associate with the countryside'. It also refers to development outside cities as 'non-sustainable' forms of development. It seems that these consequences of physical development are selected at the very least for their value relevance, as we saw in Chapter 2. The report's authors might want to suggest that these predictions are just descriptions of what the future might be like, and perhaps deny that their personal values enter the picture here, and that they are merely taking as given certain values about the qualities of the countryside which we all share but it seems to me that these are to be taken as problematic, and we have an explicit **value** claim, a normative **evaluation**, that the further loss of wildlife, tranquillity and beauty would be undesirable (see Table 3.1).

Table 3.1 Knowledge Claims in Urban Planning

Knowledge claims in planning	Type of claim	Examples from the Urban Task Force (1999) report
Current state	Description	People have been leaving the cities
	Evaluation	Loss of rural land and 'the qualities which we all associate with the countryside – wildlife, tranquillity and beauty – are becoming seriously eroded'
	Explanation	This is caused by negative attitudes to the city, the unattractiveness of cities the 'worst of our social housing estates', and 'swathes of industrial dereliction' and the history of urban development in Britain

(Continued)

Table 3.1 *(Continued)*

Knowledge claims in planning	Type of claim	Examples from the Urban Task Force (1999) report
Predicted state	Prediction	If present trends continue, by 2021 there will be 3.8 million new households and 'if we were to build 3.8 million new dwellings at prevailing average density levels for new development this would cover an area greater than the size of Greater London'
	Evaluation	'The implications of non-sustainable forms of development go much wider. It means more traffic on overcrowded roads, more energy use, further depletion of natural resources, fewer tranquil areas, loss of bio-diversity, increased air pollution, and intensified social polarisation'
Desired state	Evaluation	An urban renaissance – more people living in cities
	Prescription	An urban renaissance will be created by 'higher density, compact developments in existing urban areas, using recycled land and buildings' 'Successful urban regeneration is design-led'

Source: examples based on the Urban Task Force report, 1999

The key argument in the Task Force report, then, is that the current situation is, and the predicted future situation will be, highly undesirable. Therefore, as the Urban Task Force report asserts, for 'a combination of compelling reasons' (Urban Task Force, 1999: 46), people need to be encouraged to live in urban areas rather than outside them. This is **the desired state (or planned state)** that the report advocates – an 'urban renaissance'.

But how can this be done? Here we have a further value claim, a **prescription** about what policies will bring about an urban renaissance: design-led regeneration. This is based on a prediction that attention to the design of the physical environment will create more attractive cities, in which people will want to live, this will reduce the demand to leave the city therefore protecting rural land from development. It draws on the theory that the unattractiveness of the city (and the relative attractiveness of the countryside) is a factor in making people leave the city. The report refers to some evidence to support their theory – the experience of Barcelona and unspecified cities in Germany and The Netherlands. Here too the authors could argue that they are not giving their personal opinions about what we ought to do, but merely suggesting what we, as a society, could do if we value wildlife, tranquillity and beauty in the countryside. But it seems to me that – in the context of a report commissioned and prepared by the government of the day, in which the Chair of the Task Force was described by the (then) Deputy Prime Minister as an 'evangelist of urban renaissance' (Urban Task Force, 1999: 3) – this is a prescription.

However, the report acknowledges that design will not alone be sufficient to bring about the future that is planned. There needs to be investment in health, education, social services, community safety and jobs. 'But design can help support the civic framework within which these institutions function successfully' (1999: 49). For planners the task is to help create these high density developments, and one mechanism that should be used for this purpose is 'the spatial master plan'

The final knowledge claim in planning debates is about the **outcome** of the policy. This would refer to the situation in 2021 after the policy has been implemented. The report has little to say about this. What is the measure of success? Success of the policy, another evaluation, could be measured by more people living in cities, or by what seems to be the ultimate aim of the policy, the reduction in the loss of wildlife, tranquillity and beauty outside cities. This 'test' of the prescription would require some description of the situation in 2021, with an explanation of why the policy had (or had not) 'worked'.

BOX 3.1

TYPES OF RESEARCH QUESTION

- Descriptive research questions or 'what' questions seek answers which describe a situation or event or a pattern of behaviour or a set of practices
- Explanatory research questions or 'why' questions seek explanations or understandings of a situation, event, behaviour, practice or policy or they seek predictions, assessments of the consequences of situations, events, behaviours, practices or policies.

Research questions

Underlying the main types of knowledge claim highlighted above in planning debates, there are two more specific types of claim which are of interest when we are thinking about developing some research: descriptive and explanatory claims. It is useful to think of each of these claims as an answer to one of two types of research question: What? and Why? (see Box 3.1)

To illustrate the nature of research questions, let us consider the provision of green space in cities. Though more recently attention has changed to the problems associated with urban sprawl and to the advocacy of the 'compact city', planners have for long been concerned with problems of high density 'overcrowded' cities (see for example, Howard, 1898). This topic or broad policy question is selected because open green space in cities is something that land use planning systems can in principle influence or take action on, it is an *actionable* factor in Hakim's (2000) terms. There could be many questions about the 'supply side' of open space. How much open space is there? What types of open spaces are there?

These questions are essentially seeking descriptive answers and are 'what' questions. Of course, in answering them we need to decide on how to define 'green space' in cities and how to measure it. Are we interested in public open space to which everyone has access, at least in principle, or do we include private open space, like gardens or land previously used for industrial purposes (so-called brownfield land) but now 'green' and used informally by the local population and their children. The importance of these definitional issues is explored again in Chapter 5.

But there are further questions to which our planning researcher might want to know the answer. Why do we have the current provision of open space? Why does the provision of open space vary between cities?

On the 'demand side' of the policy issue, there could be another whole range of questions. Here we might be interested in the use that people make of open space in cities. Who uses urban open space? Are older or younger people more likely to use it? Are men or women more likely to use it? What do they use it for? Walking the dog? Running? Playing games? Communing with nature? Where do they use it? How often do they use it? When do they use it? Answers to these questions tell us something about the behaviour of urban residents. All these questions too are aimed essentially at obtaining descriptive answers. But they don't help us to understand or explain the behaviour of urban residents and why people use open space in these ways. Hence the need for additional 'why' questions. On the assumption that our descriptive research reveals that some people use urban open space and others do not, we might want to know why that might be? Or to give another plausible finding from descriptive research, why do people use open space in different ways at different times of the week? The distinction between *explanation* and *understanding* in why questions is between attempts to make characteristics or regularities in behaviour intelligible (see Blaikie, 2000: 75) through identifying causes or discovering reasons, respectively. There is a debate about how clear-cut this distinction actually is (see Chapter 6) but we will adopt it for the time being. Once we start looking at causes or reasons then we need to decide which of the many possible causes or reasons are going to be included in the research and investigated.

However, planning researchers are often not just content to describe a situation or explain why it has come about. There will be questions about how to promote change, policy questions. Here there could be questions about the effects of the provision of open space. What are the consequences of using open space? What are its effects on the physical or mental health of those who participate? How could we encourage more people to take exercise and make use of urban open space? These are the questions which often motivate planning researchers to want to investigate an issue. Blaikie (2000) calls these types of questions 'how' questions which he distinguishes as a separate type of research question. I prefer to see this type of question as one which can be answered by researchers on the basis of their answers to descriptive and explanatory research questions when they make tentative recommendations about policy or practice.

Such questions can be answered on the basis of evidence gained from research in two ways. The first, and most commonly used way of tentatively answering such a question, is to make some recommendations based on an understanding of why people behave in the way that they do. If we have found that some people use open space for exercise, and the explanation is that these people were more likely to have taken part in sports at school, then one possible recommendation might be to advocate some changes in schools and encourage more participation in school sports. This recommendation is based on some generalisation from the results of a specific study of users of open space to the population more generally. The degree to which it is permissible to make these more general claims is a subject of debate amongst researchers as we will see in Chapters 5 and 6.

The second way of answering a 'how' question is to introduce some change in policy and assess whether it has produced the desired change. Most researchers have to accept that they have little or no power to bring about change in policy, and they can only study the impact of past policies to see whether they are having the desired effect. This sort of research, sometimes called evaluation research, which looks at the consequences of past policies is a very significant potential source of ideas for planning research, as Reade (1987) and others have suggested.

The important point here is that there is a logic to the order of asking research questions in relation to the state of knowledge about a subject at any particular time. Before a situation has been satisfactorily described, it cannot be explained, and until we know something about the problem and why it exists, we cannot hope to make recommendations for changing it. It is therefore important when confronting policy questions which ask 'what can be done to improve a situation?' to ask 'what do we know already about the nature of the problem?' And 'what do we know about why that problem exists?' If these questions have not been answered satisfactorily, then they need to be addressed. This is one of the reasons why it is important to discover what has been established by previous researchers before starting research.

Generating research questions: reviewing the literature

When one is designing research, a key activity is to review the literature available on the topic in which you are interested. These days, electronic searches of databases make it very easy to conduct searches of the literature and to identify a large number of works of various kinds on a topic. One reason for doing this is, at least in the early days of work on the project, that you might not have a question which you want to investigate and you want to use the review of literature to generate or suggest some questions which you might use. Sometimes you can be lucky and you may find a review of literature which identifies research questions which need to be answered. One such review of literature was conducted by Ela Palmer Heritage (2008) commissioned by a range of bodies involved in regeneration in England. This review looked at both the academic literature and the reports produced by organisations involved in regeneration projects. The conclusion of the review was that there had been a lack of evaluation of the social impacts of heritage-led regeneration projects and that where an evaluation had been made, it tended to be anecdotal or the opinion of one or two individuals 'who may have particular outlooks or agendas' (2008: 30). Hence this review indicated that here was essentially a 'gap in knowledge' and further research was needed in this area.

Literature reviews are not always readily available, however, and where they have been published, it is often the case that the academic who produced the review has used it to go on and develop some research to answer the questions thrown up by the review. This, of course, is not to say that a further investigation would not be worthwhile.

Another way of generating a research question is to look at some pieces of published research in your area of interest, and identify the research questions which have guided these pieces of research. These articles will also contain a review of literature published up to the time when the research was conducted. Sometimes students worry that if they do this, and tie their research too closely to some previous research, they might be accused of plagiarism. But there is no harm in doing this, however, provided that you make a full acknowledgment of this in your literature review, and there can be substantial benefits when the time comes to write up the dissertation, because you will be able to compare your findings with those of the previous researcher(s).

How to recognise research questions in published research

Given that research is usually justified in relation to the state of current literature on a subject, which is discussed in detail in Chapter 4, it is therefore always very useful to ask of any piece of research: to what question is this research an answer? One would hope that in reading articles and reports of empirical research that the research question or questions that writers have addressed would be easy to identify. However, it can sometimes be difficult to identify these questions, and it can take a bit of practice to interpret what a particular writer is claiming to have investigated. Conventionally one would expect to see the research question in the introduction of a paper. If research is intending to answer that question, it would seem sensible to look for the answer in the conclusion of the paper too. Here we will focus on the introduction.

Activity 3.1 asks you to read a section of a research paper that deals with the policy issue of urban green space which we have already met in Chapter 2. The introduction to the paper contrasts the views about the importance of urban open space as seen by three groups of professionals who deal with the issue: urban and landscape designers, leisure managers, and planners. It also introduces a new approach (in the context of the time the paper was written) to urban green space, that associated with environmentalists, or as the authors put it the 'urban conservation lobby' whom they also call 'new conservationists'.

ACTIVITY 3.1

Identifying research questions

Read through the introduction to this paper by Burgess et al. (1988). Can you find a research question here? What sort of question is it (given the brief definitions above)?

> Urban green spaces are highly valued by urban and landscape designers for their contribution to the quality of life in cities. 'Access to natural open spaces is a central value in modern society' Kornblum (1978) reminds American readers while Laurie (1985) chastises some of his colleagues for expressing more interest in their commission fees than 'the social concepts of the parks or the closer relationship of man (sic) and nature which they can induce, or the community needs which parks can express and enhance' (p. 77). In leisure management, however, there is less consensus about the importance of urban open spaces and several studies (Veal, 1982; Limb, 1986) demonstrate that politicians often need to be convinced of the social benefits of access to open spaces. Further, Duffield and Walker (1983) argue that planners often regard parks and gardens as historic legacy to be maintained rather than managed in response to local requirements. Similar trends are evident in the United States where urban parks are said to 'have fallen on evil days' (Jackson, 1978).
>
> Open space supply in London as set out in the Greater London Development Plan (GDLP 1969) has been based on a hierarchical principle: parks fulfil different functions with increasing size and distance from home. Variety of park function is thus achieved through a spatial supply of sites where the most diverse functions are offered by the largest parks. The hierarchy assumes that parks of equivalent status offer the same quality of recreational experiences and that they are equally accessible to all sections of the community. These guidelines remained essentially unchanged in the draft alteration to the GLDP for there was very little empirical research to suggest that the hierarchy was not the best solution to open space provision in London (GLC, 1986).
>
> The most articulate challenge to conventional approaches to open space provision has come from environmentalists (Laurie, 1979; Dower, 1984; Mabey, 1980; Cole, 1984; Fraser, 1984). Wishing to promote a wider presence for nature in the urban landscape, particularly in public open spaces, the urban conservation lobby argues that contact with natural areas affords people a range of personal, social and cultural benefits as well as opportunities to learn about ecology. However, parks and leisure services departments, in answering this challenge, point out that urban open spaces should perform many different recreational

Policy Issues and Research Questions

> functions: they cannot be regarded exclusively as `nature reserves' (GLC, 1986). Reconciling the leisure uses of open spaces with their new-found role as nature parks threatens the validity of traditional assumptions and the integrity of a profession founded on principles of good groundsmanship rather than ecology. With budgetary cuts, job losses and the growing politicisation of leisure provision and services (Coalter, et al., 1986), it is not surprising that parks departments regard the environmental challenge as a threat to their professional integrity (Winning, 1986).
>
> Neither the 'new conservationists' (Micklewright, 1987) nor the conventional leisure managers, however, have made any sustained attempt to discover whether the beliefs, values, attitudes and behaviours of urban residents accord with the newly advocated role for public open spaces.
>
> *Source*: Burgess et al. (1988 455–6).

The key to identifying the research question in this reading is in the final paragraph. Here the authors point to the lack of evidence on the 'beliefs, values, attitudes and behaviours of urban residents' and whether this is consistent with the claims of the 'new conservationists', that is, about the importance of contact with nature in the urban environment. So on the face of it, this is essentially a descriptive objective for the research and the research question is a 'what' question or perhaps rather a series of 'what' questions. We could write it, for example, as two questions:

- 'What are the beliefs, values, attitudes of urban residents in relation to contact with nature in open space?
- 'What are the behaviours of urban residents in relation to contact with nature in open space?'

The first question, as I have re-written it, asks about beliefs, values and attitudes of urban residents. Now some researchers might make a distinction between these concepts, and differ on how they inter-relate (Robson, 2002) but here, I think, the researchers use these terms in a flexible way to focus attention on what thoughts and feelings people have, what is in their minds, when they are in contact with nature. The first question is a 'what' question in that it is demanding a descriptive answer about beliefs, values and attitudes. This is a question which has been neglected, the researchers claim. The second question is about the behaviour of urban residents in open space. This too is a 'what' question. However, just to make matters a little more complicated, it seems likely to me that the researchers would see a link between these two questions, in the sense that they would see the beliefs, values and attitudes of urban residents as providing an understanding of the behaviour of urban residents. To the question 'why do people behave in this way' in urban open space, at least part of the answer would be 'the beliefs, values and attitudes' of urban residents. So there is, if you like, a hidden 'why' question here too. This is a way of answering a why question which we explore further in Chapter 6.

Research questions, hypotheses and theories

'What' questions require descriptive answers, 'why' questions demand an explanation or some understanding of why something happened. A hypothesis is a provisional answer that sets out what you might expect to find, but a provisional answer that remains to be tested against the evidence from research. In some disciplines it is quite common for tutors to emphasise the importance of students developing a hypothesis. In my experience, this is not the case in planning and, perhaps, there should be more emphasis on it. If you are trying to answer a 'why' question, a hypothesis will help you direct and focus your research efforts. Some writers (see Greener, 2011) suggest that hypotheses are more appropriate for some types of research (quantitative research) than others. I agree with White (2009) that hypotheses should not be restricted in this way and can be used in all research projects where there is a 'why' question to be answered. The view of Popper, for example, was that advances in knowledge come when intellectual puzzles about why something happens are the subject of 'bold conjectures' or hypotheses.

A question posed by Jane Jacobs (1961) was why some public spaces in New York had high levels of use by members of the public whilst others are shunned. Her hypothesis was that the reason was that some places are subject to surveillance by many watchers who thereby deter anti-social behaviour in these places, and consequently encourage more people to use the space. She contrasted the crowded streets of Greenwich Village in New York with the planned but empty open green spaces which planners had favoured. This was a bold conjecture in the context of the time when she was writing (the early 1960s), given the conventional wisdom of the time about open space in cities. This hypothesis has generated a whole series of studies on crime and 'defensible space' in cities. Her hypothesis has thus been applied to a range of other cases, and because of this, could be seen as constituting a more general theory about behaviour in public spaces. There is a further discussion of theory in the context of empirical research in Chapter 6.

Creating helpful research questions from initial ideas

Having an answerable research question is the first condition for having a well-designed piece of research. Once you have a starting point – a topic, or an aim or a question for a dissertation – one of the challenges is to develop a researchable question of the 'what' and 'why' type, bearing in mind that you need to be able to describe a situation before you can hope to explain why it exists, and know something about why it occurs before coming up with recommendations for how to change and improve things. In this section we will look at four examples to see how they could be developed to do just that.

Example 1 'Can the target for renewable energy production be met by xxx?'

This type of question is not an unusual one to interest students for two reasons. First, it deals with an important policy issue: greenhouse gas emissions, and global warming. Second, planning processes might help or hinder achievement of the target through allowing public involvement in decisions on the development of wind-farms, for example.

In terms of the knowledge claims in planning, the target can be seen as the **planned state**, which policy aims to achieve. Applying the hierarchy of research questions to this question, we could first ask a **descriptive** question: What has been the trend in the production of renewable energy since the target was set? If this is not known already through previous investigation, then the first step would be to design some research to try to answer it. In this case, official statistics are available in the UK to answer the question (Department of Energy and Climate Change, 2014) and a dissertation could accept these statistics as the answer, though as always there might be questions about the accuracy of the statistics.

Assuming, however, that these statistics are provisionally accepted, then, the next research challenge is to answer the 'why?' question which aims for an **explanation**: why is the progress towards this target at the current level? What are the causes or factors which have led to this situation, including the impact of planning processes? Sometimes this is phrased as 'what are the obstacles to achieving the target?' There is potentially a big research agenda here. Many dissertations could be written in an attempt to answer this 'why?' question because any one dissertation can only aim to focus on some of the possible factors involved, or look at the various hypotheses which have been suggested. For example, is public opposition a factor? And does the planning system allow this opposition to be expressed? There has been much discussion of the NIMBY – not in my backyard – attitude of people towards developments (Devine-Wright, 2011). On the basis of this explanation of the current situation, **a prediction** could then be made about the likelihood of achieving the target, if nothing changes. This may be what is in the mind of the person proposing this as the title for the dissertation.

But the title might also suggest a question, in addition to the predictive one, like this 'Under what circumstances would it be possible to meet the target?' This would be looking for a recommendation or prescription on how to improve things. Assuming the hypothesis that public opposition is a factor, how could it be reduced? One hypothesis about public opposition is that opposition to proposals is strongest when the idea has not been adequately explained and that this takes time, so the prescription might be to involve members of the public early in the process. Research could, in principle, be designed to test this hypothesis.

Example 2 'To uncover whether gentrification is a positive outcome of regeneration'

Here the starting point for the dissertation is presented as an aim, setting out a goal for the project in terms of the sort of knowledge to be produced. Urban regeneration, as advocated by the Urban Task Force report discussed above, involves the building of new housing on recycled land in urban areas, that is, land that is derelict or vacant (brownfield land) following changes in the economy of urban areas (Schultze-Baing and Wong, 2012). This was seen to be desirable in the view of the Task Force because it would protect rural areas from further development and protect the peace and tranquillity of the countryside (amongst other things). One consequence of this regeneration policy is that some of the people who would previously have moved out of cities would in future be housed within them. The aim of this dissertation as spelled out above is looking at the other side of the coin, as it were, at the outcome of policy and in effect asking a normative question: whether gentrification is desirable? There has been quite a debate amongst planning academics about this issue, and it illustrates the significance of normative concerns to the discipline.

From the perspective of thinking about the development of a researchable question for a project, an aim can be a useful staging post, but as a guide to research, this particular aim does not work because it seeks a normative judgement which no amount of empirical research can deliver, though empirical research could provide 'factual' ammunition to those interested in taking sides on the issue.

If we leave aside the debate over the desirability of gentrification, and see gentrification as a descriptive term (rather than an evaluative one) then we could try to define its characteristics, and make some progress in generating research questions. If we define gentrification in this context as the difference between the social status of those moving into an area, and those living in the area before the regeneration, then a whole series of questions requiring descriptive answers is raised. What sort of housing is being built? Who moves into it? What is the difference in social status between those occupying the new housing and those currently living in the area? These descriptive research questions are clearly preliminary questions which need to be answered.

However, if the interest here is in the further consequences of gentrification, not the fact of gentrification per se, then in this case, there are questions about the consequences of richer or higher status people moving into the area. And as Atkinson and Kintrea (2001: 2280) ask 'is it worse to be poor in a poor area than one that is socially mixed'? If gentrification is a cause then there are many possible effects or consequences of gentrification that one might investigate. One issue is the attitudes and feelings of the existing population. How do they feel about the changes in their area? And is the gentrification of the area the cause of these feelings or is it something else that might have changed? Another effect might be a change in the perception and 'reputation' of the area which might it easier for people living in the area to get jobs.

In this case again, in the context of developing some ideas for a dissertation, it is helpful to dig below the level of the debate about values to explore some of the more descriptive and explanatory claims on which the debate rests. This digging suggests fruitful areas for further investigation.

Example 3 'The dissertation will consider the extent to which heritage-led regeneration can help address the issues facing coastal towns in Dorset.'

Our third example is again about regeneration. Regeneration is a concept that has been adopted in a number of policy and planning contexts with somewhat different meanings, depending on the adjective that has been attached to it. This time the focus is on heritage-led regeneration and the interest in it as a topic for students has, in part, been generated by a review of literature by Ela Palmer Heritage (2008) commissioned by a range of bodies involved in regeneration. The focus on Dorset may have been prompted by a student's home location, and by the possibility of conducting research close to home. These very practical considerations might also be reinforced by the theoretical belief that the way planning operates and its effectiveness depends on the context in which it is operating (see discussion in Chapter 6). Dorset might provide a different context physically, economically and socially from other places where coastal towns are to be found.

Heritage-led regeneration was defined by Ela Palmer Heritage as 'the improvement of disadvantaged people or places through the delivery of a heritage-focused project.' (2008: 1–2). It is interesting that the definition is sufficiently broad to cover objectives which include the improvement of the [lives of] disadvantaged people as well as the improvement of places. According to this report, there are three distinct types of heritage-led regeneration. These are:

- Area-based regeneration (for instance, physical regeneration of a town centre, conservation area, or historic landscape)
- Single building regeneration (the physical regeneration of a single building)
- Heritage project regeneration (a socially beneficial project not involving physical regeneration, but based around a historic building).

Under this definition of heritage-led regeneration, then, we have a mix of different sorts of physical development with different sorts of objectives (the improvement of people's lives or of places). Clearly, for research purposes you would need to be very clear which of these types of heritage-led regeneration would be the subject of the proposed research because they would lead to quite different decisions about the conduct of the research.

Returning to the aim of the dissertation set out above and its focus on Dorset, the inclusion of a specific geographical location is in contrast to the two previous examples we have looked at. In these examples it is, perhaps, implicit that the place being referred to is the UK, but of course the UK is not the only place where there are renewable energy targets or where regeneration is taking place in the world. So, as we will see further in Chapter 5, it is useful to think clearly about the widest set of cases ('the population' of cases) to which your results will refer, and its geographical limits, which should be included in your research question.

To make progress we need to explore the more specific claims that might underlie this broad policy question, which reads as currently stated rather like an essay question, in order to carve out a manageable and researchable dissertation question. First, we might consider the nature of the 'issues facing coastal towns in Dorset'. The way that the aim is written pre-supposes that we know already what the issues are that face coastal towns, i.e., that the current state of these towns has been adequately described in some previous research. Researchers are always keen to question evidence. A starting point for a dissertation might be to question these assumptions, with a 'what' question 'what are the main issues facing coastal towns in Dorset?' As we have seen in Chapter 2, there are many ways of framing an issue so there is scope in a dissertation for questioning the way the problems have been presented, and presenting an alternative description of the problems. Perhaps one way to do this would be to focus on the problems of people living in the towns rather than the physical appearance of parts of the towns.

There could also be scope for a dissertation which questioned the explanation given in official documents for the problems in the area, raising a 'why?' question about the causes or factors involved in creating the problems in these towns.

Something it would be useful to know in developing a dissertation is if there have been any examples of the types of heritage-led regeneration as defined above in Dorset. If there have been such examples, then, the interest in a dissertation might be the outcome of this regeneration. Did it help address the issues facing coastal towns in Dorset? An explanation of why was it successful (or unsuccessful) would be needed, working back from the outcome to the factors (or obstacles in the case of an unsuccessful outcome) involved in this situation.

If there have been no examples of heritage-led regeneration, then the interest in this question might have been stimulated by the perception that there is the potential for the heritage of these towns, so far untapped, to be used as the basis for regeneration. A dissertation could set out to describe the historic and heritage 'assets' in the towns, with a view to assessing that potential. This would not just be a list of the heritage assets but some justification based on previous research of what counts as a heritage asset. The next question here might be a 'why?' question 'why has there has been no regeneration in this area?' Perhaps the assets are different from those found in other places where heritage-led regeneration has been implemented? Or local conditions are not helpful to this type of regeneration? This dissertation would aim to provide an explanation of the lack of heritage-led regeneration in this area.

Example 4 'Can the Green Belt be disembedded?'

This question is couched in terms which stem from the planning theory literature. The idea behind this dissertation topic is that certain policy ideas have become so influential that it is very difficult to change them. They have become 'embedded'. The term used by Healey for a policy idea is 'discourse', which goes back to the arguments about the framing of problems introduced in Chapter 2. Discourse 'refers to the policy language and metaphors mobilised in framing, justifying and legitimating a policy programme or project. This vocabulary gives expression, implicitly or explicitly, to one or more frames of meaning which shapes how 'problems' and 'solutions' are perceived.' (Healey, 2007: 22). In Britain, the idea of green belts around cities as a solution to the problem of urban sprawl has this status of being 'embedded'. It has entered popular consciousness (see Natural England, 2010) and the idea of 'protecting the green belt' is mobilised to deflect the call for further development to other areas. The idea of green belts goes back to the nineteenth century to Ebenezer Howard and his proposals for 'garden cities' surrounded by green belts as a way of managing growth in large urban regions. In The Netherlands, the idea of the protection of the 'green heart' of the country has a similar status. Healey says that the idea dates back to the 1930s and has been reinforced by the idea of sustainable development and the compact city. 'They are linked to a strong and culturally-embedded notion of the defence of the countryside landscape, as embodying particular cultural values of "Englishness" (Healey and Shaw 1994)'. If we assume that the idea of the green belt is embedded, then the interest is in an **explanation** of why it is embedded, and the conditions – cultural values according to Healey (2007) – which have brought this about. The next step is to explore whether the contextual conditions, which support the discourse are vulnerable to change, and a **prediction** could then be made about the status of the policy.

Conclusion

In this chapter, I have looked at the role of research questions in research design. Many writers (Blaikie 2000; deVaus 2001; Gorard 2013) emphasise the importance of research questions to research design. They are essential to the development of a research design. Planning academics tend to be concerned with policy issues and the improvement of planning policy and practice, while some of them advocate a close relationship between the questions investigated by researchers and the concerns of practitioners. Underlying planning policy debates, I suggest that concerned parties make descriptive claims about the current situation, which – it is asserted – is problematic and needs to be changed; explanatory claims about why that situation exists; and predictive claims about how that situation will develop without a change of policy. Finally, there are prescriptive claims about how the situation will improve if a particular policy is implemented. Descriptive claims are necessarily selective, in that only some features of a situation will be described. Explanatory, predictive and prescriptive claims depend on theories which are selective in the factors that they address. Corresponding to these claims are different types of research questions: 'what' and 'why' questions. It is these questions which student researchers need to consider when planning a dissertation. They are researchable or answerable questions.

> ## Summary/Key lessons
> 1. The starting point for research design is to develop a researchable question, therefore it is important to spend some time thinking and working on the development of a research question.
> 2. A researchable question is one that can be answered by conducting empirical research.
> 3. 'What' questions seek descriptive answers and result in descriptive claims.
> 4. 'Why' questions require explanatory answers and produce explanatory claims. A hypothesis is useful as a provisional answer to a 'why' question, and can be tested through your research.
> 5. There is a logic in the order of asking these questions. Before a situation can be explained, understood or assessed as desirable or undesirable, there needs to be an adequate description of that situation. So important work needs to be done to describe the problems with which planning deals. Claims or arguments for the adoption of particular policies need to be based on some explanation or understanding of why problems exist, so that predictions can be made about the consequences of a proposed intervention.
> 6. Initial ideas, broad policy questions or topics for your dissertation need to be re-worked into a researchable question.

> **Exercise: Generating research questions**
>
> One of the most difficult stages of the research process, as we saw in the examples given in this chapter, is to move from some initial ideas for research to develop a clear focus for the project, developing some answerable research questions. This activity asks you to do just that. Taking your provisional topic or question for your dissertation:
>
> 1. Write down your provisional topic as clearly as you can at this stage.
> 2. Analyse your topic in relation to the categories in Rydin's typology of claims in planning (shown in Figure 3.1). There can be claims about:
>   - the current state of the world – the nature of the current problem;
>   - the predicted state – what will happen if nothing is done about the problem;
>   - the desired or planned state – what the planning system should aim to achieve in future;
>   - The outcome state – what outcomes have actually been achieved.
>   - Which of these claims in planning is of relevance to the topic you have in mind?
> 3. What more specific types of knowledge claims underpin these claims in planning? Descriptions? Explanations? Predictions? Prescriptions?
> 4. Write down a list of the questions which need to be answered. What would seem, at this stage, to be the key research questions which need to be answered?

Further Reading

Many text books on research methods devote some attention to research questions but I would single out three books which take a rather similar approach to research questions to the one taken here which you could fruitfully read:

Blaikie (2000) has a chapter on research questions, and contains advice on developing and refining research questions: Blaikie, N. (2000) *Designing Social Research.* Cambridge: Polity Press.

White (2009) provides very useful guidance on how to develop research questions from topics and what makes questions 'researchable': White, P. (2009) *Developing Research Questions.* Basingstoke: Palgrave Macmillan.

Andrews (2003) makes a helpful distinction between main research questions and subsidiary questions: Andrews, R. (2003) *Research Questions.* London: Continuum.

References

Atkinson, R. and Kintrea, K. (2001) 'Disentangling Area Effects: Evidence From Deprived and Non-Deprived Neighbourhoods', *Urban Studies* 38 (12): 2277–98.

Becher, T. and Trowler, P. R. (2001) *Academic Tribes and Territories*. Buckingham: The Society for Higher Education and the Open University Press.

Blaikie, N. (2000) *Designing Social Research*. Cambridge: Polity Press.

Burgess, J. Harrison, C.M. and Limb, M. (1988) 'People, Parks and the Urban Green: a Study of Popular Meanings and Values for Open Spaces in the City', *Urban Studies* 25: 455–73.

de Vaus, D. (2001) *Research Design in Social Research*. London: Sage.

Department of Energy and Climate Change (2014) *Digest of UK Energy Statistics*. London: National Statistics.

Devine-Wright, P. (2011) *Renewable Energy and the Public: From NIMBY to Participation*. London: Earthscan.

Ela Palmer Heritage (2008) *The Social Impacts of Heritage-Led Regeneration*. London: Ela Palmer Heritage.

Goldstein, H. A. and Carmin, J. (2006) 'Compact, Diffuse, or Would-be Discipline?', *Journal of Planning Education and Research* 26: 6–79.

Gorard, S. (2013) *Research Design: Creating Robust Approaches for the Social Sciences*. London: Sage.

Greener, I. (2011) *Designing Social Research*. London: Sage.

Hakim, C. (2000) *Research Design: Successful Designs for Social and Economic Research*. London: Routledge.

Healey, P. (2007) *Urban Complexity and Spatial Strategy*. London: Routledge.

Healey, P. and Shaw, T. (1994) 'Changing Meanings of "Environment" in the British Planning System', *Transactions of the Institute of British Geographers* 19 (4): 425–38.

Howard, E. (1898) *Tomorrow: A Peaceful Path to Real Reform*. London: Swan Sonnenschein; republished in facsimile (2003) with a commentary by P. Hall, D. Hardy and C. Ward.

Jacobs, J. (1961) *The Death and Life of Great American Cities*. New York: Random House.

Natural England and Council for the Protection of Rural England (2010) *Green Belts: a Greener Future*. London: Natural England and CPRE.

Reade, E. (1987) *British Town and Country Planning*. Milton Keynes: Open University Press.

Robson, C. (2002) *Real World Research*. Oxford: Blackwell.

Rydin, Y. (2007) 'Re-Examining the Role of Knowledge Within Planning Theory', *Planning Theory* 6 (1): 52–68.

Schultze-Baing, A. and Wong, C. (2012) 'Brownfield Residential Development: What Happens to the Most Deprived Neighbourhoods in England?', *Urban Studies* 49 (14): 2989–3008.

Urban Task Force (1999) *Towards an Urban Renaissance. Final Report of the Urban Task Force, Chaired by Lord Rogers of Riverside.* London: Spon.

White, P. (2009) *Developing Research Questions.* Basingstoke: Palgrave Macmillan.

4

A JUSTIFICATION FOR YOUR RESEARCH QUESTION

Key questions

What practical and academic justifications exist for a research question?

What is a literature review?

How does a literature seek to persuade readers of the academic benefits of answering a research question?

Key concepts

Practical justifications for research, academic debates, arguments, literature reviews, current state of knowledge

Overview

In the previous chapter, I argued that research in planning, as in other subjects, needs to be guided by one (or more) research questions, questions which the research is aiming to answer. This chapter addresses a question which someone else (someone assessing your dissertation, for example) might raise about any piece of research: Why is it worthwhile spending time and effort answering this particular research question? The research question therefore needs to be justified in some way. There are two ways in which researchers aim to justify their research. The first is in academic terms. You need to develop an argument using the existing literature to show that the question you are proposing to answer has not so far been answered, or has not been satisfactorily answered. This helps to explain why considerable knowledge of the academic literature is displayed in published papers and why students are expected to make reference to the literature in dissertations.

It is worth saying at this point that literature reviews in dissertations are often rather poor, because I suspect it is not clear why they are required and in particular it is not clear that the review should develop an argument about the limitations of the existing literature. It is also worth saying that being able to handle the existing literature in a mature way is something that impresses the examiners of a dissertation.

A second type of justification for conducting research is that the answer to the question might be of some practical benefit; it might help to improve a problem in planning or a policy of some sort. Some planning academics want to see a very close relationship between the research they conduct and the problems faced in the world of planning practice, whilst others want to adopt a somewhat more distant relationship. Increasingly, however, planning researchers are being asked to justify their work in terms of some payback to policy (see Chapter 9).

The first section of this chapter analyses two examples of the sorts of practical justifications that are used in academic papers. The next section examines literature reviews and conventional academic justifications for further research. The final section looks at the structure of a literature review, and how the structure helps develop the argument for further research.

Practical justifications for further research: Two examples

If we are interested in the way that academics justify their research, it is useful at this stage to look at some examples. Luckily in our field there is some convention about where these justifications are expected to be found when presenting research. The examples we are going to look at are taken from the introductory sections of two pieces of published research that we have already discussed. It allows us to see the practical justifications that writers give for conducting their research. To do this we have to be able to understand or interpret what is being said, and often to get behind the words on the page, as it were, to understand the logic of the argument that is being developed.

The first example is taken from Atkinson and Kintrea (2001). The topic of interest here is 'area effects' or whether poor people, living in areas where there are concentrations of other poor people, suffer additional disadvantages to those they face from being poor (and would not experience if they lived in other areas). Or as the authors express it elsewhere (Atkinson and

Kintrea 2001: 2278): 'the outcome in life-chances and opportunities that might vary if one lived or grew up in different types of area.'

In the introduction to the paper they note that in Britain in the 2000s under a Labour Government, there was a focus in policy on the '"worst estates" and socially excluded areas containing some of the most intractable problems for public policy.' (2001: 2277). They also note that underlying this policy is a belief that these area effects do exist. In other words, this is the theory behind the current policy. Research which could evaluate this theory would be relevant and useful research. And to emphasise the possible importance of these effects, they remark (2001: 2278): 'Nothing is more stark than the possibility that someone will die younger by virtue of where they live (Shaw et al., 2000) or that a person's address affects their chances of getting a job (Dean and Hastings, 2000). The importance of this problem in Britain at present is intensified by the widespread recognition that spatial segregation between the poor and the better-off has become greater in the past 10 or 20 years (Lee and Murie, 1997; SEU, 2001a).' The implicit argument here then is that there are two reasons why we should be interested in this question. First, it gains its importance because the current government thinks it is important. A second reason is that it appeals to our values. We would all agree, presumably, that nobody should die any younger than they have to, nor be denied a job just because of where they lived. Our values should therefore lead us to support this research.

Our second example is from the paper by Burgess et al. (1988). We have already looked at this in Chapter 3 in order to identify the research questions which the authors are aiming to answer (see Activity 3.1). Here we are interested in the arguments that they make to support the investigation of this question. If we turn to the introduction we can see that they discuss the topic of urban open space in relation to some existing literature which deals essentially with the benefits that the use of open space provides, or is assumed to provide, for people and society. The issue in debate is a practical one 'What are open spaces for?' And the professional concern is with how they should be managed. The introduction uses the literature on the topic to contrast the perspectives of different professional groups about the benefits. Urban and landscape designers, as exemplified by Laurie (1985) seem to see a wide range of benefits from parks: 'social concepts of parks', the 'relationship between man and nature' and 'community needs' though it is not clear to the non-expert reader what these benefits mean. Leisure managers, or at least some politicians involved in decision-making, are 'less convinced of the social benefits of access to open spaces' whilst planners, it seems, see parks and gardens as landscapes having an essentially historic interest and so places to be protected or maintained rather than 'managed in response to local requirements'. Planners also have developed the idea of a hierarchy of open spaces within a city where small and more readily accessible open spaces close to home have a more limited range of functions than the larger and more distant parks and spaces. 'The hierarchy assumes that parks of equivalent status offer the same quality of recreational experiences and that they are equally accessible to all sections of the community' (Burgess et al., 1988: 456). This professional debate has been joined by environmentalists who want to use open space as a way of introducing nature into cities. This adds a further element to the mix of interests involved and to conflicts over professional roles in relation to open space management.

Reconstructing or reinterpreting this in terms of our approach to justifying research questions, the underlying argument of the introduction would thus seem to be something like the following: The management of open space is an important issue on which most professional groups agree (though different professional groups disagree about why it is important), hence this topic is an important and justifiable one for researchers to investigate. But there is a debate amongst professionals about how to improve the management of parks and open spaces; the debate is, in our terms, a debate about a 'how' question, so research can help to shed light on this policy debate.

These two examples illustrate the point made in Chapter 2 that subjects and questions, are selected for study because they are 'value relevant', that is, they deal with issues or problems which are thought to be 'important'. This importance could relate to the values of the researcher(s) or to some wider body of people such as the government of the day and its policies, or to professional groups such as planners who are involved in dealing with the issue. But the people who might be interested in the question could equally be particular members of the community, the disabled, for example, or any group whose interests are thought to be neglected. This means that in thinking about your research question, you too should think about why it is important to you, and whether it is of wider importance. Might answering the question help to understand some problem or lead to some change in the way that the problem is tackled? As we will see in Chapter 9, some planning researchers think that the interests of planning professionals – the problems they have to deal with – should be the starting point for any research investigation.

Reviews of literature: Justifying research in academic terms

The word 'critical' is often used to describe the ideal literature review in a dissertation, and often it is said that literature reviews are not critical or at least not critical enough. By critical it is meant that a review seeks to develop an argument about the limitations of current research, and provides a justification for further research. Given the importance I attach to research questions, and the purpose of a literature review which is to review the state of knowledge on a question, it makes sense when reviewing the literature to use your research questions as a framework for the review. This means that the literature to be used in the review should relate to the specific question you are investigating (see Figure 4.1). Often a literature search will identify a large number of publications which have something to say about the subject, particularly if one searches professional publications as well as academic journals. Many of these may develop theoretical arguments or may be works which advocate a particular approach to dealing with a planning problem. These publications may be useful sources of hypotheses which could be tested in subsequent research. But from the perspective of a critical review of the literature it is also important to assess how far any publication is based on some original research investigation. Even when a paper is based on research, it may be unclear how the research was conducted. At other times, we may know something about the methods which were used but not how or why they were used. Gorard (2013) argues that in a literature review search, any sources which are not based on research – which are statements of opinion or theory – should be dropped from the review process and similarly with reports of research which do not explain how the research was conducted. When these considerations are taken into account, the number of relevant papers might be small. Often in planning there may be only one or two previous research papers available for close examination and critique.

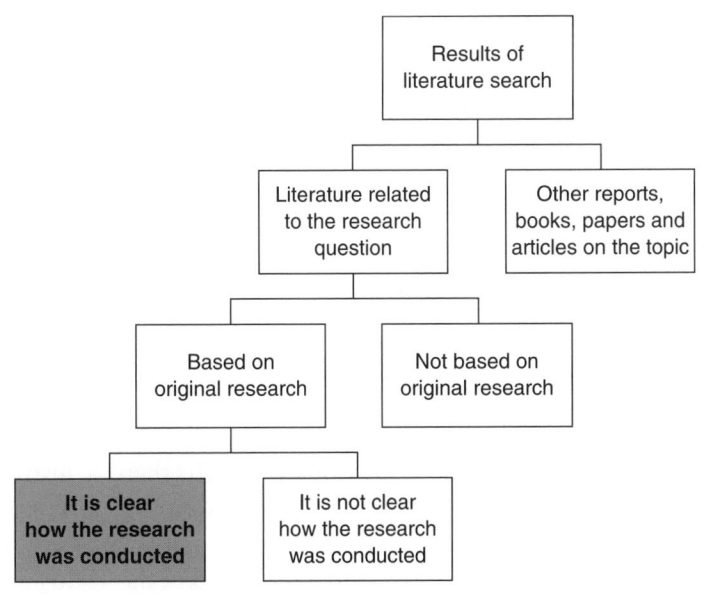

Figure 4.1 Classifying the Documents from a Literature Search

Box 4.1 sets out a number of arguments that researchers typically make about the limitations or deficiencies in the existing literature. In the paper by Burgess et al. (1988: 456) discussed in the previous section, the claim of the authors is that 'Neither the "new conservationists" (Micklewright, 1987) nor the conventional leisure managers, however, have made any sustained attempt to discover whether the beliefs, attitudes and values and behaviours of urban residents accord with the newly advocated role for public open spaces'. In other words, the authors claim that there is what might be called a 'gap in knowledge' (argument 1 in Box 4.1), that they don't have any evidence to inform the policy debate. Actually, they don't quite say that. They say that there has not been any 'sustained attempt' to produce any evidence by these professional groups.

BOX 4.1

ARGUMENTS TYPICALLY DEVELOPED BY RESEARCHERS TO JUSTIFY FURTHER RESEARCH

1. No one has looked at this before, it is a neglected question. There is a 'gap' in the literature.

2. Past studies are 'limited'. There are four versions of this criticism.

    2.1 Times or the context have changed so that even though there have been studies in the past, they are now outdated and need to be revised.

    2.2 There is a debate about a topic. A debate is raging between 'pro' and 'anti' camps on the importance of X and its effect on Y, or the meaning of X.

    2.3 Past studies have been conducted in limited settings or contexts.

    2.4 Past studies have neglected an important factor.

3. Past studies have been 'flawed' in terms of the way that the research was conducted. These are methodological arguments. Aspects critiqued can include the sampling methods and the cases selected for study, the methods of data generation and methods of analysis.

If a literature search reveals some previous research, then, a justification for further research could be that 'times have changed' or at the very least that it is worthwhile to see if a further study would back up any past claims. For example, if a search reveals a review of literature conducted in the 1980s that claimed that planners thought about parks and gardens as items of historic heritage to be maintained and protected rather than spaces to be used for community benefit, then, the question could be raised about whether they still think like this (argument 2.1 in Box 4.1). Research could be conducted to test the claim.

A second justification could be that there is a continuing debate in the literature about the topic (argument 2.2). Atkinson and Kintrea in the quotation below point to a debate between commentators on 'area effects', effects which are claimed to affect the lives of the poor living in areas of concentrated poverty:

> The literature on area effects has mainly derived from US cities and the plight of an urban poor concentrated in small areas that create additional impacts which prevent them from escaping poverty. The mechanisms for this additionality are found in processes such as burdens on local service provision, poor reputation that is projected onto individual residents, poor-quality or absent private services, lower standards of public service provision and the socialisation processes in poor neighbourhoods [...]. Nevertheless, the propositions about area effects remain contentious and social scientific knowledge is still being assembled. While some commentators, such as Kleinman (1998), are critical of the area effects thesis, more conclude that area effects do matter (in particular the wide ranging review by Ellen and Turner, 1997). However, little evidence on area effects exists for British cities to validate either position fully.' (2001: 2278)

Let us analyse their argument. First, they note that the literature is mainly derived from research in US cities. The next sentence suggests mechanisms which have been proposed to bring about these area effects. In terms of our discussion of types of claim in planning, we have a range of consequences or effects – area effects – and the literature suggests a range of hypotheses about situations or mechanisms or causes that might contribute to those effects. On the assumption that we know that there are area effects, these hypotheses are proposed as possible answers to the 'why question?' 'why do area effects exist?'

But the authors go on to say that there is a debate in the field about the very existence of area effects – 'the propositions about area effects remain contentious' – citing the opposed views of Kleinman, and Ellen and Turner. One reason why this debate might exist is because they note that 'social scientific knowledge is still being assembled' and by implication more evidence might help to resolve the debate. Finally, they say that there is 'little evidence on area effects for British cities'. So the argument here, then, for further research is essentially that we do not have enough evidence to say whether 'area effects' exist in British cities.

We might ask why, if we have US evidence for area effects, we need further British evidence? The authors do not address this point. It could be because the authors see the aim of social research as being the development of generalisations that apply widely across space, and further research conducted outside the US would allow us to see if such a generalisation is supported by the evidence. We will look at this interest in generalisation again in Chapter 5. Another possibility is that the authors think that the situation in British cities could be in some way different from that in the US. For example, some of the possible causes of area effects might not be so evident in British cities. Perhaps public sector services are better funded in poor areas in British cities? Hence the **context** in which poor people live in British cities would reduce the chances that area effects exist (argument 2.3). Another way of looking at the different contexts in which social life is lived is to say that there is another factor whose influence has been neglected in past research and which needs to be taken into account (argument 2.4).

A final type of argument used by academics is to raise questions about the way that previous research has been designed and conducted and on the findings which have been produced (argument 3). This could be as simple as suggesting that the way that questions were posed in a questionnaire had an impact on the answers given by respondents to a more fundamental debate about the conduct of research. We saw in Chapter 2, for example, the methodological debate between researchers on the value of thinking about research design in terms of 'control' and those who argue for 'naturalism' in research design, that is, the belief that research ought to be conducted in situations which are as normal and natural as possible. And Burgess et al. (1988) argued that they held a much more positive evaluation of the type of research results that they would obtain on the significance of open space in people's daily lives from adopting the principles and practices of group-analytic psychotherapy, and conducting in-depth discussion groups, than from conducting structured interviews.

The demand on students to review the literature is less onerous than might be expected of an academic seeking to publish in journal. As Bell (1993: 33) says, a dissertation is not expected to give a definitive account of research but to show 'some evidence of reading of relevant literature' and 'some awareness of the current state of knowledge in the subject'.

The structure of a literature review

A literature review should aim to develop an argument about the state of current research and establish the need for further research. An example of a short literature review from a research proposal is shown in Box 4.2. In a dissertation the literature review may be longer and could go into more detail about the nature of previous research but the interest here is in how the review is structured. First, the opening paragraph sets the policy context for the proposed research, by outlining the way that planning policies aim to retain village services, and thus (implicitly) suggest that the issue to be investigated is an important one. It also sets out the assumption that lies behind this policy approach: that village services will be supported if most new development in rural areas (i.e., housing) is directed towards larger settlements.

BOX 4.2

EXAMPLE OF A SHORT LITERATURE REVIEW

Village services in England are in decline and, for decades, planning policies in England have sought to retain rural services by directing most development in rural areas to larger rural settlements where new residents can benefit from, and support the services and facilities of that settlement, thus contributing to rural sustainability (Countryside Agency 2002a).

Recent research in remoter rural areas of England and Wales has shown that housing growth over the 1990s was concentrated within settlements (2000–30,000 population) rather than in the open countryside (Brown et al., 2005). Service sector employment was also growing in these settlements, but the link between housing growth, population growth and service provision in rural settlements has remained until recently an assumption. Some recent work has begun to question this assumption. A longitudinal study of service provision and housing growth over the period 1981–2001 in Devon showed that there was slight negative relationship between housing growth and change in service provision at parish level so that higher levels of housing growth were associated with a somewhat faster decline of village services taken as a whole though the association was rather weak (Wilson, 2004). The study also revealed no relationship between service retention and distance from larger towns, and service retention and whether the settlement had been designated as a local service

(Continued)

> *(Continued)*
>
> centre. These somewhat surprising findings highlight the importance of understanding the mechanisms that support local services.
>
> One possible mechanism of support for services generated by an influx of population is increased community involvement. This can take a number of forms: finance, management, labour, premises and involvement at strategic level. Literature on rural in-migration points to the potential for engagement in community activities as one motivation for rural living (Champion, 1997). Moseley (2000) has argued for the importance of community involvement as a mechanism in some situations and Barton et al. (2004) claim that such involvement is better able to meet the needs of vulnerable local groups. Small scale case study work in Devon (Wilson, 2004) supports the first proposition, though pointing to variation depending on the service concerned. However, clear and wide ranging evidence on the effects of community involvement does not exist. Moreover, the conditions which promote community involvement have also not been researched. It has been suggested that the housing mix in villages and small towns, for example, allowing more affordable housing, could be a key variable (Wilson, 2004) but community spirit, a high degree of local social interaction and attachment to place seem to be characteristics of wealthier areas (see Forrest and Kearns, 2001).
>
> The aim of the research is therefore to assess the impact of community involvement on service retention in sparsely populated rural areas and the conditions which shape community involvement and, in turn, to provide policy guidance on the role of community involvement in service delivery; and on whether future policy responses might be warranted.
>
> *Source:* Farthing, 2007

The second paragraph looks at the aggregate evidence for the success of this policy (Brown et al., 2005), and some recent evidence based on a 'longitudinal study' in the rural county of Devon (Wilson, 2004) which questions its success. This leads the authors to the conclusion that we need to know more about the 'mechanisms that support local services'. So the research question raised here is effectively 'why does the rate of service decline in villages vary?'

The third paragraph suggests the hypothesis that community involvement in some villages (but lack of community involvement elsewhere) could help us to understand why these villages retain their local services, a hypothesis 'supported by small scale case study work in Devon' by Wilson (2004) and by Moseley (2000). This is effectively, in terms of the types of justification for further research identified in Box 4.1, the argument that an important possible factor has been ignored. The final paragraph, therefore, argues that the proposed research aims to test the hypothesis that community involvement will have an impact on service retention in villages. It also aims to discover under what conditions local communities get involved, that is, what are the factors which affect this.

> **Summary/Key lessons**
>
> This chapter has been devoted to the idea that research questions need to be justified, and to an exploration of the types of justification to be found in published research. I suggested that nowadays academics are expected to conduct research that has some practical benefit as well as research which has an academic justification.
>
> 1. You can justify your research question as having some (potential) practical benefit by showing that it is relevant to some problem which is important in its own right, and that the research is likely to make a contribution to understanding that problem, and perhaps offer a solution for it.
>
> 2. You can justify your research question in academic terms by showing that you are familiar with the current state of knowledge in the field, a knowledge derived from your reading of the existing literature on your question.
>
> 3. In order to write an effective literature review you have to develop an argument about the current state of knowledge about the research question, which should lead the reader to the conclusion that further research is required.
>
> 4. This chapter has highlighted a number of typical arguments that are to be found in the literature, arguments which you may find helpful in developing an argument for further research.

> **Exercise: Reviewing the literature**
>
> Reading and reviewing the research literature is not confined to the research design phase of research but continues throughout the whole dissertation process, but this exercise is designed to get
>
> *(Continued)*

(Continued)

you started on that process. First, taking your initial research question, it asks you to conduct a library search. In most universities, search facilities access a large number of databases and searches typically bring up many hundreds and sometimes thousands of books, articles and reports. Usually, subject librarians are very happy to help students if you are having problems developing appropriate search terms from your question. For this activity, you need to divide the books, articles and reports into the following categories:

- Policy documents.
- Texts which are essentially opinion pieces on policy issues, though they may be based on practitioner experience. These may be particularly represented amongst articles in professional magazines.
- Works of theory. These may be found in academic or scholarly publications/journals. They do not report on empirical research.
- Literature reviews.
- Texts which report the results of empirical research, and provide some description of the methods of research used. These too will be mainly found in academic journals.

The first two categories may be useful for giving a practical justification for the dissertation you will write, including the possibility of testing the theory behind current policy and evaluating the likely effectiveness of policy. The third category could also be useful in providing hypotheses for organising your research. These first three categories therefore should not be discarded but classified and saved. Amongst the last two categories, find initially just two articles based on research relevant to your proposed dissertation question which you think needs to be addressed. Read the introductory sections of the papers and:

1. Identify the research questions they are aiming to answer.

2. Assess their arguments for further research against the list of those given in Box 4.1. Note: there may be more than one argument in any one paper.

3. Write you own short (critical) review of these articles, giving your justification for some further research to answer your research question that you might carry out building on this work. This will obviously be provisional, and will certainly change as your knowledge of the literature expands.

Further Reading

Advice on how to review research papers and research reviews is given in:

Locke, L.F., Silverman, S.J. and Spirduso, W.W. (2010) *Reading and Understanding Research*, 2nd Edition. Thousand Oaks, CA: Sage.

Texts which discuss how to conduct literature reviews:

Bell, J. (2010) *Doing Your Research Project*, 5th Edition. Buckingham: McGraw Hill/Open University Press.

Fink, A. (2014) *Conducting Research Literature Reviews: From the Internet to Paper*, 4th Edition. London: Sage.

Hart, C. (1998) *Doing a Literature Review: Releasing the Social Science Imagination*. London: Sage.

Ridley, D. (2012) *The Literature Review: A Step by Step Guide for Students*. London: Sage.

References

Atkinson, R. and Kintrea, K. (2001) 'Disentangling Area Effects: Evidence from Deprived and Non-Deprived Neighbourhoods', *Urban Studies* 38 (12): 2277–98.

Burgess, J., Harrison, C.M. and Limb, M. (1988) 'People, Parks and the Urban Green: a Study of Popular Meanings and Values for Open Spaces in the City', *Urban Studies* 25: 455–73.

Bell, J. (1993) *Doing Your Research Project*. Buckingham: Open University Press.

Brown, C., Farthing, S.M., Smith, I. and Nadin, V. (2005) *Dynamic Smaller Towns: Critical Success Factors*. Cardiff: Welsh Assembly Government.

Dean, J. and Hastings, A. (2000) *Challenging Images: Housing Estates, Stigma and Regeneration*. Bristol: The Policy Press.

Ela Palmer Heritage (2008) *The Social Impacts of Heritage-Led Regeneration*. London: Ela Palmer Heritage.

Farthing, S.M. (2007) *Community Involvement and the Support of Village Services in England*. Unpublished ESRC research proposal, UWE, Bristol.

Gorard, S. (2013) *Research Design: Creating Robust Approaches for the Social Sciences*. London: Sage.

Healey, P. (2007) 'Re-Thinking Key Dimensions of Strategic Spatial Planning', in G. de Roo and G. Porter (eds) *Fuzzy Planning*. Aldershot: Ashgate. pp. 21–41.

Laurie, I.C. (1985) 'Public Parks and Spaces' in S. Harvey and S. Rettig (eds), *Fifty Years of Landscape Design*. London: The Landscape Press. pp. 63–78.

Lee, P. and Murie, A. (1997) *Poverty, Housing Tenure and Social Exclusion*. Bristol: Policy Press.

Micklewright, S. (1987). *Who are the new conservationists? An analysis of the views and attitudes of the membership of two new Urban Trusts*. Discussion Paper in Conservation No. 46, Department of Biology, London: University College.

Moseley, M.J. (2000) 'England's Village Services in the late 1990s', *Town Planning Review* 71 (4): 415–33.

SEU (Social Exclusion Unit) (2001a) *A New Commitment to Neighbourhood Renewal: National Strategy Action Plan*. London: Cabinet Office.

Shaw, M., Dorling, D., Gordon, D. and Davey Smith, G. (2000) *The Widening Gap: Health Inequalities and Policy in Britain*. Bristol: Policy Press.

Wilson, H. (2004) *Villages and Service Retention: Does New Housing Help?* Unpublished Masters dissertation, Faculty of the Built Environment, UWE, Bristol.

5

DESCRIPTIVE QUESTIONS: SCOPE, CLAIMS AND SAMPLING

Key questions

What is the scope of my research?

What are data sources? What data sources should I use?

How can I select ('sample') the cases to study? What is the significance of representativeness in a sample?

Key concepts 🔑

Definitions, Data sources, Sampling units, Cases, Validity, Reliability, Representativeness, Empirical generalisation, Probabilistic sampling methods: Simple random sample, Systematic sampling, Stratified sampling, Cluster sampling. Non-probabilistic sampling methods: Snowball sampling, Quota sampling, Convenience sampling, Volunteer sampling, Judgement or Purposive sampling

Overview

If the starting point for a research design is the generation of a researchable question, which can be justified as one which is worthwhile to investigate, the following stages of research design are concerned with developing some convincing way of answering that question. This chapter examines the initial stage in this process. It deals with decisions on the **scope** of your research questions and the way that you might **sample** the **cases** to be investigated. It explains that scoping your research questions helps focus your research and makes the sampling or the selection of the specific cases you aim to investigate much easier. It discusses the reasons why the representativeness of your sample of cases is an important issue in research, and how this can be achieved, through probability sampling. Practical constraints, however, often mean that non-probability sampling has to be used. The type of research question I examine in this chapter is descriptive or 'what' questions, research questions where the purpose of the research is to provide a descriptive answer. 'What' questions may be investigated because the answer to the question, or the claim that you will make, is valuable in its own right, given what we know about the subject, or you may pose such a question as a precursor to posing a further 'why' question, the subject of the following chapter.

Scoping research questions

When we think about the scope of a piece of research, the way that research questions are posed is very important. Some researchers, and you may be one of these, start a project with, and typically aim to investigate, some precisely defined questions. You might have conducted a literature review which has revealed that there has been a good deal of previous research on the topic and, although further research might be needed, some of the core concepts have already been identified, and findings have been reported from previous studies.

But if you are investigating a topic about which the literature review suggests that there has been little or no previous research it would be sensible to start with a more open-ended exploratory question. Open-ended questions also have methodological justifications, influenced by the epistemological perspective of interpretivism. The argument here is that the researchers wish to avoid imposing their own interpretations of a situation on those involved in that situation, and to obtain the participants' views and perspectives (see Chapter 2, and the explanation given by Underwood for her research on planners in a London Borough). Researchers like Burgess et al. (1988) have also adopted this sort of open-ended question in the sense that they saw their research questions as ones 'to be explored and developed in the research process' (Mason, 1996: 15). They also, of course, claimed that there was something of a gap in the existing literature on the subject. Hence on both accounts, a more open-ended question seemed sensible.

Descriptive Questions

One problem with open-ended questions, though they might work for more experienced researchers with time to conduct their investigations, is that they do not provide by their nature much guidance on what exactly the research ought to be describing. They may also seem very ambitious for a small scale study. A useful way of avoiding this problem is to think about the scope of your research, including clarifying the definitions of the core concepts in your research, and the time and place to which it refers as far as you can. Box 5.1 raises scoping questions that should be asked of any research question but which are in this case applied to the proposed research question: What do people use open space for?

BOX 5.1

SCOPING YOUR RESEARCH QUESTIONS

1. What is the scope of the core concepts?

Are you interested in open space which is 'green'? How 'green' does it have to be? In some cities, people may have access to space which is not green but has 'hard landscaping' on which they can walk and play games, for example. Is this land to be counted as part of urban open space?

Are you interested in public open space to which everyone has access, at least in principle, or do we include private open space, like gardens or land previously used for industrial purposes (so-called brownfield land) but now 'green' and used informally by the local population and their children?

Is it open space *within* cities? As it stands, this would seem to be the meaning of the question. But you might be interested in the use of open space by urban residents, whether that open space is within or outside cities, for example space just outside the urban built up area of the city but within the administrative boundaries of the city.

And then there is the question of 'use'. What sorts of behaviours are to be investigated? There is a vast range of behaviours and uses that might be of interest. Is this leisure use or working use too? And would sitting somewhere and contemplating a piece of green space count as 'use' too?

2. What aspect of the topic are you interested in?

Are you interested in the behaviour of people using open space? Or the amount of time per week that people devote to these different behaviours? Or the experience of the use of open space? Or the attitudes and beliefs of those who use open space? Or all of them?

(Continued)

> *(Continued)*
>
> **3. What is the time frame for the description?**
>
> Is the interest in the current use of open space? Or is your interest in change over time in the use of urban open space? If so, over what timescale?
>
> **4. What is the geographical location for the description?**
>
> Open space in the whole country? Or in particular localities or regions?
>
> **5. How general is the description to be?**
>
> Do you want to describe patterns of use for different sub-groups of the population? For example, are you interested in descriptions of the use of open space by different age groups? Comparing older or younger people? Or men and women?
>
> **6. How abstract is your interest?**
>
> Are you just interested in the use of open space? Or are you interested in it as a reflection of something else? For example, as a way in which social capital might be built up in communities through shared activities in open space, or as a way that women's activity patterns are restricted by fear of male violence?
>
> *Source*: adapted from de Vaus (2001)

Each of the questions in Box 5.1 raises important considerations in refining and clarifying a piece of research. One important issue is to think about the core concepts in your question, and the definitions that you will use in your research. Definitions are important because we need to be as clear as possible about what we mean by the phenomenon we are researching. A number of commentators on planning have pointed to the often rather vague or fuzzy definitions in the field (Campbell, 2003; Taylor, 2003; de Roo and Porter, 2006). Taylor (2003) is particularly critical of the way that a whole series of different and sometimes conflicting objectives are wrapped up in the concept of 'sustainable development'. Campbell (2003) gives as examples: 'community', 'participation', 'social capital', 'inclusion'. She suggests that we might assume that these are all understood in the same way by users but in fact they might be interpreted differently. The significance of this in research terms is that different definitions of the phenomenon of interest will be likely to lead to quite different results, and when reviewing the literature it is important to establish which definitions have been used, and how they relate to the definition you have in mind.

The answers to these questions will have consequences for the decisions you have to make about selecting the sample of cases which you will investigate. Cases are 'the phenomena located in place and time' (Hammersley, 1990: 28) about which data will be obtained. The cases you can investigate in the time available for research, which I have suggested will be quite limited, are likely to be much more restricted in number than the total cases which you think might exist actually or potentially.

Sampling: Data sources and methods

The importance of paying attention to sampling has been underlined by Blaikie (2000: 197), 'Sampling is frequently the weakest and least understood part of research designs. The type of sample selected, and the method used to do so, can have a bearing on many other parts of a research design, and these decisions determine the type of conclusions that can be drawn from a study.'

An important first step in thinking about sampling is to think about the different data sources from which you could obtain data to answer your research question. The concept of a data source is sometimes used to describe a repository of secondary data, like the census or other official statistics from which data can be accessed. Data sources in this context has a different meaning, they are 'those places or phenomena from or through which you believe data can be generated' (Mason, 1996: 36). Much data in planning research is generated from people, but publications, administrative records, maps, plans, diagrams, and laws can all be seen as data sources for research. These data sources can also be used in conjunction with each other in any particular study. It is useful to try to think of data sources independently of methods of data collection, because data can sometimes be generated by a number of methods.

To continue with the open space example, are you interested in the different types of behaviour? If so, then obvious **places** which would be data sources are existing areas of open space, parks and green spaces in cities. Here different activities – playing football, jogging, dog walking, sitting quietly on a bench etc. – take place in a 'natural' setting so that people's behaviour could be observed by a researcher who could claim that s/he was not influencing the behaviour observed.

In practice, some activities would be easier to describe through observation than others. People playing football, for example, would seem to be easy to spot in the cultural context of the UK. But observation of someone walking on the open space might be impossible to categorise beyond the fact that they are 'walking'. What is classified as walking might cover people doing so because they are aiming to go shopping and are crossing the space to travel to the shop, or they may be walking to take some exercise, or they are taking their children to get some exercise ('let off steam', as it is known), or to lose weight, or as a situationist political gesture, as a way of getting in touch with the environment (in a way which is not possible in a car, for example). Here the data source would be the minds of the walkers involved, or in their interpretations of what they are doing, and in order to get at these, you would need to ask questions.

Asking questions would be necessary, too, if you were interested in the experience of the use of open space or their attitudes and beliefs about it. Now there are a number of different ways of doing this. You could ask them to complete a questionnaire, but as we saw in Chapter 2, Burgess et al. (1988) rejected this way of generating data about attitudes and values in relation to open space in cities. They advocated 'qualitative methods' and they chose a specific form of group interviewing as their method of data generation.

The time frame for the description of behaviour in open space is an important consideration. Current use in parks and open spaces is observable but there are likely to be changes in use over the seasons and over longer timescales. Most small-scale research cannot extend beyond a few months. So it will not be possible to study change over time unless you ask people about their current and past behaviour and experiences. A retrospective study faces the potential difficulties of people not being able to remember very reliably. And there is a sampling issue here too. Who do you ask? People currently using open space? If so, you may miss people who used to use it but no longer do so. Or people who live in the area where open space is available? There are problems here too. People who live in the area now are not the same people who lived in the area in the past. There will have been change through mobility, through the ageing of the population and births and deaths.

Sampling and the selection of cases to study

Once you have established the potential data sources you need in order to generate the data which will answer your descriptive research question, the next task is to think about the precise 'cases' you aim to investigate, and therefore to think about sampling. Here you need to think about the practicalities of research and the difference between the cases that you want to find out about, and the units you might have to sample.

Sampling units and cases

Sometimes the units you sample might not correspond with the cases you wish to examine. You might be interested in the behaviour (or practices) of planners when they are dealing with development proposals (rather than, say, producing plans or researching policy issues). In this situation they will be dealing with some, often diverging, interests from those proposing the development, local residents, and other members of local government. In a paper entitled 'What do planners do in the US?', Hoch (1996) is clearly interested in this topic. There are a very large number of planners in the US, and they deal with many development proposals, so that the population of potential cases of planner behaviour in relation to development proposals is large. But if we wanted to select a sample to investigate, it is pretty obvious that there is no listing of all the actions taken by planners in relation to these development proposals, from which you could sample some cases for investigation.

A practical approach is to start with something that is 'sampleable', in this case the planners as the data source, and use interviews with them as the means of generating data about their practices in relation to development proposals, which is what you are really interested in. You would need to identify a sample of planners in the US to interview, and these would be the sampling units selected, but it would be the behaviour of the planners in relation to the development proposals that would constitute the cases to be investigated. In Hoch's paper this would seem to be the approach he took, though the actual sample of cases investigated in total is not clear. He talks about his research on US planners, and selects accounts of their behaviour from just two planners, the implication being that these represent a very small sample of the cases he investigated. Their stories give details of four cases of developments with which the planners were involved, the problems they faced in these cases – lack of fairness or political favouritism, and the action they took to counter these problems and encourage practical democracy.

Validity and reliability

Mason (1996) has pointed out that sampling and the selection of cases to study are closely tied to questions of validity and reliability, concepts which inform the quality of the research conducted. Validity, in this context, concerns the extent to which in a piece of research the researcher is measuring what they say they are measuring. Are interviews with planners telling us about their actions in dealing with development proposals or more about their attitudes to developers or the public? If planners are talking about their own actions, for example, do they rationalise their behaviour after the event and give a positive version of what went on? Or do they describe what they would ideally have liked to do in those situations? If these accounts are thought to be inaccurate, then this will affect the validity of the description we develop. We may be worried about this but accept that this may be the only way of obtaining data about their behaviour. When reliability is at issue, the concern is usually with the uniformity of the way that, in this case, different planners are asked about the development proposals they have been involved in. An inconsistent approach may lead them to answer in different ways (and thus affect the validity of the research).

Representativeness and empirical generalisation

The widest set of potential cases from which your sample of cases is to be selected is called the **population**. The reason for selecting a sample rather than trying to cover the population is that: (a) it will often be unlikely that you could generate data about the population from the data sources you have identified because there are too many of them, indeed, there may be an infinite number of cases; or (b) some of them are inaccessible; or (c) you want to describe them in detail and, with a large sample of cases, this would not be practical within the time available.

To continue with the open space example, if you were interested in people's experiences of the use of open space, then, in any city or country there would be a very large number of 'experiences' you could potentially describe. This is because there are many people and many green spaces in cities, and each visit to a green space would provide an experience. Similarly, if you were interested in describing the characteristics of episodes of spatial strategy-making in city regions, or urban development proposals or the 'activities and practices of planners as they go about their work', the population of potential cases could be very large. However, some studies may have a smaller number of possible cases from which to generate data. If you are interested in the discourses which structure behaviour in spatial strategy-making then the number of discourses may well be small.

What is the relationship between the sample you select for study, and the wider population from which your sample has been drawn? If your interest is in describing behaviour or experiences, then, you may want your sample to be representative of that population.

Why might you be concerned with the representativeness of your sample?

You may be concerned with representativeness so that you can claim that the evidence from your sample can be generalised to the population. This would be using your sample to make an **empirical generalisation** about the population. Hoch (1996: 238), for instance, does generalise, if in a guarded way, at the end of his paper about the practices of planners dealing with development proposals in the US: 'We fail to see and we may even disdain, the subtle but pervasive political influence of planners who attend to fairness, the rules of civil society, political legitimacy, and their professional craft. That is, however, what planners do in the United States – not everywhere and not always, but remarkably often.' How often 'remarkably often' is, is not established and there could certainly be questions about the extent to which these cases establish the claim.

You might want to be able to generalise from your sample, if you are interested in describing 'typical' behaviour or experiences, experiences of open space use in cities, say, or the 'average' or 'mean' time that people spend exercising per week in parks and open spaces. Or you might want to break these typical or average experiences or behaviours down between men and women or young and old for various policy reasons, because, for example, there are concerns about obesity in the population at large, and you want to see which groups might need to be encouraged to exercise more (in the belief that exercise is a way of combating obesity). In general, the more you wish to describe the behaviour of subgroups of the population, the larger the sample of cases you will need to select.

Not every description you might wish to make will have to aim to be representative at national level, your population could be of more local or restricted nature. It is perfectly acceptable to describe planning practices in a specific place, indeed, some argue that many writers on planning have assumed that planning is a global activity, unvarying in its characteristics wherever it is practiced, and consequently these writers have paid insufficient attention to the context within which planning operates (Watson, 2002). But while the practices of planners in the context of heritage-led regeneration in Dorset could be an appropriate population to which to generalise, based on a sample of the practices actually studied, even this degree of generalisation is rejected by some researchers, who are merely happy to describe what happened at a particular place and time.

Why you might not be concerned with representativeness?

You may question the need to generalise from your sample of cases, believing that 'it is virtually impossible to imagine any human behaviour that is not heavily mediated by the context in which it occurs. One can easily conclude that generalizations that are intended to be context free will have little that is useful to say about human behavior' (Guba and Lincoln, 1982: 62, quoted in Gobo, 2008: 196). Here your research could be intended to give what is called an 'idiographic' account of some complex piece of behaviour, requiring detailed examination of the social processes and the context in which it takes place and you are not concerned with generalisation.

Other more practical reasons for not being concerned with representativeness, is that it would be too costly to conduct research which could be claimed to be representative because you only have a limited time available so the best you can do is investigate a few cases. You may also want to conduct some initial exploration of a social practice because your review of literature suggests that not much is known about it. Finally, it may not be possible to use probabilistic sampling methods which are designed to allow generalisation from a sample to a population, because there is a difficulty in finding a list of the population from which you can randomly select the sample. This is a significant problem in planning research (see below for some examples of the problem of existing lists for the sampling of residents).

Sampling methods

Sampling methods are conventionally divided into probabilistic and non-probabilistic sampling. If your sample is selected at random from a population (probability sampling), there are statistical methods which allow you to generalise to the population, with varying degrees of confidence, depending essentially on the size of the sample you can afford to investigate. Researchers who use quantitative methods are typically interested in the representativeness of their sample cases and the degree to which the description that they have produced from the sample investigated can be generalised to a wider population. Qualitative researchers, like Hoch discussed above, may also be interested in this issue. He is particularly clear about the wider population – the practices of planners in the US – that his selected cases are meant to represent, though often, as Hammersley (1992) points out, qualitative researchers do not spell out what the aggregate of cases is, a criticism which could also be extended to many quantitative researchers too.

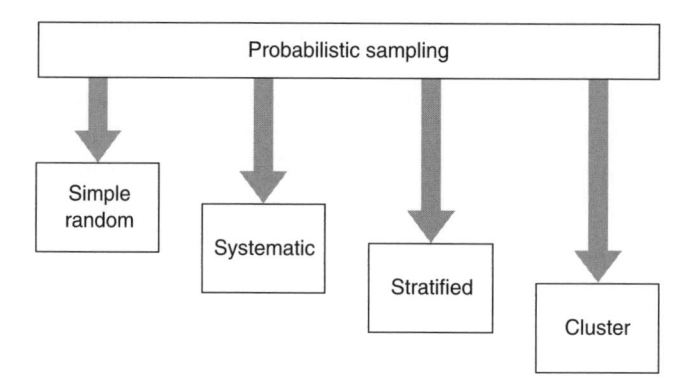

Figure 5.1 Types of Probabilistic Sampling

Probabilistic sampling methods

There are various methods of probability sampling (see Figure 5.1). According to Blaikie (2000), for example, the first of them sets the standard against which all other sampling methods are judged, though I would add only if the aim is to generalise to the population from which the sample has been selected. A **simple random sample** is one in which each sample of a given size from a population has the same chance of being selected (Blaikie, 2000). This, as with other methods of random sampling, requires a list – called a sample frame – of the population from which the sample can be selected, and the list to be numbered so that random numbers can be used to identify the cases to be sampled.

Systematic sampling is an approximation to the simple random sample method of sampling that requires you to be able to list the population of interest again. If, for example, there are 500 residents in a neighbourhood and you want to draw a sample of 50 people to interview about their use of open space then you would use a sampling ratio of 1 in 10. You would use a random method to determine the first case (amongst the first 10) to be selected on the list and then work though selecting each tenth subsequent case for your sample. You might use a list of residents as your sampling frame and the list from which you would draw your sample. The electoral register in the UK would give you the names and addresses of some residents (it excludes those who are ineligible to vote, and those who have asked for their names to be taken off the list) which can be purchased. In my experience, only about two thirds of those eligible to vote are listed. An alternative is to sample from the postcode address file, a list of residential addresses approximated by the addresses for 'small users' in each postcode area. Here there may be more than one resident at each address so some random sampling method within each address would be necessary, perhaps asking for the person whose birthday is nearest the date of questioning to answer the questions.

Stratified sampling is used when you want to ensure that a particular group is represented in your sample in at least the same proportion as the population, something which is not guaranteed with simple random sampling. You may be interested in ensuring that the use that young people make of open space is properly represented. This depends on you being able to identify young people from the rest of the population on the sample frame. If you can do this then, it would be possible to use stratified sampling. If young people represent 100 out of the population of 500 people then you could select 10 of your sample at random from the 100 young people and 40 from the rest of the population. In practice, there is no easy way of sampling young people as a group.

If you were particularly focussing on the behaviour and interests of young people, then, you might over-sample young people so that instead of having only 10 in your sample, you would select perhaps half the sample – 25 cases from young people and the other half of the sample from the older population. This would be disproportionate stratified sampling and might allow you to compare the behaviour and motivations of younger and older people, though the sample sizes here are quite small.

The importance of sample size with probabilistic sampling methods is that the larger the sample you have obtained, other things being equal, the more likely you are to find that any differences between your sub-groups are 'statistically significant', thus allowing you to make an empirical generalisation to a larger population with a known 'confidence level' (see Chapter 8). One of the other things that is usually 'not equal' is that the non-response to a survey based on a questionnaire can be very large, a problem which is highly likely to undermine the representativeness of the sample you have to work with and also of any wider generalisations you make.

Cluster sampling This method is used when it is impossible to obtain a sampling frame for the population you are interested in. To continue with the example above, if you are interested in the views and behaviours of young people, then, you might think that sampling them via school is a potentially viable way of doing so. A school would constitute a cluster of young people and you could select a sample within the school to constitute your cases for investigation. This has the advantage of getting at the cases you want but the disadvantage that the young people in the school you choose might not be representative of all young people. Another example of the use of cluster sampling could be in the study of the homeless in a city. You might select a hostel for the homeless as your cluster but this too might result in what would be considered a 'biased sample' because you would not be including in the homeless category those who choose not to stay in hostels, and perhaps sleep on the streets.

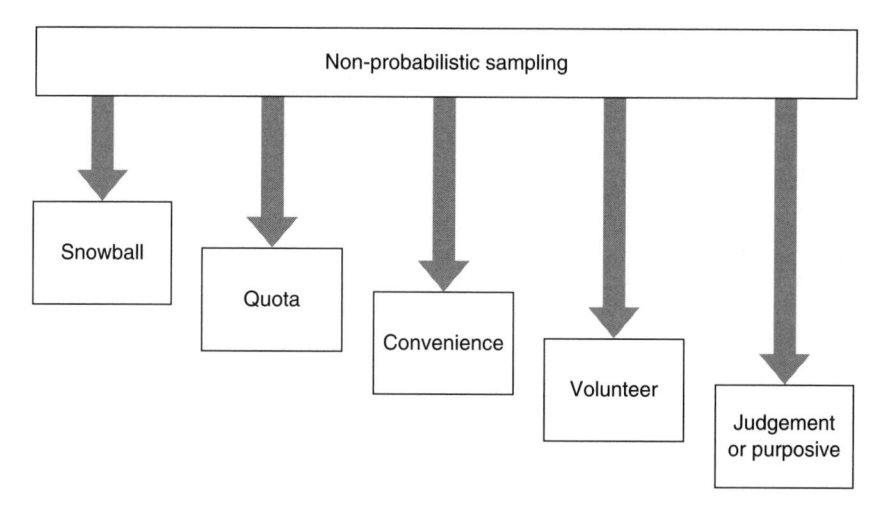

Figure 5.2 Types of Non-Probabilistic Sampling

Non-probabilistic sampling

However attractive the idea of random sampling might be, if one wants to generalise to a population from the sample of cases you investigate, it is very often the case that it is difficult, too time-consuming, or virtually impossible to identify all the members of the population from which you wish to sample. For many practical purposes planning researchers have to use another, non-probabilistic method of selecting the cases for investigation (Figure 5.2). Those using qualitative research methods typically use non-probabilistic sampling, and may not consequently be able to say much about representativeness.

The research by Burgess et al. (1988) illustrates two of these methods. If you look back to the extract from Burgess et al. (1988) in Chapter 2, you will see, first of all, that their sample of individuals who participated in the 4 group interviews lived in the London Borough of Greenwich. In another paper

(Burgess et al., 1990) where the different researchers in the team explain their interest in participating in the project, we see that Harrison was influenced by the perception that the debate in the 1980s about nature conservation and landscape protection via the planning system had neglected the 'unofficial countryside found in towns and waste places – the landscapes accessible to most people' (1990: 144) and neglected, too, the voice of 'the ordinary "consumer" of wildlife'. So the findings from the study can be seen to relate to the wider population of ordinary 'consumers of wildlife' living near open spaces in cities in Britain. The focus on Greenwich was somewhat accidental, in that two members of the team, Harrison and Goldsmith, were actively opposing the building of a bridge across the river Thames, a project which was threatening several open spaces in the borough. Harrison (Burgess et al., 1990: 144) wanted to focus on 'the attitudes and values of a cross-section of people living in one London borough'. Their sampling method involved the recruitment of individuals to participate in their four group interviews based on the neighbourhoods in which people lived in Greenwich. The neighbourhoods differed in socioeconomic and ethnic characteristics, housing types and open space supplies. They used what is known as **snowball sampling** as a method of recruitment, in which they first made contact with a wide variety of community groups in each neighbourhood and were then 'passed on to friends and neighbours who might be interested in the project' (Burgess et al. 1988: 457 footnote 2). The advantage of this approach is that you speed up the process of finding willing participants in the research, but the disadvantage is that the groups who participated in the group interviews are likely to be composed of friendship networks, and may not have been representative of the population of the borough. There was an Asian women's group but not an Asian men's group, for example.

In order to get some measure of the generalizability of the findings from the group interviews or, as Burgess et al. (1988) put it, the extent to which 'the values expressed in the groups were shared in the wider community' they conducted a household survey. This is a strategy suggested by Hammersley and Atkinson (1995) as one that qualitative researchers might use for this purpose. As a way of selecting the sample they used **quota sampling**, a method in which the researchers identify the characteristics of the sample to be selected in advance. For example, you might divide the sample to be selected into two categories according to age (young/old) and two categories according to gender (male/female) on the grounds that you think that these characteristics will have an impact on the way that people use open space. This would give four sample categories and you might decide to select 25 respondents in each sub-group giving a total of 100 respondents to be selected. The criteria used by Burgess et al. (1988) are given in the extract in Box 5.2.

Descriptive Questions

BOX 5.2

EXAMPLE – QUOTA SAMPLING AS USED BY BURGESS ET AL. (1988)

We wished to explore the extent to which some of the values expressed in the groups were shared in a wider community and so we undertook a household survey in the borough. One of the most persistent themes in all four groups was the extent to which the supply of open land in particular localities affected the ways in which people perceived and used open spaces. In consequence, we rejected a random sample of households and chose instead a quota sample based on the same areas in which the group members lived. We sampled from two neighbourhood types as defined by the CACI Acorn Types (CACI, 1983) in Eltham, Plumstead and Thamesmead. In each case, one neighbourhood was characterised by high levels of owner-occupation and higher socio-economic groups, the other by high levels of rented accommodation and lower socio-economic groups. This allowed some comparison to be made between neighbourhoods whose residents might be expected to have differential access to more distant open spaces, both in the urban area and beyond it. Two further samples were taken from an area in Woolwich: one of white, the other of Asian households. This gave a total of eight sub-samples from which 25 households were targeted. In the event, slightly more interviews were achieved in some sample groups and a total of 212 interviews were completed.

Source: Burgess et al. (1988: 458–9)

Burgess et al. did not use age and gender, which are rather conventional demographic criteria, but three different ones. First, they wanted their quota sample to cover people living in areas with different levels of open land, this being one of the criteria used to divide neighbourhoods for snowball sampling in the first phase of the research and which they argued was confirmed through the group interviews as being an influence on the way that people perceived and used open space. Second, within these localities, they wanted to divide their sample units between those who were restricted to the use of local open space because they lacked access to transport, and those who could access more distant open spaces. They did not measure this directly but assumed that different types of neighbourhood as measured in the CACI Acorn Types, which have different levels of owner-occupation and of socio-economic groups, would also be associated with different levels of car ownership and thus of mobility. Sampling within these contrasting types of area would be likely to produce a sample with these different characteristics, although this is by no means guaranteed. Finally, they wanted to obtain respondents representing different ethnic groups (white/Asian). For convenience, because the Asian population was over-represented in one neighbourhood in the borough (Woolwich) they wanted to select respondents on the basis of ethnic origin in this locality. So they ended up with eight selection categories, and as they decided to sample the same number in each of the sub-sample categories, as illustrated in the Table 5.1, this gave a target sample size of 200 respondents. They do not report here how they selected the respondents for interview within these areas. Whatever the method, the researchers continue their work until the quota of interviews has been completed.

It is interesting that they rejected probabilistic random sampling. They did so because a random sample of households in Greenwich would not necessarily have selected cases which would have had the experience of living in the different types of area, in terms of open space provision, that they wanted to reflect in their sample. This criticism is true of random sampling; a random sample may have under-sampled or over-sampled people living in 'open space rich' and 'open space poor' localities. This is a problem that could have been overcome by the use of probabilistic stratified sampling as we saw above. I suspect that in practice, however, it would have been difficult to develop an adequate sampling frame for the population of the Borough of Greenwich, and the researchers saw quota sampling as 'economical, easy to administer and quick to do in the field' (Blaikie, 2000: 205).

Table 5.1 Framework for Quota Sampling in Greenwich Neighbourhoods

Open space provision	Social characteristics of neighbourhoods and target quota sample size	
Rich variety of open spaces (Eltham)	Higher access to open space 25	Lower access to open space 25
New parks and wild remnants of scrub and marsh (Thamesmead)	Higher access to open space 25	Lower access to open space 25
Two large commons but few local parks (Plumstead)	Higher access to open space 25	Lower access to open space 25
A common and some local parks (Woolwich)	Asian 25	White 25

Source: Based on Burgess et al., 1988: 457

Convenience sampling is a method of sampling which, as its name suggests, uses a convenient sample of cases to examine an issue. These cases were readily accessible to the researcher when needed. The final selection of cases in quota sampling as described above can be seen as a method of convenience sampling within the framework of the categories set up in advance.

Volunteer sampling arises when those who participate in the study volunteer to do so, in response to an advertisement or general request to play a role in the research.

Judgement or purposive sample is when the researcher selects a 'typical' or 'interesting' case or cases for study. An example of this purposive sampling strategy, involving the selection of a variety of cases, is to be found in the study by Brindley et al. (1996: iv) of 'the varieties of planning practice in the Thatcher years' in Britain. The cases they selected for study were based on a theory in which the nature of planning practice in a locality is influenced by two factors. First, what was perceived to be the nature of the urban problem (or how much pressure for development there was) in an area. This factor led them to distinguish three levels of market pressure: buoyant areas, marginal areas, derelict areas. Second, the attitude of key actors to the market, which was divided between market critical and market-led attitudes. These two criteria produced six varieties of planning practice, and the authors selected cases of planning practice which met these criteria for detailed description. Here I suspect, as with the quota sampling used by Burgess et al. (1988), the final selection of cases within the six broad categories of planning practice they identified was to use convenient cases known to the research team. With their category of *popular planning*: 'planning by local communities in their own neighbourhoods. It involves both the formulation of planning proposals and their implementation by local community organizations' (1996: 74), there were probably not many more cases beyond Coin Street in London.

Table 5.2 Framework for Purposive Case Selection: Styles of Planning in Great Britain

	Attitude to market processes	
Perceived nature of urban problems	Market-critical	Market-led
Buoyant area: minor problems and buoyant market	The Cambridge area	Colchester, Essex
Marginal area: pockets of urban problems and potential market interest	Coin Street, London	London Docklands
Derelict area: comprehensive urban problems and depressed market	Glasgow Eastern Area Renewal Project	Stockbridge Village, Knowsley

Source: Adapted from Brindley et al., 1996: Table 2.1

Summary/Key lessons

In this chapter I have suggested that, having developed a researchable question, an important step in research design is to focus your research question and to think about cases you might investigate, and the justification that there might be for a particular method of sampling:

1. You can focus your research question by clarifying and defining the nature of the **core concepts** in your question and setting limits to the scope of your research interests by defining the time frame and geographical focus for your research. This makes decisions on the selection of the specific cases you will investigate, and about which you will generate data, much more straightforward.

2. It is important to distinguish between the **cases** which you are interested in studying, which may not be immediately accessible, or observable, and the **data sources**, that is the people or places from which information about the cases may be obtained through some method of data generation.

3. Given that it is normally impossible to investigate every case of a given phenomenon (the **population**), a key decision in moving your design work on is to think about the **sample** of cases to be investigated. Data sources may be sampled in order to obtain data on the cases you are investigating, the data sources are then **sampling units**.

4. In selecting a sample do you want the sample to be 'representative' of that population? Unless the sample is intrinsically interesting the attempt to answer a 'what' question often seeks to describe some case(s) of behaviour or events or practices which is/are representative. That is, you may well want to make some **empirical generalisation** to a broader population on the basis of the research.

5. Where the aim is representativeness, and there is some feasible way of selecting a random sample from that population, then **random sampling** provides a sensible strategy to adopt. However, in many research situations, random sampling is not possible and you may have to use alternative **non-probability** methods of sampling.

Exercise: Focusing your research question

Apply the questions in Box 5.1 to your own proposed research questions. In addition to the definition of core concepts, it is important to think about the time frame for research, the geographical location, how general your description is to be, and how abstract your interest is in the topic.

Sampling of cases

Think about the answers to the following questions:

1. What 'data sources' are available to help you answer your research question?
2. What wider population are your cases to be selected from? How important is it that your cases should 'representative' of this wider population?
3. What methods of sampling might you use? Probabilistic or non-probabilistic?
4. What specific 'cases' might you be interested in investigating?

Further Reading

For an example of a piece of planning research which used a sample frame of planners in the United States and was based on probability sampling, a simple random sample, see Hoch, C. (1988) 'Conflict at Large: a National Survey of Planners and Political Conflict', *Journal of Planning Education and Research* 8 (1): 25–34.

The paper by Burgess et al. (1988) on which I draw in this chapter illustrates a number of methods of non-probability sampling: Burgess, J., Harrison, C.M. and Limb, M. (1988) 'People, Parks and the Urban Green: a Study of Popular Meanings and Values for Open Spaces in the City', *Urban Studies* 25: 455–73.

White (2009) provides very useful guidance on refining research questions: White, P. (2009) *Developing Research Questions*. Basingstoke: Palgrave Macmillan.

Books which discuss sampling and the selection of cases in the context of research design are:

Blaikie, N. (2000) *Designing Social Research*. Cambridge: Polity.

de Vaus, D. (2001) *Research Design in Social Research*. London: Sage.

Gorard, S. (2013) *Research Design: Creating Robust Approaches for the Social Sciences*. London: Sage.

Greener, I. (2011) *Designing Social Research*. London: Sage.

References

Blaikie, N. (2000) *Designing Social Research*. Cambridge: Polity.
Brindley, T., Rydin, Y. and Stoker, G. (1996) *Remaking Planning: the Politics of Urban Change*. London: Routledge.

Burgess, J., Harrison, C.M. and Limb, M. (1988) 'People, Parks and the Urban Green: a Study of Popular Meanings and Values for Open Spaces in the City', *Urban Studies* 25: 455–73.

Burgess, J., Goldsmith, B. and Harrison, C. (1990) 'Pale Shadows for Policy: Reflections on the Greenwich Open Space Project', *Studies in Qualitative Methodology* 2: 141–67.

Campbell, H. (2003) 'Talking the Same Words but Speaking Different Languages: the Need for More Meaningful Dialogue', *Planning Theory and Practice* 4 (4): 389–92.

de Roo, G. and Porter, G. (2006) *Fuzzy Planning: The Role of Actors in a Fuzzy Governance Environment*. Aldershot: Ashgate.

de Vaus, D. (2001) *Research Design in Social Research*. London: Sage.

Gobo, G. (2008) 'Reconceptualizing generalization: Old Issues in a New Frame', in P. Alasuutari, L. Bickman and J. Brannen (eds) *The Sage Handbook of Social Research Methods*. London: Sage. pp. 193–213.

Greener, I. (2011) *Designing Social Research*. London: Sage.

Guba, E.G. and Lincoln, Y. S. (1982) 'Epistemological and Methodological Bases of Naturalistic Inquiry', *Educational Communication and Technology Journal* 30: 233–52.

Hammersley, M. (1990) *Reading Ethnographic Research: A Critical Guide*. London: Longman.

Hammersley, M. (1992) *What's Wrong with Ethnography?* London: Routledge.

Hammersley, M. and Atkinson, P. (1995) *Ethnography: Principles in Practice*. London: Routledge.

Hoch, C. (1996) 'What Do Planners Do in the United States?' in S.J. Mandelbaum, L. Mazza and R.W. Burchell, (eds) *Explorations in Planning Theory*. New Brunswick, NJ: Rutgers, the State University of New Jersey. pp. 225–40.

Mason, J. (1996) *Qualitative Researching*. London: Sage.

Taylor, N. (2003) 'More or Less Meaningful Concepts in Planning Theory (and How to Make Them More Meaningful): A Plea for Conceptual Analysis and Precision', *Planning Theory,* 2 (2): 91–100.

Watson, V. (2002) 'Conflicting Rationalities: Implications for Planning Theory and Ethics', *Planning Theory and Practice* 4 (4): 395–407.

6

EXPLANATORY QUESTIONS: STARTING POINTS, CLAIMS AND SAMPLING

Key questions

What are the starting points for answering a 'why' question?

What are the different ways that you can explain why something happened? What criticisms are made of causal analysis in planning?

How can you establish the existence of a causal relationship? What wider claims can you make about this on the basis on your research?

How can you select the cases for study?

What are case studies?

Key concepts

Causal explanation, Understanding, Meanings, Theoretical generalisation, Principle of induction, Falsification, Association, Internal validity, External validity, Judgement or purposive sampling, Critical case sampling, Maximum variation sampling, Theoretical sampling, Thick description, Case studies

Overview

The previous chapter examined the scoping of research questions, and the issues involved in sampling cases to be investigated to answer descriptive questions. This chapter discusses 'why' or explanatory questions where the purpose is to make whatever is the subject of the research intelligible or less puzzling. The first part of the chapter discusses briefly the different starting points for answering such a question: some researchers start with a hypothesis while other researchers are more open-minded about the answer that might emerge from the research. The next sections explore in some detail the difference between seeking a causal explanation or an understanding of a situation, the criticisms that are levelled at causal analysis of social life, and the question of the wider claims or theoretical generalisations that might be made on the basis of a piece of research. Finally, the way in which a sample of cases might be selected is reviewed.

Starting points

The starting point for any piece of research which poses an explanatory or 'why' question is pretty obviously that there is some puzzle thrown up by previous research which needs to be explained. There may be some evidence from a review of literature that there is a difference in behaviour between people or differences in patterns of social life. For example, if some descriptive research has documented differences in the amount of affordable housing provided in different places in Britain, then the puzzle here would be in finding out why this has happened. You want to work back from the current situation to find some explanation for why it has come about. Another possibility is that there is evidence that something has happened and you want to know what effect it has had. In this case there might be an interest in assessing the impact of policy, in examining the outcome of policy. Has a policy had the effect intended, or the effect I am interested in? This sort of question is of key concern in planning policy debates. Has building new housing in rural settlements helped those settlements retain local services? Has the provision of local services with new housing developments reduced the amount of travel undertaken by people living in those areas?

Where, as in the former situation, the question is rather an open one, there could be many different factors or explanations for the variable delivery across space of affordable housing, and this research question therefore does not provide much focus or guidance on what sort of research to conduct, and what sort of data to generate. Questions about the impact of policy in relation to the objectives set for the policy do provide much more help in this respect.

Explanatory Questions

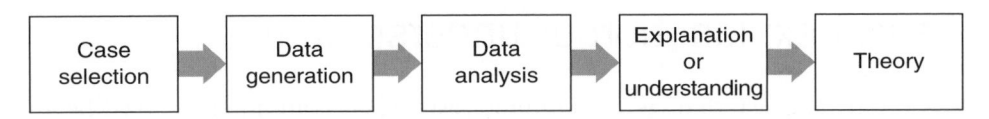

```
┌───────────┐   ┌───────────┐   ┌───────────┐   ┌─────────────┐   ┌────────┐
│   Case    │──▶│   Data    │──▶│   Data    │──▶│ Explanation │──▶│ Theory │
│ selection │   │generation │   │ analysis  │   │     or      │   │        │
│           │   │           │   │           │   │understanding│   │        │
└───────────┘   └───────────┘   └───────────┘   └─────────────┘   └────────┘
```

Figure 6.1   Inductive Approach to Explanation and the Development of Theory

Where the question is open, some researchers adopt, and advocate, an open-ended **inductive** exploration of the data in the cases they investigate working towards an explanation for the puzzle (see Figure 6.1). Of course, it is impossible to start a project with no pre-conceived ideas, so however open-minded you intend to be there has to be some initial set of guiding ideas to focus the research, and there is benefit in scoping your question in the same way as I suggested for descriptive questions in the last chapter. But for students, I think that there can be considerable benefits in identifying a hypothesis which you think might be the answer. The sources of these hypotheses are varied. For example, your review of the academic literature might have revealed that, in a previous paper, a particular explanation had been proposed by the researcher for differences between places. You may have decided to take this explanation and treat it as a hypothesis to be tested, justifying it in terms of the sorts of reasons for further research set out in Box 4.1. People involved in the situation as practitioners may have their own explanations as presented in papers in professional journals or elsewhere, or you may have your own idea or hunch about why it happens, and use this as basis for your research. This is a **deductive** approach to explanation (see Figure 6.2). The hypothesis provides guidance on the sorts of cases to be selected, the data to be collected and the analysis to conduct. The explanation may be supported by the evidence from the study or it may be found wanting and rejected. This approach is thought to be associated with researchers who use quantitative methods, though it is not restricted to such methods and this approach can also be used by qualitative researchers too (see Mason, 1996).

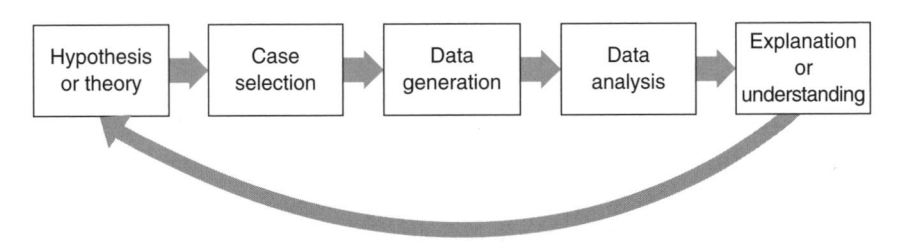

```
┌───────────┐   ┌───────────┐   ┌───────────┐   ┌───────────┐   ┌─────────────┐
│Hypothesis │──▶│   Case    │──▶│   Data    │──▶│   Data    │──▶│ Explanation │
│ or theory │   │ selection │   │generation │   │ analysis  │   │     or      │
│           │   │           │   │           │   │           │   │understanding│
└───────────┘   └───────────┘   └───────────┘   └───────────┘   └─────────────┘
      ▲                                                                 │
      └─────────────────────────────────────────────────────────────────┘
```

Figure 6.2   Deductive Approach to Explanation and the Development of Theory

Causal explanation or understanding?

I want to suggest that as a planning researcher your interest may be in explaining why something happened in the situation you are studying by identifying the factors or causes involved. Alternatively, you may be much more interested in understanding why something happened by looking at the world views or perspectives of those involved in the situation and looking at the reasons which people give for their actions and the meaning of their action in the context in which they were acting. Of course, you could look both at factors and at reasons on the grounds that how people respond to a situation and how they explain their intentions in acting in a particular way may be shaped by contextual factors of which they are unaware. The assumptions you make here will take your research in different directions.

Rydin (2007: 53) makes a strong case for the role of causal explanation in planning research. She argues that:

> Knowledge differs from information and data in that the specification of a causal relationship is central to knowledge. This is why knowledge is of such central relevance to planning. Since planning seeks to create specific impacts, planners need to understand how such impacts follow from specific planning actions; they need to understand the causal relationships between action and impact.

If we see an explanation as an answer to a 'why' question relating to a specific case or cases investigated in a research project, it is convincing as an explanation because it draws on a theory. What is theory? Theories 'are concerned with why one type of phenomenon tends to produce another (other things being equal) wherever instances of that type occur.' (Hammersley, 1990: 48). They thus are concerned with causal relations and the derivation of laws. Explanation in this model works on the logic of 'If C then E. If no C, then no E.' (Fay, 1996). This is sometimes described as the constant conjunction model of causation. Laws have in principle universal applicability. But this is where the problem with theory in planning and social science more generally is said to arise, say the critics (see Fischer, 2003).

Those who challenge the idea of universal applicability highlight the meanings, the self-understandings and intentions behind social action. The objects of social science, it is said, are intentional phenomena (Fay, 1996). We understand them because we understand the meaning of the action concerned. As we saw with people using open space, we need to understand what it means to the person involved when we see people walking or running across a park. Are they going shopping but crossing the space to get to the shop? Or are they taking exercise to keep fit? These meanings can change over time as new ideas develop and new sets of intention are created. Jogging is a recent activity. 60 years ago it would not have been possible to study jogging because it did not exist as a recreational activity. Applying for planning permission did not exist before the development of state control over land use. The point here is that at best causal generalisations can only apply to particular historical periods. Flyvbjerg (2001: 39) makes this point when he argues that theory – in the sense of universal, context-free theory – does not exist and probably never will. The social context changes what it means to engage in an action. So perhaps the idea of theory whose applicability is restricted to certain historical periods is what he means by the description of the theory he uses, which he sees as 'soft' theory or 'non-predictive theory'. (Nevertheless, this does not stop him drawing on Nietzsche and Machiavelli from earlier historical periods for theoretical inspiration!)

Identifying causes

The ideal logic for identifying causes is, in the view of researchers who see social research as a scientific activity, to use experimental methods as employed in the natural sciences (see Preece, 1990). But in social research, it is extremely rare to have the degree of control over the subjects of research to be able to use experiments, and there are ethical reasons why one should not experiment on people. If something is thought to be good, then everyone should be given the opportunity to benefit from it. Sometimes public programmes provide opportunities for researchers to examine the effect of changes introduced by the programme, perhaps through the funding of pilot programmes (see Deyle and Slotterback (2009), for an example), or through the gradual implementation of the policy which allows some comparison of areas where the policy was implemented first with areas not the initial subject of the policy (see Hopton and Hunt (1996) for an example in relation to housing improvement in an area of damp housing).

But usually the best that can be hoped for, for those who are interested in causal analysis is that there will be some 'natural experiment' that might be investigated in order to detect the impact of a particular factor. This usually involves making a comparison between places or groups of people who have experienced different exposures to a particular factor. Planning research is often concerned with assessing the outcome of policy (see Chapter 3). In rural planning policy, for instance, some settlements may have been designated as key settlements and have, over a number of years, experienced considerable housing growth whilst others have had very restricted housing growth. If the aim of the policy is to retain local services in the key settlements, then one could compare the decline of services in the two types of settlement to see if the key settlements have fared better in this respect.

Sometimes planning researchers are interested in assessing, in advance of the implementation of the policy, whether a particular policy might have the beneficial effects predicted for it. Is a policy which is proposed to increase social mix in areas where there is currently an overwhelmingly deprived population likely to change the lives of those living in the area? Atkinson and Kintrea (2001), whose work we examined in previous chapters, identified neighbourhoods which had higher and lower levels of poverty (or deprived and socially mixed neighbourhoods as they called them) and attempted to establish some of the differences between the experiences of those living in these areas. The starting point of the research was a range of hypotheses about possible area effects derived from theories in the literature, particularly in the review by Ellen and Turner (1997). These area effects work through 'mechanisms' which have both primary and secondary outcomes and lead to the 'wider reinforcement of deprivation'. For example, the mechanisms which produce or cause the concentration of poor people in an area in turn cause an area to have a poor reputation and thus stigmatise the area and the people living in it as a primary outcome. The hypothesis therefore predicts that if an area has a concentration of poor people it will get a poor reputation. This was tested by examining the experience of residents in the two types of neighbourhood. Atkinson and Kintrea (2001) asked the residents of deprived and mixed neighbourhoods whether they thought their area had a poor reputation and whether they found it difficult to get jobs as a result of the poor reputation of the area. The results were also consistent with the theory: many of the residents of the deprived areas reported a poor reputation whilst those living in the mixed areas were very much less likely to report this. Some of the difficulties of this type of approach to causal analysis are examined again in Chapter 8.

Theoretical generalisation

How do we know as researchers whether there is a causal link between the factor we think accounts for, or explains, the regularity we are interested in? You cannot see a causal relationship but 'Causes and effects are ideas used to encapsulate a firm impression that we have about the way the world works' (Gorard, 2013: 61). And to claim a causal relationship is to make a universal claim about what will happen whenever the causal conditions are met.

Although we can never be certain that we have established the existence of a causal relationship, various attempts have been made to set out the conditions which would need to be met before we could have some 'reasonable' belief in the existence of such a relationship. One key element is an association between the two phenomena, that is, as set out above, if one thing is present then the other is also present, and when one is absent the other is absent. Some researchers argue (though this is often implicit in what they say about their research) that the more evidence that we have that the supposed cause is always linked to the effect, then the more certain we can be that there is indeed a causal relationship between the two. This is the **principle of induction** (see Chalmers, 1999). This means that the plausibility of a causal claim is unlikely to be convincing on the evidence of one piece of research alone, rather the plausibility has to be judged in the light of this piece of research and all the other work reported in the literature. There is thus a cumulative impact of research findings on this model. Bradford Hill (1965) quoted in Hopton and Hunt (1996), a paper on the health effects of improvement to housing, set out the criteria as shown in Box 6.1.

BOX 6.1

CRITERIA FOR ASSESSING THE EXISTENCE OF A CAUSAL RELATIONSHIP

- Strength of association, consistency in observing the association in different circumstances or groups of people
- That the association should be specific (specificity), (and cannot be accounted for by other obvious variables)
- That one variable should be consistently present before the other (temporality)
- That an increase in one variable is associated with an increase in the other
- That there is a plausible explanation for the association
- That there is experimental evidence for the association

Source: adapted from Hopton and Hunt (1996)

The first four of these deal with the nature of the association between the variables. Atkinson and Kintrea (2001) argued in their justification for further research (as we saw in Chapter 4) that there was American evidence for the existence of area effects but there was little evidence for such effects in British cities. They could be seen as arguing for evidence of an association to meet the first of Bradford Hill's criteria: evidence from the 'different circumstances' of Britain, or the different 'groups of people' to be found in Britain. This, in turn, might be interpreted as a call for 'more evidence' to provide further inductive support for the belief in a causal relationship. And it is certainly possible that the mechanisms that produce area effects do not work in all contexts. This emphasis on the context within which mechanisms may or may not operate is a view of causation which is associated with the 'realist' model (see Pawson and Tilley, 1997) or the retroductive model of causation (see Blaikie, 2000). Atkinson and Kintrea (2001) identified national, regional, city and neighbourhood contexts which may affect the operation of the mechanisms affecting the production of area effects. Differing contexts may also affect the success of planning interventions. Careful negotiations with landowners for the provision of some affordable housing on a housing site which is to be developed can be successful where land values and development pressures are high but the same approach to negotiation can be noticeably less successful where the context is one of lower land values and lower development pressures (Farthing and Ashley, 2002).

Time order means that in the case of an association between variables, causes have to come before effects, and not the other way round. So concentrations of poor people have to come before the bad reputation in order for the concentration of the poor to be the cause of a bad reputation. But when we are measuring the two things at the same time, as Atkinson and Kintrea (2001) were in their research, then we do not know whether the bad reputation followed or preceded the concentration of poor people. It is possible that a place might get a poor reputation, and then only the least powerful people (the poor) would accept housing in such a place (see Figure 6.3).

When we are dealing with the social sciences, we are looking for the social mechanisms by which a concentration of poor people might get a poor reputation. One possibility might be reports of crime in the local media, and the assumed association of criminal activity with these areas.

As everyone is always taught (or should be), association or correlation does not mean causation. The criterion about experimental evidence is that this method is supposed to give the researcher control over the situation so that it will eliminate the impact of other factors, allowing the researcher to concentrate on the factor (or independent variable as it is commonly expressed) of interest and its impact on the factor to be explained (or the dependent variable). In these circumstances, the study is said to have **'internal validity'** (a term introduced by Campbell and Stanley (1966)).

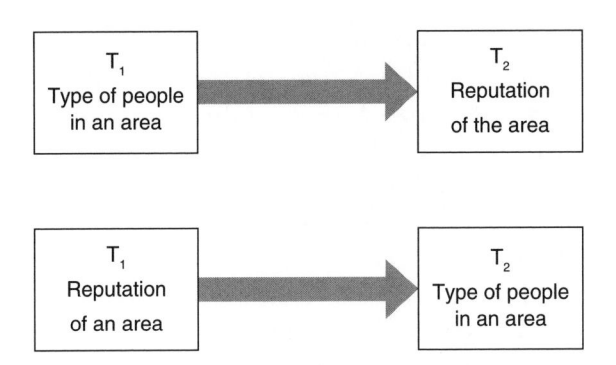

```
       T₁                            T₂
  Type of people      ──────▶      Reputation
    in an area                     of the area


       T₁                            T₂
    Reputation        ──────▶    Type of people
    of an area                     in an area
```

Figure 6.3 The Importance of Time Order in Casual Analysis: Alternative Explanations for an Association between the Type of People Living in an Area and an Area's Reputation

If you are using a 'natural' experiment then in addition to the factors of interest there may well be other factors, confounding factors, which get in the way of your interpretation of the evidence. These have been described as threats to 'internal validity' by Cook and Campbell (1979) who listed a series of such threats. The complexity of the factors involved in the situations studied by social researchers is well known, and Atkinson and Kintrea (2001) acknowledged some of these in their study. First, the fact that in addition to different levels of poverty, the neighbourhoods they selected for study were at different distances from jobs and services so some of the 'area effects' could be due to these factors and not to poverty per se. A second confounding factor was the possibility that the characteristics of the poor people in the different neighbourhoods were not identical so that some of the apparent area effects could be due to these differences rather than the concentration of poverty. As Gorard (2013: 69) concludes 'This means that the results of our experiments in social research are not generally clear-cut. We have to judge whether our findings are substantial enough to be worth taking note of'. It is therefore worthwhile, in any piece of research where a causal explanation is offered, to be aware of likely problems in your study and to acknowledge them.

There is a problem with the logic of induction, with the collection of more evidence to support a theory, though many social researchers tend to ignore it in their research practice. The problem is that we can never be certain that the relationship we have observed many times is universal or 'generalisable', that is true for all times and places, (or even generalizable, in the more restricted sense discussed above, to the conditions existing in our current historical period). Another study might always be observed which contradicts the claimed causal relationship. This problem is sometimes described as the problem of **'external validity'**.

This consideration feeds into the idea behind 'falsification' as an alternative approach to the logic of research, associated with the philosophy of Karl Popper (see Chalmers (1999) for a helpful discussion of this approach). If we can find just one case where one thing is present and the other is absent, if we find one case where there is a concentration of poor people but the area does not have a poor reputation, then, we know that we are not dealing with a simple causal relationship. A concentration of poor people in an area might still be a necessary condition for a poor reputation to be established for an area, and for the people who live in it, but it is not sufficient alone to produce a poor reputation. Hence we can falsify our theories. The logic of this thinking is to argue that rather than looking for evidence which will support our belief in the link, which is the logic of induction, we should instead try to look for situations where the association does not hold. This will have an impact on the cases which we aim to sample in our research (see below) and lead us to try to develop hypotheses about the other factors which might be involved in the situation. Social research can thus develop by eliminating hypotheses that have been shown to be false. Amongst planning researchers, Flyvbjerg (2001) is an advocate of this approach to social research.

Whilst there are arguments against the logic of the inductive approach – the more evidence we have, the better the approach – there are arguments against the practice of the falsificationist logic. How do we know that any piece of evidence, which appears to falsify a hypothesis, is to be trusted? One could always criticise the research rather than the hypothesis.

The debate about the justification of claims to knowledge by either invoking an inductive approach (the argument that 'the evidence is building up') or the falsification approach (the argument that 'the theory has been falsified') goes back to the point made in Chapter 2 about the 'provisional' nature of research findings and the judgements made by groups of researchers about the plausibility of research findings, especially ones that challenge key hypotheses or assumptions associated with a particular theory. What this means is that empirical research can never give us absolute certainty about causal relationships (or anything else). The research you conduct might be consistent with previous hypotheses or it might be inconsistent with them. But you need to be aware of the complexity of real life situations, that there are many factors involved, many of which may interact with each other, and research will be unable to control for all these possible threats to the validity of its findings. You need to be aware of, and acknowledge, therefore, the necessary limitations of what you have been able to do.

Understanding social life

Planning researchers such as Innes (1990) who emphasise the need to 'understand' or make sense of social life argue that research does not give us direct access to 'social reality' but only to interpretations of reality which reflect the concepts and frames of reference which we employ.

The aim of researchers who adopt this view of social research (Hammersley, 1990) is to 'make sense' of the actions and responses of people to the situations they face. To the question 'why did they act in this way?' the answer is because of the way they interpreted the situation they were in, and the way that they responded to that situation in what they saw as an appropriate manner. Hence the emphasis is on understanding the beliefs, values and attitudes in the minds of those involved in the situation and providing 'rounded understandings' (Mason, 1996) which take account of complexity, detail and context. The world views of the public for whom planners plan have been neglected, it is asserted, and this ought to be the subject of research. Watson (2003) argues that planners make assumptions about the values, beliefs, and rationalities of those for whom or, with whom, they plan, but these assumptions she claims frequently do not hold. A similar perspective lay behind the research of Burgess et al. (1988) into the views of ordinary people about nature and open space in cities, views which had not previously been examined. And those who take this approach emphasise the diversity of perspectives or ways of orienting to the world to be found in contemporary cities (Sandercock, 1998) and the multiple perceptions of urban experience and its significance, which need to be understood if the behaviour of different individuals and groups is to be explained.

The world views or the 'assumptive worlds' (Young and Mills, 1981) of policy actors, decision-makers and planners themselves are also key to understanding the nature of policies which are developed in an area. In policy contexts, Innes (1990: 23) uses the concept of 'myth' to describe 'a usually traditional story of ostensibly historic events that serves to unfold part of the world view of a people or explain a practice, belief or natural phenomenon.' More recently still the term 'discourse' has been used to describe a world view or a more general way of thinking in the minds of policy actors 'the policy language and metaphors mobilised in focusing, justifying and legitimating a policy programme or project' (Healey, 2007: 22). 'Planning teams are often not just embedded in particular policy communities, but they are also tied together both by particular traditions that provide ways of thinking about issues and priorities, and by particular practices of manipulating knowledge' (Healey, 2007: 242–3).

The term 'discourse' is also used by scholars who are interested in finding out not just what the world views of policy actors, decision-makers and planners are, not just describing what is in their minds, and why they therefore act in the way they do but *why* they think in the way they do in the first place. Here there has been an interest in the role of official discourses enshrined in planning documents, particularly in the case of UK planning in the documents produced by central government and the devolved administrations, which are aimed at guiding the practice of planners. I discuss this further in Chapter 7 in the section on documents.

Whereas 'control' is a key methodological concept for those trying to study cause and effect relationships, there are two methodological arguments linked to this ontological perspective. The first introduced in Chapter 2 is 'naturalism'. Here the argument is that we need to study people in naturally occurring settings that exist independently of the research process, so that the behaviour we observe is 'natural' too or at least not primarily influenced by the artificiality of the situation in which people are observed (which is the criticism made of experimental methods and structured approaches to research). The aim of the researcher is to get close to the actors involved in the setting but minimise his or her impact on the situation studied so that what has been discovered might be generalised to other similar settings, though not all researchers aim at generalisation. What people do reflects the context (the 'natural' context) in which they act. This is why a researcher like Forester (1993) who is interested in how planners learn about the world in which they practice is interested in listening to the stories which are told in meetings in the natural setting of the planning office. Or why Underwood (1980) spent time in the planning office in a London Borough listening to what planners were saying in meetings.

A second argument concerns the importance of 'exploration' or 'discovery' as the basis for credible social research. This is a justification for formulating a research question in an open-ended way, as we saw in Chapter 5. We need to explore the perceptions and interpretations of the people being studied: 'in the social world we cannot know what a phenomenon is until we know what it is believed to be' (Innes, 1990: 32). Researchers need to find out from the accounts of those involved in a situation what is happening rather than imposing their own interpretations or pre-suppositions on the situation or running the risk of theoretical over-simplification (Forester, 1993). In comparison with the deductive approach to research described above, this would be described as an inductive approach to research starting with the evidence.

Theoretical generalisation

It is not agreed whether researchers who emphasise the understanding rather than the explanation of social life are aiming to draw theoretical conclusions from their work. There are a number of problems. First, as we saw above, because social life changes and the way that people think about their actions, and the meaning given to their actions changes, the objects of social understanding change over time. Hence in this sense universal generalisations that one might make about social life cannot exist because they do not apply to all times. However, the scope of the universal claim when one is making a theoretical generalisation from the case or cases studied to a range of possible cases applies only to cases in which the conditions covered by the claim exist, i.e., all possible *relevant* cases.

The second problem relates to the question of whether the understanding of behaviour that comes from exploring what is in people's minds, from exploring their beliefs, values and attitudes and the reasons people have for their action is equivalent to a causal explanation (see Hughes and Sharrock (1997)). There is no agreement here. Some seem to take the view that they are not (Allmendinger, 2002). Fay (1996: 97) argues that reasons can be causes. 'Agents come to have a reason to act as a result of engaging in a practical reasoning process... When we explain an action by reference to the reasons for which it was done we are actually explaining it as the causal outcome of a process of reasoning'. Fischer (2003) also accepts that these 'quasi-causal' accounts of the effects of subjective factors can be accepted in interpretive policy research. If these accounts are accepted as being causal, then, in this sense too they can be seen as universally applying to actors with the same sets of beliefs or values, faced by the same situation or environment. Others (Lin (1998) quoted in Fischer (2003)) argue that the reasons which motivate action help to get at the *causal mechanisms* behind what may be the associations shown by statistical analysis.

Sampling and the selection of cases to study

Data sources and cases

As with descriptive ('what') questions, answering 'why' questions involves sampling of cases to study, and the same issue of distinguishing between data sources and the cases to which those data sources potentially give you access still apply (see the discussion in Chapter 5).

A deductive starting point for research (hypothesis testing)

Where you start your project with a specific hypothesis that you wish to test, and if as is usually the case, experimental methods are not possible, then the general approach to sampling can be described as **judgement**, or **purposive sampling**. The representativeness of a sample in relation to a population, in comparison with answering descriptive questions, is less of a concern.

One specific purposive method of sampling which you could use to test a hypothesis is to select what has been called a **'critical case'** (Flyvbjerg, 2001). There are two types of critical case: 'the most likely' and the 'least likely' case. If one has a hypothesis, and one looks at the 'most likely case' that is a case where the theory predicts that something will be found, but in fact the prediction is not supported by the evidence of this case then this could be seen as representing a 'falsification' of the theory. A study which is commonly quoted as being an example of this approach to sampling is the study by Goldthorpe et al. (1968–69) which was concerned with the impact of increasing prosperity on the attitudes of working class people – the 'embourgoisement thesis' which predicted that increasing prosperity would lead to the adoption of middle class attitudes by the working class. This was tested in the critical case of Luton, which was a town where at the time working class employment in manufacturing was high and well paid. Here, if anywhere, it was argued, if working class attitudes are predicted to change, evidence of this change would be found. Attitudes were not found to have changed and the hypothesis was accepted as having been falsified. Here it should be noted that the word 'case' as applied to Luton refers to a setting or situation rather than to cases in the sense of the phenomenon of interest which in this study was the attitude of working class workers. The setting of Luton is one in which the research team was most likely to find the sort of employees who constitute prosperous working class people.

The 'least likely' critical case is one where evidence to support a hypothesis is thought least likely to be found. This might be because the context of the case within which the hypothesis is tested might work against the hypothesis. Flyvbjerg's (1998) study of the politics of planning (or the relationship between rationality and power) in Aalborg, Denmark, a state widely seen as a model democracy, can be seen as an example of a context where if a vote is taken to adopt a particular planning policy for a city, then that policy will be implemented. This is a situation in which the wishes of the elected representatives are least likely to be subverted, so if they are, then it is likely to happen everywhere else.

A further example here is the theory that the local provision of services and facilities in neighbourhoods will encourage people to use local facilities and in turn encourage them to walk or cycle to those facilities, as claimed by a planning policy document of the 1990s (Department of the Environment, 1994). If one studies situations where there are some local services and facilities (such as shops, schools, health centres) and others where these services and facilities are absent but in all of these situations the local population is young and prosperous with high car-ownership rates and likely to have very mobile and geographically dispersed life styles, then they will have substantial choice of where they shop or use services. In this situation, the local provision of services and facilities is least likely to be successful in attracting local trips and encouraging walking and cycling. If, however, we find that this does happen in this situation then this helps to support or confirm the theory (Farthing and Winter, 1997).

Another variant of purposive sampling is the **maximum variation** case sampling method, where the variation between the situations studied is due to variations in the factor which is thought to be the cause. The research by Atkinson and Kintrea (2001) on area effects could be interpreted as illustrating this approach where they selected two areas (one in Glasgow and one in Edinburgh) which were in the top 5% of the most deprived neighbourhoods in Scotland (representing situations where there was a concentration of poverty) and two areas where there was a lower concentration of the deprived. The cases are again not the areas but the experiences and behaviour of residents of the contrasting areas. There may also be a sampling decision to be made about the cases to select *within* the two areas. It may be possible to survey all the residents of the area, but it may also be necessary to select a sample, in which case the decision has to be made about the method to use.

Atkinson and Kintrea (2001) aimed to select a random sample of 200 addresses from the postcode address file in each of the areas they studied, which would then give them access to the sampling units – residents – who could report on selected aspects of their behaviour or experiences. This has the advantage of providing, in principle, a representative sample of residents. Of course, the real interest is not in comparing a representative sample from each area but in comparing the behaviour and experiences of residents of the same type in each area (the poor). The experiences of life and behaviour of residents amongst the deprived are likely to vary with age and gender so it might have been better to attempt to control for this possibility by only selecting one type of resident to investigate.

In so far as the research situation is controlled in this way, this increases what is called the 'internal validity' of the research, the conclusion that the differences in behaviour of deprived residents or of residents of new housing developments are due to the factor of interest, and not to other factors which could be influencing behaviour. But by looking at the behaviour of a specific group of residents, for example, questions may be raised about the extent to which the claimed causal relation would apply to other residents of the areas concerned or to those elsewhere. This is the issue of external validity which raises questions about the role of various factors which might be necessary for the causal mechanisms to work.

An inductive starting point for research

Those adopting an inductive approach to research start a project without a specific hypothesis to test but with a broader question in mind. Only as the focus of the research becomes clearer does the issue of theory and the mechanisms involved arise. Researchers using both quantitative and qualitative methods of research may adopt an inductive approach to the development of an explanation. In a context in which local planning in England gives local authorities the power to determine applications for development and gives applicants a right of appeal to the Planning Inspectorate if their application is refused, Wood (2000) was interested in the local authority's 'negotiating style'. A local authority could adopt a style which was 'soft' in which they would negotiate with applicants over the details of applications. He called this a 'regenerative style', adopted in the interest of getting development in the area. The alternative was to adopt a 'hard' or 'defensive' approach and refuse applications without much attempt at negotiation. Their negotiating style was measured by the rate at which local planning authorities in England refused permission for development. He was interested in exploring how the local authority's negotiating style related to the environment within which they operated and in particular the 'development pressure' they faced 'that is how keen applicants are to pursue their application for development in the face of refusal' (Wood, 2000: 98). This he measured by the appeal rate. The data he used in his quantitative analysis was secondary data, that is, data collected by the government and the Planning Inspectorate for other purposes and made available for analysis, and the data covered all planning authorities and developers in England but was a sample in the sense that it referred to the behaviour of all planning authorities and all developers in England over a specific historic period (1988–94), raising questions about whether it could be applied (or generalised) to their behaviour in earlier or in subsequent periods. Using a scatterplot (see Figure 6.4), he established an association between these variables. In the scatterplot each point on the graph represents the data for one local planning authority. The line of 'best fit' in the graph indicates the general association between the two variables. Most of the points are close to this line, though there is some variation about the line, and a few are scattered more widely. One might logically expect such a general relationship to appear with a lower appeal rate (appeals as a percentage of all decisions) being found where more applications are approved. But it is this variation about the 'best fit' line which was of interest. Authorities above the line had a higher appeal rate then might be expected. This led Wood to hypothesise that they had adopted a hard negotiating style with less flexibility in negotiations and with policies being more rigidly adhered to. Those below the line were apparently adopting a 'softer' or 'regenerative style' of negotiation.

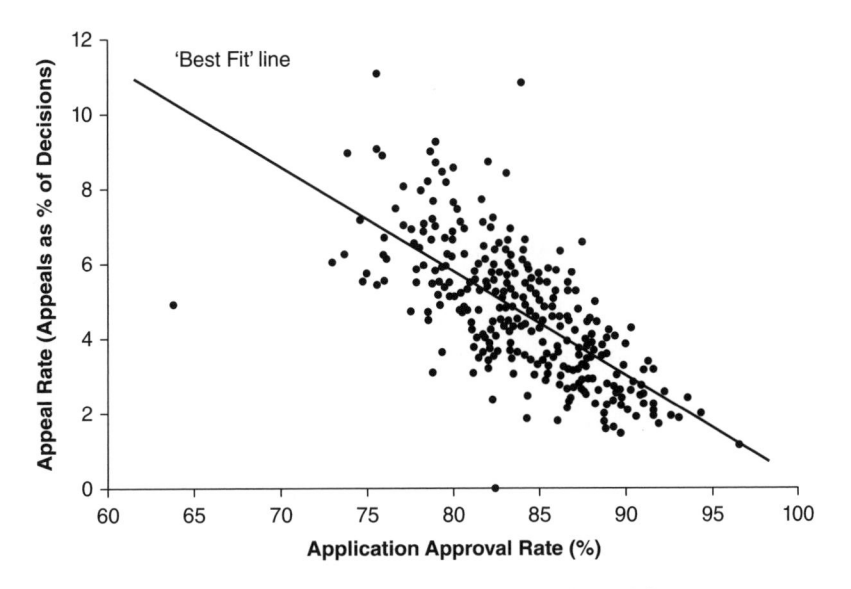

Figure 6.4 Development Application Approval Rate vs. Appeal Rate
(*Source*: Wood, 2000) © Liverpool University Press. Reproduced with Permission.

This naturally raises further 'why?' questions about causal relationships. Why is a harder approach adopted towards negotiations when there is high development pressure? Is one factor causing the other? Or is there some third factor which might be influencing both negotiations and development pressure, such as the existence of landscape designations like green belts? These are areas where one might expect a harder negotiating style by an authority since these designations are intended to discourage development. And, of course, these are the very areas where development is particularly attractive and development pressure would be high. This was a factor which Wood suggested would need further investigation in subsequent research.

Whilst Wood (2000) is an example of an inductive starting point for research using typical quantitative methods of research, those adopting qualitative methods of research also frequently do so. For example, a body of research in planning, called the practice movement (see Watson, 2002) is interested in the 'activities and practices of planners as they undertake their planning tasks'. One situation of interest to these writers is the existence of conflict over planning policy and over particular development proposals which expose planners to the 'politics of planning'. How do planners respond to this situation? This is of particular interest because the training of planners, it is perceived, has not equipped them with the skills to deal with this type of situation. In some ways it might seem that conflict is endemic in planning practice, so that if one is interested in studying planning in situations of conflict then there would be many situations or cases from which to select in any piece of research, and there would not be any problem in finding a case to investigate.

One strategy that could be employed, however, is to focus on **extreme or deviant cases.** The extreme or deviant case is selected 'which can be especially problematic or good in a more closely defined sense' (Flyvbjerg, 2001). This could be used in an exploratory way to find out what is happening in this extreme case and to develop some hypotheses in an inductive sense. One case used by Forester (1993) was the situation in a small city which followed a local election in which the mayoral challenger, who lost narrowly, had run a campaign vigorously attacking the successful incumbent's planners. Despite the ubiquity of conflict over planning matters, this would seem to be an extreme case raising questions about the reasons for this political saliency of planning, and the responses of planners to the situation. Here Forester argues that listening to the planners' meeting is 'a way of getting inside the "organizational mind" of the planners, getting to know both how they perceive the situations they are in and how they begin to act on the problems they face.' From this the planners learn about planning practice and 'they reconstruct selectively what the problems at hand really are', how far they were to blame and what they aim to do in future to avoid these problems. Forester's theory is not a theory of political conflict, or what makes some situation more conflictual than others. It is a theory in the sense discussed above that it is about developing an interpretive understanding of planners and their world view, with what is called *thick description*, and as he says this 'embodies and enacts the play of power'. By 'power' he means, in the context of debates over planning, the way that planners define the problems to be solved; 'the selective focusing of attention, the expression of self, the presumptions of "us" and "them", and the creation of reputations – the shaping of expectations of what is and is not possible, the production of more (or less) politically rational strategies of action, the shaping of others' participation, and much more.' (1993: 201–2).

A deviant case might be seen as a situation where agreement (rather than disagreement) can be achieved over planning matters. Fischler (2000) argues that Innes' study (1996) of eight cases of consensus building in planning in California is an example of an inductive approach to theory building. The cases might be seen as 'good' in the sense that they are cases where consensus was achieved amongst the parties represented. The study of successful cases only will allow the possible identification of hypotheses about factors which might be necessary for the consensus to be developed but could not, without an examination of unsuccessful cases, hope to test which factor is essential for success. For a critique of this approach to research, called by some the comparative method, see Hammersley and Atkinson (1995).

Perhaps the most well-known approach to the development of theory for inductive researchers is grounded theory (Glaser and Strauss, 1967) which uses what is called **theoretical sampling** where the initial case is selected for theoretical purposes and additional cases are added to help develop the emerging theory through a process of constant comparison. Of course all the types of sampling discussed in this section are informed by theoretical thinking, so that reserving this label for the approach can be somewhat misleading. Flyvbjerg (1998: 7) suggests that he developed a 'grounded theory of the relationship between rationality and power' resulting in 10 propositions, though this is not grounded theory in the sense of the process advocated by Glaser and Strauss (1967) since he only investigates one case – the Aalborg case.

Henricksen and Tjora (2013: 4–5) illustrate the use of theoretical sampling (see Box 6.2) in their study of community which was guided by the rather open question 'how does (or doesn't) community in the urban neighbourhood occur?'

BOX 6.2

EXAMPLE – THEORETICAL SAMPLING IN A STUDY

This article is empirically based on 10 housing and community sociology projects in the period 2006–11. They were initiated on the basis of a theoretical interest in the community question, as well as an invitation

(Continued)

(Continued)

from the municipal administration of the city of Trondheim to develop research to increase our knowledge about, and address the problem of, 'student ghettoisation' [...]

In the overall design of the whole array of projects we have been applying theoretical sampling (Glaser and Strauss, 1967) by which preliminary results and reflections from one study have informed the questions and empirical sample for the next. For example, the study of well-established dwellers was needed for us to get a deeper understanding of neighbourliness in a neighbourhood that had evolved organically over time, and that was not well enough represented in the first stages of data generation.

In the survey and the first studies, we were struck by the fact that many people would put a significant emphasis on the role of neighbourhood community and at the same time avoid investing 'too much' time and interacting extensively with neighbours. Observation from Bay Garden confirms this: even though it was the middle of the summer and warm weather, we only observed people who spent time (and being available for others) in the common area on two occasions. We also found that the residents of Bay Village in particular used the term 'idyllic village life' to describe it. Most of the residents here knew each other quite well, including names, work and family situation. In all the other neighbourhoods we examined, people would know many of their neighbours by face, but only a very few by name. Of all our 92 in-depth interviews about housing and neighbourhood (excluding those about meeting places) only a handful of participants stated that they had become friends with their neighbours. While it was no surprise that neighbourhood relations are maintained as weak social ties (as suggested by Fischer (1982) and Schiefloe (1985) among others), our sociological curiosity was triggered by the participants' emphasis on neighbourhood relations as important. Do the relatively subtle forms of communication between, and the weak social ties among, neighbours have more significant social value than often anticipated? It was necessary for us to dig into the details of neighbourhood interaction, including those very small moments of recognition—a nod of the head in the local supermarket, small informal chats in a hallway, more explicit acts of communication, as well as organised gatherings. Our observation has documented such practices and how they vary, of which much is familiar from the sociology of Erving Goffman (1963, 1967, 1971; Kendon, 1988) and from the tradition of

> ethnomethodology (Garfinkel, 1967). Our contribution in this article is not replicating the detailed observation of these contributors of detailed interaction studies, but rather the use of in-depth interviews, to identify the nuances of participants' accounts of interactive (or non-interactive) neighbourhood experiences and how they put meaning into these practices.
>
> *Source:* Henriksen and Tjora (2013: 4–5)

Although starting with the word 'how' this is an example of an explanatory or 'why' question, it is effectively asking about the causes of community. And the authors were interested in the role of interactions between residents in this process. It is not clear in this report of the research whether they started the project with the idea that they would focus their investigations on interactions or whether this emerged during the course of the research.

The 'cases' that they studied were various middle-class neighbourhoods in the city of Trondheim. There are three important points in terms of understanding grounded theory in this account of the study. First, the process of analysis of the data they collected was continuous. Second, that the selection of the next case or neighbourhood to study – for example, the one containing the 'well established dwellers' was selected because they needed to understand neighbourliness in a different setting or set of circumstances from those they had already studied in order to develop their theory about neighbourliness. Third, the methods they used to study the issue varied depending on whether they were establishing what people thought about the importance of neighbourliness (depth interviews) or testing this against what they actually did (observation of behaviour). From this process of sampling and analysis, they developed a theory about the type of community which develops in a neighbourhood, the type of community being a result of the existence of interaction pretexts in a neighbourhood and the level of activity in the neighbourhood. An interaction pretext is defined by Henricksen and Tjora (2013: 9) as 'a common reference or concern that legitimises an encounter, small-talk or a conversation, on the basis of passing-by or gathering in a shared physical space.' Children playing and pet ownership are examples of interaction pretexts. Tasks carried out in neighbourhoods such as outdoor tasks also provide interaction pretexts. The level of activity is concerned with how much common activity there is in a neighbourhood.

Case studies

What are case studies in planning research? Many dissertations and theses in planning are labelled as case studies. There are a number of different understandings of the term case study both in the planning literature, and more generally in the social sciences. Blaikie (2000) in his survey found six different definitions. Some definitions refer to the fact that the cases are studied using *multiple methods of data collection or generation* (Yin, 2008). Others see case studies as a type of *research design*, distinguished from a range of other designs, including experiments, surveys, archival analysis, and history. Mitchell (1983: 192) suggests that the idea of a case study should be restricted to studies with a theoretical intention: 'a detailed examination of an event (or series of events) which the analyst believes exhibits (or exhibit) the operation of some identified general theoretical principle'. This obviously excludes descriptive case studies from the definition.

I think that it is best to see 'cases' as referring to the situations, events or the behaviours of interest in a study. A case study would then be the examination of one of those cases, for example, a case of an attempt to develop a consensus on a planning problem. This could be studied in some detail. There could be multiple case studies in this sense within a piece of research, each of which would be studied with somewhat less detail because the resources for the research are spread more thinly. There would be no expectation about the methods of research to be employed. What are sometimes referred to as case studies might more appropriately be designated as 'settings'. The Goldthorpe et al. (1968–69) study of Luton, as described by Flyvbjerg (2001) is not a case study of Luton as a town, it is a study of the attitudes of well-off working class people who happened to be living in the setting of Luton.

Summary/Key lessons

Explanatory research questions are raised when there is a puzzle about why something happens or has happened or about the consequences of something having happened. This chapter started by arguing that a helpful way of characterising the differences amongst urban planning researchers in answering such questions is to contrast the views they take on the nature of what constitutes a satisfactory explanation and the starting points for the accounts they give (an inductive or deductive approach)

1. I hope that I have alerted you to the recognition that you can't design a piece of research to explain why something happened or explain the consequences of something having happened without adopting some position on what a satisfactory explanation might be like, and whether you think it is sensible to make theoretical generalisations. Though there are many differences between researchers in these matters, I have suggested that some apply what they see as a scientific model to social study and who emphasise the search for causal factors, factors which in principle should apply to other situations (people, places, social contexts etc.) beyond the cases studied (theoretical generalisations).

2. I have explored the difficulties which face all researchers in providing evidence to support a claim that a causal relationship has been established. Such claims, I tried to show, can neither be conclusively proved nor conclusively disproved though judgements can be made about their plausibility and I encouraged an honesty about the limitations of your research when making claims. I take up this point again in Chapter 8.

3. I have examined some of the arguments that have been used to criticise the use of causal analysis in planning by those who are interested in understanding what is in people's minds as a way of accounting for their actions. The emphasis for these researchers is on the meaning of social actions, and the understanding we have of people's actions because we understand the meaning of the action in the cultural context in which it took place. The emphasis on the importance of context here tends to restrict the extent to which such researchers might be concerned with generalisation. Too much, I consider, should not be made of this difference: many believe that looking at the reasons people have for action is in practice equivalent to a causal explanation. Explanations can be composed of a mix of causes (or factors) impinging on the situation in which people found themselves, and the reasons they had for responding in the way they did, which were founded in their understanding of that situation.

4. I have argued that a deductive approach for answering an explanatory research question starts with a possible hypothesis or tentative explanation in mind which is to be tested against the evidence from the research.

- Hypotheses might be justified by reference to your analysis of the academic literature, be suggested by articles in professional journals, or might be derived from your own hunches about why something has happened.

- You might find this a fruitful approach because it gives a focus and direction to the design of the rest of the research process. When you have a hypothesis you can select cases for study which allow you to test your hypothesis in different circumstances from those studied by previous researchers but also cases which might constitute a critical test for the hypothesis or cases selected because they vary in terms of the factor thought to be the cause.

(Continued)

(Continued)

5. An inductive starting point for answering an explanatory research question by contrast starts without a specific hypothesis or theory and thus without attempting to pre-judge what the explanation might be.

- The justification you might use for this approach is the absence of previous research, and the novelty of the phenomenon being investigated. Or else the methodological principle might be that of the importance of exploration in social research, the need to avoid imposing your own perspective on the topic being investigated. In this case you will start with the data as revealed by the cases investigated to develop your explanation.
- In contrast to the deductive approach, there is less guidance on the selection of cases to sample. You might adopt an extensive strategy, select a large number of cases, and search for some associations between the phenomenon of interest and other factors. Or you might start with a more intensive strategy and look at one or a few cases in depth, cases which are examples of the phenomenon you are interested in explaining. Further cases could be selected according to the principles of grounded theory, testing your tentative explanation on new cases or cases in a new setting.

6. Finally, I have argued that it is best to see a 'case' as in 'case study' as referring to the situations, events or the behaviours of interest in a study rather than studies as such.

Exercise: Answering an explanatory question

Having reviewed the literature on your topic, and identified an explanatory or 'why?' question to be answered, you need to ask yourself the following questions:

1. Do you have some initial hypothesis which would answer your question (a deductive approach)? If so, what is it? Or do you aim to start with an open mind on the question (an inductive approach) and allow the explanation to develop from your research inquiries?

2. Are you aiming to explain the situation by reference to causal factors or are you interested in understanding the world views of the actors involved in the situation, the meaning of their actions and the reasons they acted in the way they did given the context in which they found themselves? Or both?

3. What 'data sources' are available to help you answer your research question?

> 4. What wider population are your cases to be selected from? How important is that your cases should be 'representative' of this wider population?
> 5. What methods of sampling might you use? Probabilistic or non-probabilistic?
> 6. What specific 'cases' might you be interested in investigating?

Further Reading

Research meeting the criteria for 'true' or controlled experiments is difficult, if not impossible, to conduct in planning situations. However, some examples of planning research which have attempted to emulate these methods can be found in:

Preece, R. (1990) gives an illuminating explanation of how experimental methods, originally developed by agronomists, might be applied to research aimed at evaluating the impact of different development control policies in different places. Preece, R. (1990) 'Development Control Studies: Scientific Method and Policy Analysis', *Town Planning Review* 61: 59–74.

A series of pilot studies of participation in planning in Florida enabled Deyle and Slotterback (2009) using what they called a quasi-experimental design to test the effect of participation in planning processes on group learning about planning problems. Deyle, R. and Slotterback, C.S. (2009) 'Group Learning in Participatory Planning Processes: An Exploratory Quasiexperimental Analysis of Local Mitigation Planning in Florida', *Journal of Planning Education and Research* 29: 23–39.

The implementation of a housing improvements programme involving the heating systems of dwellings in an area where problems of damp in housing were endemic gave an opportunity for Hopton and Hunt (1996) to examine the impacts of the heating of housing on the health of children. Hopton, J. and Hunt, S. (1996) 'The Health Effects of Improvements to Housing: A Longitudinal Study', *Housing Studies* 11 (2): 271–86.

The differences between inductive and deductive starting points for research, and ways of developing or testing theory are discussed in a number of texts. De Vaus (2001) is a useful reference if you wish to follow up the ideas introduced in this chapter about the different starting points for research, the testing and generation of theory and about causal relationships. De Vaus, D. (2001) *Research Design in Social Research*. London: Sage.

For a strong statement about the distinctive nature of accounts of social life provided by 'understanding' as opposed to 'causal explanations' following the natural science model, see: Hughes J. and Sharrock W. (1997) *The Philosophy of Social Research*, 3rd Edition. Harlow: Longman.

Both Fay (1996) and Fischer (2003) argue that reasons that people give for their behaviour can be treated as causes: Fay, B. (1996) *Contemporary Philosophy of Social Research: a*

Multicultural Approach. Oxford: Blackwell; Fischer F. (2003) *Reframing Public Policy: Discursive Politics and Deliberative Practices.* Oxford: Oxford University Press.

On the concepts of empirical and theoretical generalisation in the context of ethnography, though the ideas can be applied to all research, see Hammersley, M. (1990) *Reading Ethnographic Research: A Critical Guide.* London: Longman.

The arguments for and against the foundation of our knowledge in falsification and inductivism, are reviewed in Chalmers, A. (1999) *What is This Thing Called Science?* Buckingham: Open University Press.

Sampling and case studies are discussed in:

Flyvbjerg, B. (2001) *Making Social Science Matter.* Cambridge: Cambridge University Press.

Flyvbjerg, B. (2006) 'Five Misunderstandings About Case Study Research', *Qualitative Inquiry* 12 (2): 219–45.

Gomm, R., Hammersley, M., and Foster, P. (2000) *Case Study Method.* London: Sage.

On grounded theory see Strauss, A. and Corbin, J. (1998) *Basics of Qualitative Research: Techniques and Procedures for Developing Grounded Theory*, 2nd Edition. London: Sage.

References

Allmendinger, P. (2002) 'Towards a post-positivist typology of planning theory', *Planning Theory* 1 (1): 77–99.

Atkinson, R. and Kintrea, K. (2001) 'Disentangling Area Effects: Evidence From Deprived and Non-Deprived Neighbourhoods', *Urban Studies* 38 (12): 2277–98.

Blaikie, N. (2000) *Designing Social Research.* Cambridge: Polity.

Bradford Hill, A. (1965) 'The Environment and Disease: Association or Causation?', *Proceedings of the Royal Society of Medicine* 58: 295–300.

Burgess, R. (1984) *In the Field: an Introduction to Field Research.* Hemel Hempstead: Allen and Unwin.

Campbell, T. and Stanley, J. (1966) *Experimental and Quasi-Experimental Designs for Research.* Chicago: Rand McNally.

Chalmers, A. (1999) *What is This Thing Called Science?* Buckingham: Open University Press.

Cook, T.D. and Campbell, D. (1979) *Quasi-Experimentation.* Chicago: Rand McNally.

Department of the Environment, Welsh Office (1994) *Planning Policy Guidance: Transport.* London: HMSO.

Deyle, R. and Slotterback, C.S. (2009) 'Group Learning in Participatory Planning Processes: An Exploratory Quasiexperimental Analysis of Local Mitigation Planning in Florida', *Journal of Planning Education and Research* 29: 23–39.

Ellen, I. and Turner, M. (1997) 'Does Neighbourhood Matter? Assessing Recent evidence', *Housing Policy Debate* 8: 833–66.
Farthing, S.M. and Ashley, K. (2002) 'Negotiations and the Delivery of Affordable Housing through the English Planning System', *Planning Practice and Research* 17 (1): 45–58.
Farthing, S.M. and Winter, J. (1997) 'Coordinating Facility Provision and New Housing Development: Impacts on Car and Local Facility Use', in S.M. Farthing, (ed.) *Evaluating Local Environmental Policy.* Aldershot: Avebury. pp.159–79.
Fay, B. (1996) *Contemporary Philosophy of Social Research: a Multicultural Approach.* Oxford: Blackwell.
Fischer, F. (2003) *Reframing Public Policy: Discursive Politics and Deliberative Practices.* Oxford: Oxford University Press.
Fischler, T. (2000) 'Case Studies of Planners at Work', *Journal of Planning Literature* 15 (2): 184–95.
Flyvbjerg, B. (1998) *Rationality and Power.* Chicago: University of Chicago Press.
Flyvbjerg, B. (2001) *Making Social Science Matter.* Cambridge: Cambridge University Press.
Forester, J. (1993) 'Learning from Practice Stories: the Priority of Practical Judgement', in F. Fischer and J. Forester (eds), *The Argumentative Turn in Policy Analysis and Planning.* Durham NC: Duke University Press. pp. 186–209.
Glaser, B.G. and Strauss, A.L. (1967) *The Discovery of Grounded Theory.* Chicago: Aldine.
Goldthorpe, J., Lockwood, D., Beckhofer, F. and Platt, J. (1968–69) *The Affluent Worker,* vols I–III. Cambridge: Cambridge University Press.
Gorard, S. (2013) *Research Design: Creating Robust Approaches for the Social Sciences.* London: Sage.
Hammersley, M. (1990) *Reading Ethnographic Research: A Critical Guide.* London: Longman.
Hammersley, M. and Atkinson, P. (1995) *Ethnography.* London: Routledge.
Haughton, G., Allmendinger, P., Counsell, D., and Vigar, G. (2010) *The New Spatial Planning.* London: Routledge.
Healey, P. (2007) *Urban Complexity and Spatial Strategies.* London: Routledge.
Henricksen, I.M. and Tjora, A. (2013) 'Interaction Pretext: Experiences of Community in the Urban Neighbourhood', *Urban Studies* 50 (10): 1–14.
Hopton, J. and Hunt, S. (1996) 'The Health Effects of Improvements to Housing: A Longitudinal Study', *Housing Studies* 11 (2): 271–86.
Innes, J. (1990) *Knowledge and Public Policy: The Search for Meaningful Indicators.* New Brunswick: Transaction Books.
Innes, J. (1996) 'Planning through Consensus Building', *Journal of the American Planning Association* 62 (4): 460–71.
Lin, A. C. (1998) 'Bridging Positivist and Interpretivist Approaches to Qualitative Methods', *Policy Studies Journal* 26 (1): 162–80.

Mason, J. (1996) *Qualitative Researching*. London: Sage.

Mitchell, J.C. (1983) 'Case and Situation Analysis', *Sociological Review* 31 (2): 187–211.

Pawson, R. and Tilley, N. (1997) *Realistic Evaluation*. London: Sage.

Rydin, Y. (2007) 'Re-Examining the Role of Knowledge Within Planning Theory', *Planning Theory* 6 (1): 52–68.

Sandercock, L. (1998) *Towards Cosmopolis: Planning for Multicultural Cities*. Chichester: Wiley.

Underwood, J. (1980) 'Town Planners in Search of a Role: a Participant Observation Study of Local Planners in a London Borough', *Occasional Paper No. 6*. Bristol: School for Advanced Urban Studies.

Watson, V. (2002) 'Do We Learn From Practice?: The Contribution of the Practice Movement to Planning Theory', *Journal of Planning Education and Research* 22: 178–97.

Watson, V. (2003) 'Conflicting Rationalities: Implications for Planning Theory and Ethics', *Planning Theory and Practice* 4 (4): 395–407.

Wood, R. (2000) 'Using Appeal Data to Characterise Local Planning Authorities', *Town Planning Review* 71: 97–107.

Yin, R.K. (2008) *Case Study Research: Design and Methods*. London: Sage.

Young, K. and Mills, L. (1981) *Public Policy Research: A Review of Qualitative Methods*. Bristol: School for Advanced Urban Studies.

7

METHODS OF DATA GENERATION IN RESEARCH

Key questions

What methods of data generation are available to answer your research question?

What range of considerations do you need to take into account in making decisions on the methods to use?

Key concepts

Interviews, Questionnaires, Ethnography, Observation, Documents, Official statistics

Overview

The previous two chapters were based on the assumption that it is a good idea to try to separate out the cases you might be interested in from the potential data sources, that is, the people and places from which you might generate data about those cases, and to do this *independently* of thinking about the methods that you might use to generate the data. In this chapter the focus is on the methods for data generation, an essential step in the research design process. Recent discussion in the literature on knowledge in planning has sought to broaden the range of methods that researchers might use – an 'epistemology of multiplicity' for planning (Sandercock, 1998) – going beyond the traditional quantitative methods of research to include qualitative methods of various kinds. Some of this is driven by an ethical desire to adopt methods of research which are seen as allowing those involved in a situation to describe the nature of their experience of that situation in their own words, and to emphasise the multiplicity of perspectives on any situation including the nature of the problem (as discussed in Chapter 2).

From a research design perspective there are two important questions about methods. First, what methods are available? Second, why use a particular method for generating data? In practice, there are a limited number of methods for data generation. I do not think that it is particularly helpful at this stage to see the choice of methods as being between quantitative and qualitative methods, though in practice many researchers tend to favour particular methods in their research careers. The methods described in this chapter are interviews and questionnaires, observation and ethnography, and the use of documents. The chapter starts with a discussion of the issues that you need to take into account when thinking about which methods will be appropriate for your research. It then examines why you might want to use each of the main methods identified for your own project.

Key issues in the choice of methods

There is no simple answer to the question of which method or methods to use in any project. The decision involves taking account of a range of issues, and balancing these to come to a considered judgement (see Figure 7.1).

Throughout this book I have emphasised the importance of research questions to the design of research. This applies equally to the selection of methods of data generation and, for any piece of research, it is important to select a method that will allow you to answer your **research question**, and therefore pay attention to the **purpose of your research**. Are you aiming to explore an issue in planning about which little is known, with a rather open-ended question which makes few prior assumptions about the issue? Or do you aim to describe a situation in some detail with a more focussed question? Or do you aim to help account for some feature of the world with a specific hypothesis about a factor involved or to assess the impact of planning policies or of the actions taken by planners? Or to provide a rich contextual understanding of the response of policy-makers to a problematic situation?

Methods of Data Generation in Research

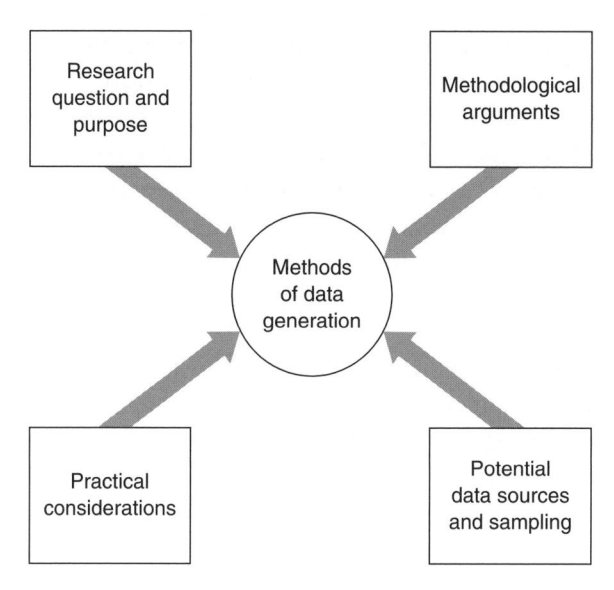

Figure 7.1 Influences on the Choice of Methods of Data Generation

The data you need to answer a research question ought to be a primary consideration here. We saw in Chapter 5 that it can be useful to distinguish between the data that you need to generate from the cases you are interested in investigating and the **potential data sources**, that is, a place or phenomenon through which your data could be generated. This has an impact on the method you might use. You can observe behaviour (or practices) in public spaces, for instance the behaviour of planners and politicians in meetings open to members of the public, but not that in private places, in, say, the pre-meeting between the chair of the planning committee and the chief planning officer, unless you can negotiate access to those places. If you cannot gain access to the pre-meeting yourself, then you may have to ask questions and rely on a report by someone involved in the pre-meeting on what took place. Or you may have to accept that you may never be able to find out about this, in which case you may need to change your research question to one that can be answered.

Also of considerable importance are other **practical considerations**, by which I mean principally the time available for you to conduct research, and the money you have at your disposal. If we accept the rule of thumb about the division of the time available for research allowing about a third of the time to be devoted to planning and developing the research design, a third of the time to conducting the research and a third of the time to analysis and writing, then most students will have a very limited time available for data generation. There are monetary costs associated with all methods of research, including travelling expenses to conduct face-to-face interviews or the costs of dispatching and paying for the return of postal questionnaires. Budgets will also limit the number of cases that might be investigated as well as the depth to which a case can be investigated, and there is a trade-off between the two: a few cases might be studied in depth or a larger number of cases might be studies with less detail, so what is feasible may turn out to be more important than what might be desirable given your research question.

Finally, there are the assumptions you make about research in urban planning, which might suggest that a particular way of conducting research is methodologically superior to the alternatives. As introduced in Chapter 2, there are theories (or assumptions) – sometimes called data theories, sometimes described as methodological theories – about the relationship between the way that research is conducted, including importantly the methods of data generation that are used, and the reality that the research is designed to capture. There is likely to be a difference between (a) the data that you generate through your methods and (b) the reality you are interested in capturing. Ideally, the impact of the research process on the data generated will be negligible. The degree to which this is not the case is sometimes called **'reactivity'**- the reaction of those researched to the researcher and the research methods used. If there is a substantial impact of the method used, then there could be reasonable questions about the relationship between the data produced and the reality the researcher is trying to assess. This is the question of validity introduced in Chapter 5.

Are we observing what we think we are observing? If the researcher is aiming to measure normal, habitual behaviour or typical views and thinking, as Underwood was trying to do in her study of planners in a London borough, discussed in Chapter 2, or Forester and Hoch were in their work on planning in the USA, and if the research process allows this, then, the research has what is called **'ecological validity'**.

The idea of ecological validity is closely linked to the argument over 'naturalism' in the research process. We need to study people in naturally occurring settings that exist independently of the research process, so that the behaviour we observe is 'natural', too, or at least not primarily influenced by the artificiality of the situation in which people are observed (which is the criticism made of experimental methods and structured approaches to research).

The aim here is to encourage the researcher to minimise his or her impact on the situation studied, and also to encourage the researcher to think carefully about this impact, to engage in reflexivity, both during and after the research. This has consequences for the methods of data generation used, as we will see.

A contrasting methodological position on methods, introduced in Chapter 2, is to acknowledge that the methods used by a researcher may have an impact on the results that the researcher obtains but that this impact can be controlled by thinking about the **'biases'** that might be introduced into the research process and thinking about how these biases might be minimised through adopting a consistent approach. This might involve, when questioning people, for example, 'following a standard protocol, asking questions in precisely the same way each time and in the same order' (Fielding, 1993: 151) and efforts to avoid 'leading the respondent' to answer a question in a particular way in an interview. The extent to which this is achieved is said to deliver **reliability** in the research process.

Interviews and questionnaires

What are interviews and questionnaires, and why use them?

Interviews and self-completion questionnaires are very familiar to planning students, and might almost be seen as 'default positions' when it comes to thinking about the methods to be used in dissertation. We do not need to spend much time in describing them. Both are methods which pose questions to respondents (data sources) about facts, behaviour, beliefs and attitudes, and their use assumes that these people are in a good position to know the answer to these questions. For an interview there is an interviewer who asks the questions and usually records the answers (even in the minimal case of switching on a device to record the interview) but for a questionnaire the questions are set in advance and they are answered by the respondent and the answers are recorded by the respondent. There is not just one sort of interview: they have different characteristics and it might be best to see interviews as a 'family' of methods. A number of dimensions are recognised in the literature (see Figure 7.2).

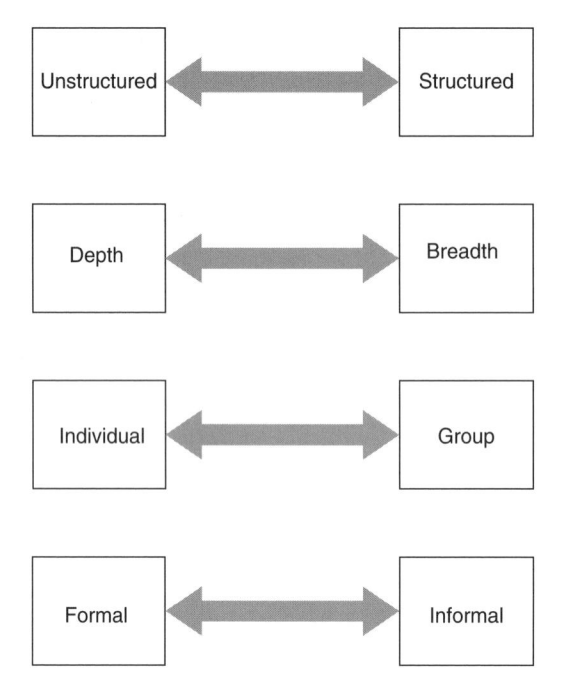

Figure 7.2 Characterising the Variation in the Types of Research Interview

Unstructured vs. structured interviews

The differences are often characterised in terms of the degree of structure that they have, with a range of types from, at one end of the spectrum, unstructured interviews, through semi-structured to structured interviews at the other end. This interest in structure relates to the degree to which the interviewer has control over the topic and the specific questions asked in the interview. The more structured the interview, the more control the interviewer has over the process, and the less freedom the interviewee has to set the agenda for the questions or topics which are explored.

You may be interested in using structured interviews if your literature review has suggested that a specific hypothesis can be tested, for example, in a new setting and that this requires the point by point comparison of responses to a number of questions or variables for a number of cases. You need to be certain that it is feasible for you to use interviews, for example, you have the time to conduct the interviews you need. You may also use structured interviews if your methodological preference is for 'control' of the research process to produce valid and reliable information.

The interviews conducted with residents of the four neighbourhoods in the research of Atkinson and Kintrea (2001) are examples of structured interviews where, though they do not go into great detail and they describe the method as a 'questionnaire survey approach', one can assume that there was an interview schedule setting out the questions to be asked by the interviewers of the residents. Each resident would be asked the same questions, except where certain questions might not be appropriate to a given respondent. Here the answer to 'filter questions' would direct the interviewer to skip certain questions, given a particular response. An illustration of questions which might be excluded from a particular interview, might be questions about the nature of current employment, if someone is unemployed. Though they use the term 'questionnaire' it is probably best to see questionnaires as the instruments used when the answers to questions are completed by the respondent rather than the interviewer (as in a postal questionnaire).

You may be interested in conducting less structured interviews because your literature review suggested that there has been little research on a topic, so a rather open-ended research question might be appropriate and it would be useful to explore with people involved in a situation their experiences and understanding of what is happening in order to inform future more structured descriptive work. With a semi-structured interview, the major questions which are of interest in the research are asked in the same way in each interview but the order in which the questions are asked may vary, and the interviewer is free to prompt and to probe for further details. Finally, in an unstructured (or non-standardised) interview you may start with a list of topics which you want the respondent to talk about but vary the order of the topics from interview to interview and, of course, follow up issues which are raised by the respondent so that the list of topics for discussion can evolve from one interview to the next. This flexibility in the unstructured interview is a valuable asset. Interviews which I and colleagues conducted with planners in the late 1980s in areas where large scale housing development was taking place revealed that the topic which we thought would be of interest – the quality of the design and layout of new housing areas – was very much secondary to a concern over 'managing growth', that is, managing the political relationships with the local population, and local politicians as well as other tiers of government in the area before and during the process of development.

You might equally be convinced by the methodological argument about the need for the research process not to be 'artificial', and take the view that the more structured the interview, and the more control over the situation imposed by the interviewer the more artificial the research situation and therefore the less likely the responses that people give to the questions asked will reflect what they really think, feel and believe or reveal much about what they do in everyday life. Interviews here are concerned with establishing 'meaning', with what is in the minds of the person who is the subject of the interview (see Gomm, 2004).

Some researchers see structured interviews as being appropriate for some types of questions, but not others. Questions can be classified as seeking to find out what people know, what they do, and what they think and/or feel. This leads to questions concerned with facts, with behaviour, and with beliefs or attitudes (Robson 2002: 272) respectively. Atkinson and Kintrea (2001) restricted their questions to their respondents very largely to 'facts' (what their tenure of housing was; whether they owned a car; whether they were employed; who else lived with them; whether they had friends and family living in the same neighbourhood) and to 'behaviour' (whether they had left their neighbourhood during the previous weekday, and what they were doing when they did so) but not to attitudes. They suggest that the justification for restricting the questions they asked and the data they obtained was that 'they were considered suitable for a quantitative approach in contrast to some of the more attitudinal outcomes which would be better tackled by qualitative or ethnographic methods' (2001: 2283–4). By 'quantitative approach' in this context we can read structured interviews. Similarly, as we saw in Chapter 3, Burgess et al. (1988: 456) claimed that questionnaires or structured interviews were 'widely acknowledged to be an inadequate mechanism for revealing values and emotions' whilst 'qualitative methods are more suitable for exploring attitudes and values about open space because such approaches are grounded in the contexts of people's daily lives (Burgess, 1984; Glaser and Strauss, 1967).'

However, more structured types of interviewing have been used to measure attitudes to town and country planning in England (McCarthy and Harrison, 1995) and have been used to study the quality of life in cities. A substantial body of research by psychologists and others has been conducted using structured methods and attitudinal scales, and standard texts on research methods, such as Robson (2002), advocate these methods.

Depth vs. breadth interviews

Another dimension on which interviews as a research method are seen to diverge is in the depth with which a topic is investigated during the course of an interview. This is linked to the difference between semi-structured and unstructured (often called qualitative interviews) which are seen typically to explore a topic in greater depth but involving interviews with fewer cases and structured (quantitative) interviews, which ask more limited questions but where the number of cases is much larger. There is a trade-off, given the practical limits to small scale research, between the number of cases you can investigate and the depth with which an issue can be explored.

Individual vs. group interviews

This distinction obviously relates to the number of people who are subject to the interview. Group interviews have become more common in recent years. Group interviews (or focus groups) involve a small group who are led by an interviewer. Why groups? What is often of interest in group interviews is the process by which the group works out its view, or its range of views on a topic. The research by Burgess et al. (1988) with groups of respondents on the significance of open space in people's daily lives was described in Chapter 2. Their methodological justification was that the process of group discussion, which continued over a number of weeks, allowed members of the group to get in touch with their deeper feelings and concerns about open space. Such an extended use would be difficult perhaps for a student to manage. But some researchers use group interviews for practical reasons: they are a quicker and cheaper way of conducting interviews with the same number of respondents, though methodological concerns cannot be ignored here. Because of the group dynamics involved it is likely that the results one gets will be different from those obtained from a series of individual interviews, i.e., what people will say in a group will differ from what they might say in an individual interview. There are practical disadvantages too – not everyone turns up and they will need to be interviewed separately if their participation is essential to the research.

Interviewing can be an expensive way of conducting research in terms of time and possible travelling expenses, on the assumption that it is probably only possible to conduct two to three interviews in any day. Telephone interviews can overcome this problem and this is where questionnaires may also be useful, as they seek answers to questions in a structured way. They are widely used in planning research and in student dissertations, a fact that Greed (1994) decries. They can be used as an alternative to face-to-face interviewing, though not a perfect one, and they have the practical advantage that they are a simple, cheap and much less time consuming than interviews or an extended period of observation as methods of generating data (de Leeuw, 2008).

Ethnography and observation

What is ethnography?

As with most aspects of social research there is some difference of opinion between writers on what constitutes ethnography, and this is reflected in the literature on ethnography in planning. Greed (1994: 125) argues that 'the boundary between ethnographic research and other forms of qualitative research is appropriately "fuzzy" and the source of much debate'. Some, such as Hammersley (1990) see ethnography as a broad concept, overlapping with a term like 'qualitative method' and characterised by a number of different ways of conducting research (highlighting the use of observation and interviewing to generate data) whilst the researcher is 'in the field'. As Greener (2011) says, such a definition is too broad to be useful, whilst other definitions which see ethnography as linked to anthropological practice go too far the other way. Greener (2011) opts for a middle range definition, not dissimilar to those to be found in the planning literature.

Forester's (1993: 188) description of ethnography in planning is a useful place to start in thinking about some typical features of the process. 'Typically, such work involves not only interviews with planners and analysts but also observations of and perhaps even participation in various formal and informal meetings in the "policy process", including, for example, planners' and analysts' own staff meetings.' One aspect which is widely agreed, and captured in Forester's characterisation, is that behaviour is studied in everyday contexts or in the real world or natural settings. For planners, these everyday contexts or natural settings include meetings of various kinds which are attended in the course of their working day. Of course, planning researchers do not need to restrict their ethnographic studies to the behaviour of planners. They could equally well study the behaviour of residents in selected areas of a city, or the behaviour of people who work in the development industry, though in the latter case there might be barriers to access.

In order to study these everyday contexts, the researcher has to be present or participate in the setting, and this means finding some way of gaining access to that setting. This can be either covert or overt. Some researchers choosing covert roles have taken employment, or joined political parties or other organisations as members in order to pursue their research. Some may already have a position which allows them to participate in a setting. Blowers (1980) used his role in local politics in Bedfordshire to study the politics of local planning policy. Similarly, Kitchen (1997) used his role as a planner in Manchester to report on the practice of planning. In this latter case, there is a choice of either revealing that you are also playing the role of a researcher or keeping this role covert. For an outsider, if participation is to be overt, then, access will need to be negotiated with whoever is the 'gatekeeper' to the setting. Forester is well-known in planning circles in the US, so his participation and observation could only be overt.

With participation there is, as Fielding (1993: 158) explains, the need to present the ethnographer's 'self' to those involved in the setting. As he says, 'a useful observational tactic is the cultivation of an impression of naïveté and humility so that members feel obliged to explain things that seem obvious to them'. Underwood's participant observation study of planners in a London borough, introduced in Chapter 2, saw her adopting the role of a new entrant to the department so that she could find out about the working relationships in the department.

Participation allows observation of what is happening, and observation is usually a significant part of the process of data generation. With covert participation, something that looks like an interview might threaten to 'blow the cover' of the researcher. But overt participation also gives opportunities for interviews with those in the situation being studied. In describing the interviews she conducted in the extract given in Chapter 2, Underwood distinguished between formal and informal interviews carried out during her period in the field in the London borough. The distinction here is between formal interviews which are planned in advance and presented as interviews, and informal ones which arise without pre-planning perhaps but which arise opportunistically during the process of work and which were more like conversations. The advantage of conducting interviews is that it allows the researcher to seek explanations from participants of what was happening in any situation. There is a flexibility in the choice of methods of data generation in ethnographic research so that the balance between observation and interviewing can vary, with the 'ethnographic studies' conducted by Henriksen and Tjora (2013) in various neighbourhoods in Trondheim, for example, being based substantially on in-depth interviews with residents and only a small amount of observation.

In what circumstances would ethnography be a useful way of generating data in a study?

Research purpose and question

Ethnographic research is useful when there is an interest in a detailed, fine-grained understanding of a social context (Greener, 2011) and also when the issue being investigated is a new one, and there is little prior research to guide research. My ethnographic study of four planning offices in England which had recently introduced computers to assist with the processing of planning applications is a useful illustration (Farthing, 1986). Systems for this purpose were being developed, and planning staff wanted to know whether they should invest in such systems, and if so, whether any systems were more appropriate than others. There was a demand for short courses and workshops to acquaint planners with the issues involved, and I wanted to produce some 'relevant research' which would be grounded in the concerns of planners. A review of the literature at the time (mid-1980s) revealed that there was little published research on the use of computers in planning, except for their use in the development of forecasting models for urban and regional change. There was nothing on the methods that were used for administrative purposes. Therefore the research question posed was the rather open-ended one 'what was the impact of these new systems on the processing of planning applications?' The aim was to undertake an exploratory study to provide an in-depth 'immersive' description of how those involved understood and made sense of what was happening in situations where systems were being used for the first time. At that time in Britain, as in more recent times, central government concern with planning was with planning delay, the way that planning was seen to act as a barrier to development because of the time it took to make decisions on planning applications – 'locking up jobs in filing cabinets' as one Secretary of State put it. One possibility was that the use of computers could speed up this process, but there might also be other benefits from having access to data bases of past planning applications in helping to understand the nature of development pressures in an area. Three months was spent in the field observing staff meetings and the use of the computer systems in the different places and in interviewing planning and administrative staff about what they were doing, and how the computer had affected their working patterns.

Data sources and sampling

For the 'computers in planning' research, the appropriate data sources from which data could be generated were **places** – the planning offices where computers had been introduced – which gave access to the behaviour of planners and others which could be observed, whilst learning the language of practitioners and administrative staff, and studying the relationships between them during the day-to-day work involved in dealing with planning applications for development. The data sources were also the **people** in the planning offices, particularly those involved in implementing the systems, but also those whose jobs were affected by the new systems, who could report on their behaviour and how and why it had changed with the introduction of computers. This gave access to the varying perspectives of those involved in the situation. The primary sampling units were thus the places. The selection of the four cases was based on the type of system implemented since this was seen as being of concern to the professionals and this choice was thought to be a significant determinant of how well the systems worked.

Practical reasons

The choice of ethnography as a method, or rather a mix of methods, of research has also to be taken in the light of **access** to the places or setting which are of interest and the **time available**. For the issue of access, some data sources are more difficult to access than others. For some there will be discouraging barriers to access and it is often said that it is easier to access relatively powerless groups than the powerful (though this has sparked a debate about how the powerful are to be identified (see Cochrane (1998)). Where access is relatively closed, students might be able to benefit from the existence of established contacts who act as gatekeepers to situations or places of interest. Some students will be working part-time in planning, perhaps, so that their own organisation could be the subject of research; yet other students may have a period during a full-time course where they are involved in projects for organisations with an interest in built environment issues organised as part of their course. These situations too might provide opportunities to conduct ethnographic studies. Work during holiday periods could create networks of contacts who act as gatekeepers and who might facilitate some interesting studies.

Ethnographic studies can take a considerable period to complete. Kitchen (1997) spent 17 years immersed in the world of planning practice in Manchester. The research by Henriksen and Tjora (2013) was conducted over a period of five years; that by Underwood in the planning office in London took six months; that by Tait (2011) two months. Such lengths of time would mean that many students would be unable to contemplate ethnography. However, Greed (1994: 126) is an advocate of ethnography, and she argues that it can be done in a dissertation and that the length of time is less important than the 'research mentality, and approach adopted, and in the way the research is structured'. She also points out that the style of interviewing in ethnographic work is more attractive to students because it is 'more open and natural' than asking closed questions. But an ethnographic study will require students to organise themselves and their work effectively for the period they will be working on the dissertation.

Methodological reasons

Finally, the choice of an ethnographic method could be justified on the grounds of the methodological arguments developed above and in Chapter 6 about the importance of studying behaviour in natural settings rather than in the artificial context of the completion of a questionnaire.

Documents

What are documents?

Macdonald and Tipton (1993: 188) define documents as 'things which we can read and which relate to aspects of the social world'. All research studies use documents in one way or another. Obviously, a literature review will use documents – articles, chapters in books, for example – to identify the state of knowledge on the topic or question of interest, and to define the nature of the research question to be answered in the research. There may be interest in justifying research (see Chapter 4) in terms of the way that the project will address issues that are of relevance to public policy (as Atkinson and Kintrea did with their study of area effects). Here some reference to official policy documents is required to make this case. But the interest in this chapter is not in this 'scene setting' use of documents but in the use of documents for generating data about the social world.

What exactly falls under the heading of 'documents' is subject to some difference in interpretation in books on research methods. There is agreement that documents include text-based documents but not all documents are text-based. Photographs are a case in point, and are often included under the category of documents. And documents of interest to planning researchers often include both text and visual material including photographs, maps, plans and diagrams. Then there are documents which record official statistics, where most of the material is numbers, where though numbers are undoubtedly parts of text they are not words, and where the type of analysis which will be undertaken is likely to be quantitative rather than qualitative (see Chapter 8). Here I make a distinction between text-based documents and official statistics.

Text-based documents

According to Rapley (2007: 10–11) 'The most ubiquitous and accessible source of documents are *newspapers and magazine* articles. This is a *massive* potential source for most academic projects. You only have to think about the diversity of weekly and daily local and national newspapers, as well as the ever-growing numbers of general and specialist magazines we are confronted with on a day-to-day basis, to realize how much material is easily available for analysis.' Yet there have been few planning studies which have made use of this source.

Other documents, particularly those produced by national and local levels of government – Acts of Parliament, Green Papers, White Papers, Good Practice guides, plans, policy statements and so on – are important parts of the social world which planners inhabit so they are meaningful and have an intrinsic interest for many involved in planning. In the UK context, planning applications, official recommendations on whether the application should be approved, the comments submitted by those consulted on the application, and the views of interested parties both in favour or against the proposed development are a case in point here.

Why would I want to use them?

Research purposes and questions

Policy documents can be and have been used for all sorts of research purposes. Amongst these documents, development plans are of particular interest to planning researchers. They are a key part of the 'hard infrastructure' of the planning system, to use the term employed by Vigar et al. (2000), and considerable time and effort is expended in their production. In addition to an interest in the objectives and policies expressed in plans, there is also an interest in why particular policies come to be developed. For this reason, many researchers are interested in the social processes by which plans are produced and who gets involved in their production. Development plans are the principal means by which planners in Britain can influence urban outcomes, though plans do not have the legal status that they enjoy in other parts of the world (France, for example), and there is therefore considerable interest in their impact on the thinking and subsequent behaviour of planners, land owners, builders, and householders. In recent years planning researchers have become interested, influenced in large measure by the writings of Foucault, in the language or discourse that is used in policy documents, the *rhetoric of policy* (see Lees and Demeritt 1998; Lees 2003). Here the interest is as much in what the documents do not say as what they do say, in their selective focussing of attention on certain issues.

Data sources and sampling

Documents are potential data sources for generating the data that researchers require. Plans can be used to generate data about the official or formal policy in a place. Berke and Conroy (2000) were interested in how strongly local plans in the US advocated the principles of sustainable development, and why the strength of support for sustainable development varied between places. They selected a sample of local development plans from across a number of US states and subjected the content and the language of these plans to an evaluation to measure the strength with which each plan supported six sustainable development principles.

In addition to formal plans themselves, there are often a large number of background papers, analyses of various matters (population change, housing, transport, environmental issues) in a locality, and other supplementary policy documents. These can be an important source of secondary data which can be used in subsequent research (see the section below on official statistics).

Practical reasons

There may be practical reasons for being interested in using documents. You may wish to do some further research on a topic and use the same sort of document as used by previous researchers. For studies of planning history, they may be the only available source of data on a topic such as changing national policy for town planning. Hobbs (1996) used documents like legislation, national guidance and debates in Parliament to identify the changing range and nature of national planning concerns over the period 1945–96. Similarly Healey and Shaw (1994) described the way that the 'environment' has been perceived by planners and policy makers over the post-war period. In both these cases, those people who were involved in the formulation of policy are no longer accessible or alive. Even over a shorter period, say a 20-year period, in researching the history of a residential development, it may not be possible to find people to interview because they have retired or moved to other posts and can no longer be traced or contacted, or if you can track them down, the events are so remote that they cannot remember them very clearly.

Methodological reasons

It is clear that researchers conceptualise the documents from which they generate data in different ways and this will influence the way they frame their research questions and go about generating their data (May, 2001). Some may see the data and analysis included in official plans and policy documents as objective statements of fact about the trends in the population, economy and transport systems in the place that they describe. For Berke and Conroy (2004) in the research discussed above, the methodological argument would be that the text of the local plan documents they analysed represented an objective assessment of how well the plan policies promoted the concept of sustainable development.

For other researchers, the interest in documents is what they tell us about how those who produce them interpret the world. Greed (1994: 120) for example discusses how she read the journal of the Royal Town Planning profession from its inception and spent time in what she called retrospective ethnography 'perusing venerated textbooks, and investigating seminal central and local government plans and planning publications' for clues to the historical roots of current attitudes and values of the planning profession.

A third approach to the use of documents, influenced by Foucault and arguments about the selectivity and the social construction of knowledge – referred to in Chapter 2 – is illustrated by the work of Atkinson (1999) in analysing the document *Involving Communities in Urban and Rural Regeneration* (DoE 1995) and of Lees (2003) on the Urban Task Force report which was discussed in Chapter 3. They are both interested in documents as a way of uncovering or generating knowledge about policy discourses. According to Alvesson (2002: 48), 'discourse is a tricky concept, used in a variety of ways', but Rapley (2007) argues that the primary interest in discourse is in how language is used in certain contexts and what specific version of the world is being produced by describing and analysing things in a specific way in that context. Often the sense is that, as May (2001: 183) puts it, 'documents are now viewed as media through which social power is expressed.'

Mason (1996: 71) makes a distinction between documents which existed prior to the research and which are used by you as the researcher to generate data, such as a policy document on an aspect of urban regeneration (see Atkinson (1999); Lees (2003)), and those documents which are created through the process of research, either by the researcher, or by the people or bodies you are researching. An example of a document produced by a researcher during the research process is a transcript of what was said during a meeting of planners (Forester, 1996), or the story produced by a researcher from the material obtained through an interview, such as the two stories about the working experiences of two planners produced by Hoch and set out in Hoch (1996), discussed in Chapter 5. A document produced for a researcher during the course of research could be, for instance, a travel diary kept for a period of a week by a sample of people.

The significance of the difference between documents which were already existing and those created through the research process is that the researcher has no influence on the content of a document which existed prior to the research, whilst the researcher has a very significant opportunity to influence the content of documents produced through the research process. Although it would seem that the latter are selective, both types of document are selective, however. If one is using pre-existing documents, then, the selection of what is written is determined by the author and the purposes for which s/he produced it. On top of this, you as a researcher will select only some documents to study because they deal with the issue you are interested in, and within those documents you will only generate data on certain aspects of the content of those documents. Atkinson (1999) accepts that there can be different 'readings' of any existing policy document.

Documents can be used in association with other methods of research. A policy document could be complemented by interviews with those involved in developing the policy or those involved in implementing the policy, depending on the purpose of the research. In the latter case, there may be an explicit interest in the differences between the policy as expressed in the policy document and how those implementing the policy understand what the policy means, and how they act to put it into effect. The study by Haughton et al. (2010) of the new spatial planning of the 2000s in the UK and Ireland seeking to compare the policy as expressed in new 'paper plans' with delivery of physical development on the ground is a typical example. Where there is a difference between what a document says and personal recollections, then there is the question of how to integrate or to reconcile the different sources, although it may come as no surprise to planning students that there may be a difference between intentions as set out in the plan and action/implementation.

Official statistics

What are official statistics?

Vast quantities of statistics are produced by the state. Some of these are the result of carefully planned survey research, like the Labour Force Survey or the New Earnings Survey. Other data come as a by-product of the operation of the state, such as statistics on those claiming unemployment benefit or the data from the Land Registry on residential house prices. The re-analysis of these data, and indeed of any data collected by another researcher or organisation is described as **secondary analysis**. (Hakim 2000: 24).

The Census of Population, widely used in planning research, produces statistics on population, migration, housing and households for areas from the nation down to the scale of 'output areas' which were first introduced in Scotland in 1991 and in the rest of the UK in the 2001 Census. These have been used again in the 2011 census with the aim of making the minimum of changes to boundaries, these being restricted mainly to areas where there had been substantial population changes since 2001 thus allowing comparisons over this period on substantially the same geography. Output areas have a minimum of 1000 population and an upper limit of 3000 population (100 to 400 households). These data have been used extensively in planning and policy research. Census data, available every ten years, has been used to measure and describe change in the population of major cities in the UK (see, for example, Champion and Fisher, 2003). Because they are available for very small areas, and policy interest has focussed on concentrations of deprivation, they have also been used as part of construction of an index of multiple deprivation, as used by Atkinson and Kintrea to select areas for their research in the cities of Glasgow and Edinburgh. The statistics produced for the census are based on what is effectively a self-completion questionnaire that is delivered to each household in the country by enumerators. In practice, not every household completes the questionnaire and hence there is an element of 'under-enumeration' in all censuses, a problem which has been becoming more significant over recent decades; it is a particular problem for young males and ethnic minorities. This problem was dramatised as the 'missing million' in the 1991 census, blamed by some on the introduction of the community charge introduced in the late 1980s.

Many statistics published on the ONS website under the heading of neighbourhood statistics – apart from those obtained from the Census – are not very fine-grained and relate principally to large areas, particularly local authority areas. However, statistics are also available from, and about, local government. Wong (2006) describes the encouragement by the Labour government of 1997–2010 of evidence-based policy at the local level, though the impetus to improve the collection of data seemed to be most apparent in less affluent areas where the information could be used to lobby for or bid for more resources. Some statistics are collected on a regular basis by local planning authorities for the purpose of monitoring trends in key land uses. These data can often be accessed by researchers and analysed for their own purposes. Guy (2010) undertook a study which aimed to describe change over a twenty-year period in retailing in Cardiff based on data collected by Cardiff City Council on gross floor space (sq. m.) and to explain why, despite an official policy to restrict out-of-centre retail development, there had been a growth in this type of development. There are often difficulties with the use of this data. The conventions and definitions used may not match those ideally required by the researcher, and they can also change over time which can make this sort of historical comparison difficult.

Why would I want to use them?

Research questions and purposes

With the use of secondary data it is often appropriate to adapt one's research questions to those questions which can be answered with the data available. We saw in Chapter 6 the apparently inductive study of the 'negotiativeness' of local planning authorities in England based on the refusal rate of planning applications and incentive to develop based on the appeal rate for refusals by

Wood (2000). Such secondary data based on statistics on development control, produced by local planning authorities, and returned to central government had previously been used in efforts to describe and explain the operation of the planning system. Brotherton (1982) in an early study used data on the number of planning applications in National Parks in England and Wales to describe development pressures in each of the national parks and to test some hypotheses using census data for why development pressure varied.

Data sources and sampling

Official statistics come from different data sources and are obtained by different methods of data generation. Some – for example, in the Labour Force Survey – come from people as a data source and have been generated by structured interviewing. Other data is a by-product of the bureaucratic processes of government, such as the number of affordable dwellings completed in an area published by the DCLG, which comes from the 'investment management system' of the Homes and Communities Agency, the Greater London Authority, and from the records of various departments within local authorities who make returns to the Department of Communities and Local Government. This system has the danger of some degree of double counting, though there are efforts to check this where local authorities provide particularly large numbers of affordable units. Hence, you will need to decide whether these methods are satisfactory, and whether the conventions which have been adopted in generating this data reflect your research needs.

Practical reasons

There are many practical reasons why official statistics and secondary data might be used by planning researchers. Blaxter et al. (2010) give a number of practical reasons for doing so. Collecting primary data is difficult, time-consuming and expensive. It is sensible to use the data you want if it already exists. It allows you to focus your efforts on analysis and interpretation rather than the collection of primary data. Of course one has to accept that the data which is available will have been collected according to certain conventions, and definitions and these may change over time.

Methodological reasons

In the same way that the use of text-based documents in research needs to take account of the way that researchers interpret documents, the use of official statistics also raise questions of interpretation. May (2001) suggests that there are broadly three types of interpretation. An 'institutionalist' interpretation sees statistics as saying more about the organisation producing them and its priorities than any 'reality' about the world, it emphasises the social construction of statistics. A 'radical' view goes further and sees them as part of the way that government wishes to order and regulate the population. Finally, a 'positivist' view sees them as attempts to produce objective measures of the social world. In this view, a significant issue for official statistics is the reliability of the data available on which they are based. Wong (2006) describes the problems that faced those researchers compiling the Town and City Indicators Database in the early 2000s as the methods of generating various national statistics were under constant revision and adjustment with consequences for the 'local estimates' which were produced for towns and cities. Particular problems arose with figures on unemployment and on employment where there were significant differences between the number of jobs estimated from the Labour Force Survey and the Annual Business Survey. These differences in the reliability of the process of data generation raises questions about the validity of the statistics produced, and the validity of comparing changes over time and space.

The validity of data was at issue in the paper by Brotherton (1982) based on the use of planning application data (McNamara et al., 1984). This concerned the validity of measuring 'development pressure' by the number of applications per annum per thousand population. One limitation of total numbers of applications is that it does not take account of the variable character of planning applications between areas, with some applications being for major developments and others of a more minor nature. The number of planning applications per thousand population measures the propensity of potential developers to make planning applications but this is not the same as the demand for development which might be measured by land values, on the grounds that high land values might be an incentive to landowners to wish to develop their land. Nor is it the same as development activity since only some types of development require planning permission (agriculture being notably excluded). Brotherton accepted that his measure was not a measure of demand for development and only an approximate measure of development pressure. He accepted too that the term development pressure was perhaps not an ideal label for what he was measuring but that it was better than the alternatives. The debate also highlighted the way that the data gets collected. In particular they point out that the making of a planning application, and its registration by a LPA may be influenced by the way that the LPA operates. A notable factor is the degree to which LPAs spend resources on pre-application discussions or negotiations with potential applicants. This activity may result in a proposal for development not being submitted as a planning application in one LPA, on the initial advice of the planning staff on its likely acceptability, whilst in another area where pre-application discussions are discouraged the same application may be submitted as an application, and subsequently refused permission. Brotherton argues (McNamara et al., 1984) that if this hypothesis is true then one would expect lower refusal rates where there were lower applications rates, and this in fact seems to be true (though he doubts whether the pre-application discussion explanation is the correct one).

> **Summary/Key lessons**
>
> In this chapter I have suggested that there are only a limited number of methods of research. Some researchers favour particular methods and get labelled, for example if they use questionnaires, as 'quantitative researchers'. I do not think the quantitative versus qualitative distinction is very helpful in making decisions about which methods to use for a project and it is not sensible to start a project with a prior decision about the method you will use. The decision about the methods of data generation to be used in any study should:
>
> 1. Start with the question: Will it allow me to generate the data I need to answer my research question? This is the most important consideration.
>
> 2. Take account of the data sources, people or places which will allow you to generate data on whatever cases you are aiming to investigate.
>
> 3. Be realistic in terms of the time you have to do any piece of research, and also in terms of access to any research setting that interests you.
>
> 4. Be consistent with your methodological beliefs about the most appropriate way of generating data about the social world.

> **Exercise: Methods of data generation**
>
> Having read this chapter, you should now, I hope, be in a position to think about the methods of data generation which you might use to answer your research question. This exercise asks you to:
>
> 1. Identify the possible methods that you might use.
>
> 2. Make short notes on the advantages and disadvantages of these methods for your proposed project in terms of allowing you to answer your research question, the potential data sources from which you might generate the data, any practical considerations (time and money available), and the methodological arguments that you find convincing.

Further Reading

A number of examples of research in urban planning using different methods of generating data have been given throughout this chapter. These could usefully be referred to if you want to see examples of research using these methods. Sandercock (1998) provides a justification for the use of a range of methods by planners in their research role beyond, but not excluding, those taught in 'quantitative methods courses'.

There are a very large number of books on research methods in social research. Some aim to be more comprehensive in their coverage and discuss a range of methods. Examples of these which students have found helpful in the past are:

Bryman, A. (2008) *Social Research Methods*. Oxford: Oxford University Press.

Gilbert, N. (2008) *Researching Social Life*, 3rd Edition. London: Sage.

May, T. (2001) *Social Researching*. Buckingham: Open University Press.

McNeill, P. and Chapman, S. (2005) *Research Methods*, 3rd Edition. London: Routledge.

Robson, C. (2002) *Real World Research*. Oxford: Blackwell.

For a more detailed discussion of specific methods of research, the following could be consulted:

Interviews and questionnaires

Arksey, H. and Knight, P. (1999) *Interviewing for Social Scientists: An Introductory Resource with Examples*. London: Sage.

Czaya, R. and Blair, J. (2005) *Designing Surveys: A Guide to Decisions and Procedures*, 2nd Edition. London: Sage.

de Vaus, D. (2002) *Surveys in Social Research*, 5th Edition London: Routledge.

Gillan, B. (2008) *Developing a Questionnaire*, 2nd Edition. London: Continuum.

Kvale, S. (2008) *Doing Interviews*. London: Sage.

King, N. and Horrocks, C. (2009) *Interviews in Qualitative Research*. London: Sage.

Ethnography and observation

Angrosino, M. (2007) *Doing Ethnographic and Observational Research*. Thousand Oaks, CA: Sage.

Gilham, B. (2008) *Observation Techniques: Structured to Unstructured*. London: Continuum.

Hammersley, M. and Atkinson, P. (1995) *Ethnography: Principles in Practice*. London: Routledge.

Documents

Burman, E. and Parker, I. (eds) (1993) *Discourse Analytic Research: Repertoires and Readings of Texts in Action*. London: Routledge.

Howarth, D. (2000) *Discourse*. Buckingham: Open University Press.

Prior, L. (2003) *Using Documents in Social Research*. London: Sage.

Rapley ,T. (2007) *Doing Conversation, Discourse and Document Analysis*. London: Sage.

References

Alvesson, M. (2002) *Postmodernism and Social Research*. Buckingham: Open University Press.

Atkinson, R. (1999) 'Discourses of Partnership and Empowerment in Contemporary British Urban Regeneration', *Urban Studies* 36 (1): 59–72.

Atkinson, R. and Kintrea, K. (2001) 'Disentangling Area Effects: Evidence from Deprived and Non-deprived Neighbourhoods', *Urban Studies* 38 (12): 2277–98.

Berke, P.R. and Conroy, M.M. (2000) 'Planning for Sustainable Development: Measuring and Explaining Progress in Plans', *Journal of the American Planning Association* 66: 21–33.

Blaxter L, Hughes, C. and Tight, M. (2010) *How to Research*. Maidenhead: Open University Press, McGraw Hill Education.

Blowers, A. (1980) *The Limits of Power: the Politics of Local Planning Policy*. Oxford: Pergamon.

Brotherton, I. (1982) 'Development Pressures and Controls in the National Parks, 1966–1981', *Town Planning Review* 53 (4): 439–59.

Bryman, A. (2008) *Social Research Methods*. Oxford: Oxford University Press.

Burgess, R. (1984) *In the Field: An Introduction to Field Research*. Hemel Hempstead: Allen and Unwin.

Burgess, J., Harrison, C.M. and Limb, M. (1988) 'People, Parks and the Urban Green: a Study of Popular Meanings and Values for Open Spaces in the City', *Urban Studies* 25: 455–73.

Champion, T. and Fisher, T. (2003) 'The Social Selectivity of Migration Flows Affecting Britain's Larger Conurbations: An Analysis of the 1991 Census Regional Migration Table', *Scottish Geographical Magazine* 119: 229–46.

Cochrane, A. (1998) 'Illusions of Power: Interviewing Local Elites', *Environment and Planning A* 30 (12): 2121–32.

de Leeuw, E. (2008) 'Self-Adminstered Questionnaires and Standardized Interviews in Conditions', in P. Alasuutari, L. Bickman and J. Brannen (eds) *The Sage Handbook of Social Research Methods*. London: Sage. pp. 313–27.

Department of Environment (DoE) (1995) *Involving Communities in Urban and Rural Regeneration: A Guide for Practitioners.* London: Department of Environment.

Farthing, S.M. (1986) 'The Impact of Computers on the Processing of Planning Applications', *The Planner* 71 (11): 17–18.

Fielding, N. (1993) 'Ethnography,' in N. Fielding (ed.) *Researching Social Life.* London: Sage. pp.154–71.

Forester, J. (1993) 'Learning from Practice Stories: the Priority of Practical Judgement', in F. Fischer and J. Forester (eds) *The Argumentative Turn in Policy Analysis and Planning.* Durham, NC: Duke University Press. pp. 186–209.

Forester, J. (1996) 'The Rationality of Listening, Emotional Sensitivity, and Moral Vision', in S.J. Mandelbaum, L. Mazza and R.W. Burchell (eds) *Explorations in Planning Theory.* New Brunswick, NJ: Rutgers the State University of New Jersey. pp. 204–24.

Glaser, B.G. and Strauss, A.L. (1967) *The Discovery of Grounded Theory.* Chicago: Aldine.

Gomm, R. (2004) *Social Research Methodology.* Basingstoke: Palgrave Macmillan.

Greed, C. (1994) 'The Real Place of Ethnography in Planning: or is it "Real Research"?', *Planning Practice and Research* 9: 119–26.

Greener, I. (2011) *Designing Social Research.* London: Sage.

Guy, C. (2010) 'Development Pressure and Retail Planning: A Study of 20-year Change in Cardiff, UK', *International Review of Retail, Distribution, and Consumer Research* 20 (1): 119–33.

Hakim, C. (2000) *Research Design: Successful Designs for Social and Economic Research.* London: Routledge.

Hammersley, M. (1990) *Reading Ethnographic Research: A Critical Guide.* London: Longman.

Haughton, G., Allmendinger, P., Counsell, D. and Vigar, G. (2010) *The New Spatial Planning.* London: Routledge.

Healey, P. and Shaw, T. (1994) 'Changing Meanings of "Environment" in the British Planning System', *Transactions of the Institute of British Geographers* 19: 428–38.

Henricksen, I.M. and Tjora, A. (2013) 'Interaction Pretext: Experiences of Community in the Urban Neighbourhood', *Urban Studies* 50 (10): 1–14.

Hobbs, P. (1996) 'Postwar Economic Development and Town Planning Intervention', in C. Greed (ed.) *Investigating Town Planning.* Harlow: Addison Wesley Longman. pp. 19–31.

Hoch, C. (1996) 'What Do Planners Do in the United States?' in S.J. Mandelbaum, L. Mazza and R.W. Burchell (eds) *Explorations in Planning Theory.* New Brunswick, NJ: Rutgers the State University of New Jersey. pp. 225–40.

Kitchen, T. (1997) *People, Politics, Policies and Plans: the City Planning Process in Contemporary Britain.* London: Paul Chapman Publishing.

Lees, L. (2003) 'Vision of "Urban Renaissance": the Urban Task Force Report and the Urban White Paper', in R. Imrie and M. Raco (eds) *Urban Renaissance?* Bristol: The Policy Press. pp. 61–81.

Lees, L. and Demeritt, D. (1998) 'Envisioning the "Liveable City": the Interplay of "Sim City" and "Sin City" in Vancouver's Planning Discourse', *Urban Geography* 19: 332–59.

Macdonald, K. and Tipton, C. (1993) 'Using Documents' in N. Fielding (ed.) *Researching Social Life.* London: Sage. pp. 187–200.

Mason, J. (1996) *Qualitative Researching.* London: Sage.

May, T. (2001) *Social Researching.* Buckingham: Open University Press.

McCarthy, P. and Harrison, A. (1995) *Attitudes to Town and Country Planning.* London: HMSO.

McNamara, P., Healey, P. and Brotherton, I. (1984) 'The Limitations of Development Control Data in Planning Research: A Comment on Ian Brotherton's Recent Study', *Town Planning Review*, 55 (1): 91–101.

Rapley, T. (2007) *Doing Conversation, Discourse and Document Analysis.* London: Sage.

Robson, C. (2002) *Real World Research.* Oxford: Blackwell.

Sandercock, L. (1998) *Towards Cosmopolis: Planning for Multicultural Cities.* Chichester: Wiley.

Tait, M. (2011) 'Trust and the Public Interest in the Micropolitics of Planning Practice', *Journal of Planning Education and Research* 31 (2): 157–71.

Vigar, G., Healey, P., Hull, A. and Davoudi, S. (2000) *Planning, Governance and Spatial Strategy in Britain.* London: Routledge.

Wong, C. (2006) *Indicators for Urban and Regional Planning.* London: Routledge.

Wood, R. (2000) 'Using Appeal Data to Characterise Local Planning Authorities', *Town Planning Review* 71: 97–107.

8

DATA ANALYSIS

Key questions

What types of claims are made in response to research questions?

What is data analysis? How do earlier decisions affect analysis?

What types of data are there?

Key concepts 🔑

Quantitative data, qualitative data, quantitative analysis, variables, construct validity, causal analysis, dependent variables and independent variables, proxy variables, cross-tabulation, random sampling error, statistical significance; qualitative analysis, key informants, corroboration, conceptual frameworks, sensitising concepts, indexing, coding; triangulation; discourse analysis.

Overview

This chapter is about the analysis stage of research, that is, the stage of research when your primary interest is in developing an argument about the claims that can be made on the basis of the research you have conducted. As we saw in Chapter 3 there are both descriptive and explanatory claims, which can be seen as answers to descriptive research questions or 'what' questions and to explanatory research questions or 'why' questions. In some ways it is true that the whole research process is concerned with this issue, and some research approaches emphasise the interaction between data generation and analysis throughout the process (grounded theory, for example) but, often, there is an intensive stage towards the end of the period of research when the analysis of the data generated is the main concern.

Referring back to the discussion in Chapters 5 and 6, we can see claims as operating at two levels. First, there are claims or 'findings' which relate to the case or cases studied in the research. Second, there are wider claims or generalisations made on the basis of the research. When the research question is descriptive and the cases studied are thought to be representative of a wider population, a descriptive claim about these cases may be the basis of an empirical generalisation from the sample to the population. This could be, say, from research on a few cities, neighbourhoods or planners to all cities, neighbourhoods or planners.

Where the research question is explanatory, a theoretical generalisation is made when an account which is given for why something happened in the cases examined is taken as being applicable beyond these cases to all cases where such conditions apply. For example, a generalisation from the factors which affect the negotiating stance of a few local planning authorities to development applications to a theory about all such cases.

Research questions therefore affect the nature of the claims you will seek to make on the basis of your research, and the purpose of your analysis. Analysis will help you support those claims by turning your 'raw data' into 'evidence'. For this reason, it is clearly a very important part of research design but thinking about analysis tends to be neglected in comparison with the attention devoted to data generation.

The nature of the research question posed, how open-ended it is, will also affect the amount of work to be undertaken at the analysis stage, during and after data generation, compared with the earlier research design stage. In earlier chapters, I advocated an approach to research questions which narrowed the scope of such questions.

The chapter proceeds as follows. It starts with a brief review of the types of data that can be generated, data in the form of words or numbers. This affects the way that data is analysed. It then examines, in turn, examples of quantitative and qualitative analysis to answer both descriptive and explanatory questions drawn from the research of authors considered in earlier chapters of the book. The aim is to reconstruct the logic of the analysis, drawing on the authors' explanations where these are available. Typical quantitative analysis in planning research is based on the analysis of survey data. Here, there are well-developed techniques for analysing data which can be adopted, and can be recognised in the writings of researchers. There is computer software available for such analysis (e.g. SPSS, MINITAB). Techniques for the analysis of qualitative data are less well documented though there is software which can be used for this purpose (including the use of word-processing and spreadsheets). In articles produced by qualitative researchers in planning, it is not always so clear exactly how the analysis has been conducted. This can lead to issues over the accountability of the analytical decisions which have been taken. Gomm (2004: 19) argues that it is relatively easy for those who might wish to scrutinise or check the process of analysis to do so with quantitative research because there are standard procedures and 'numerical data isn't particularly weighty'. By contrast, it may be difficult to keep track of the analytical decisions made in a qualitative project, and the sheer volume of data from qualitative research means that it cannot easily be shared with others.

Qualitative and quantitative data

Making a distinction between these two types of data is important because it will affect the way that you will have to analyse the data. But the type of data you have to work with will be affected, in part, by decisions you take about the methods of data generation, and also the number of cases selected for study. For the purposes of this chapter, I am taking qualitative data to be data to be analysed which is in the form of words. It could have been generated as the result of recording and transcribing unstructured or semi-structured interviews, as a result of group interviews (as conducted by Burgess et al. (1988)) or from the text in documents of various kinds. Quantitative data is, in this definition, data in the form of numbers. Much of this data may actually have originated in the form of words but has been subsequently coded as numbers. For example, structured interviews usually ask closed questions, to which there are a limited range of answers. In the design of the interview schedule, each of these answers will normally be pre-coded so that questions about – to take an example from Atkinson and Kintrea (2001) – whether the respondent had left their neighbourhood during the previous weekday can be answered with either 'yes' or 'no', and the code for 'yes' might be 1 and the code for 'no' might be 2. Here there is no implication that not leaving the neighbourhood is twice as virtuous as leaving it, the numbers are effectively labels but a statistical package like SPSS is able to handle numbers more efficiently than words. In the analysis of quantitative data, many decisions have already been taken about how the data will be organised and labelled or coded but where the results of data generation are data in the form of words, typically decisions about indexing and coding remain to be taken.

Quantitative analysis of survey data

A descriptive research question

The example I draw on here is from research by Hoch (1988). Following some research on planning and political conflict by Forester using participant observation and by in-depth interviews with planners by Baum, Hoch (1988) was interested in how representative the findings of these earlier studies were and he undertook to conduct 'a national study of planners and threatening political conflict' in the USA 'in order to find out what planners do when they believe their economic security, political legitimacy, professional competence, or moral integrity are subject to attack.' (Hoch, 1988: 27). The first aim, and the one of interest here, is essentially to produce an accurate estimate of the how many planners had faced political conflict and of the nature of their response to political conflict. A mail survey was prepared and sent to a random sample of 5% (N = 992) of the national membership of the American Planning Association in late November 1986. A little more than one in four of the sample (26.9%) returned completed surveys (N = 267). There are often problems of low response rates with mail questionnaires and this might be expected at the design stage but Hoch comments that the response rate achieved in his survey is substantially higher than the 10% response rate often to be found in such surveys. Nevertheless, in terms of obtaining an accurate estimate of conflict and planners' behaviour in response to conflict, non-response of nearly three quarters needs to be recognised as a problem if you are trying to make an empirical generalisation (see Chapter 5) about the experience of planners in the USA on the basis of the sample analysed. The other aspect of this sample frame as a basis on which to select a sample of the population of planners in the USA from which to generalise is that it would not cover planners who were not members of the American Planning Association, and some members of the American Planning Association may not be working in an occupation that one might think of as being 'planner's work', a point acknowledged by Hoch though their responses were included in the analysis. Figure 8.1 illustrates how the population of interest, the sample frame, the random sample selected and the achieved sample (after taking account of non-response) may overlap.

Data Analysis 153

```
┌─────────────────────────────────────────┐
│  POPULATION: PLANNERS IN THE            │
│            USA                          │
│                                         │
│      a                                  │
│         ┌───────────────────────────┐   │
│         │  SAMPLE FRAME (APA)       │   │
│         │                           │   │
│         │    b          c           │   │
│         │    ┌──────────────────┐   │   │
│         │    │ RANDOM SAMPLE    │   │   │
│         │    │                  │   │   │
│         │    │   d        e     │   │   │
│         │    │   ┌──────────┐   │   │   │
│         │    │   │ ACHIEVED │   │   │   │
│         │    │   │ SAMPLE   │   │   │   │
│         │    │   │          │   │   │   │
│         │    │   │  f    g  │   │   │   │
│         │    │   └──────────┘   │   │   │
│         │    └──────────────────┘   │   │
│         └───────────────────────────┘   │
└─────────────────────────────────────────┘
```

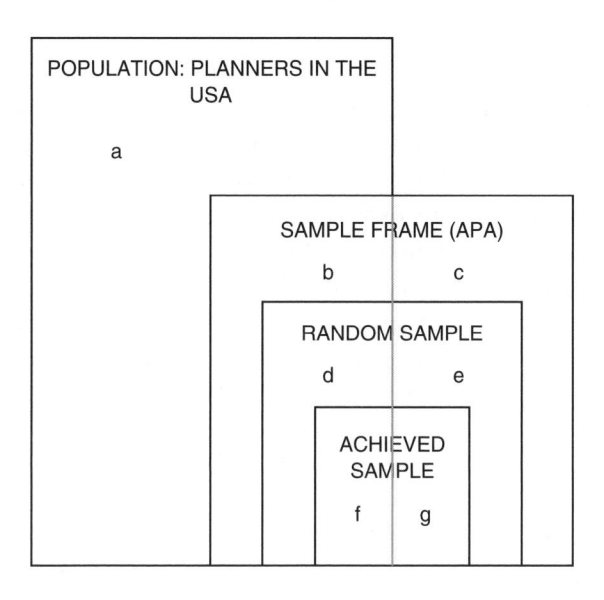

a = Planners not in the sample frame (omissions)
b = People in the sample frame
c = People in the sample frame (members of the APA) but not planners (ineligibles)
d = Planners selected at random
e = Non-planners selected at random (ineligibles)
f = Planners responding to the questionnaire
g = Non-planners responding to the questionnaire (ineligibles)

(*Source*: Based on Hoch, 1988)

Figure 8.1 Relationship between the Population, the Sample Frame, the Random Sample and the Achieved Sample used for Analysis

The nature of the conflicts planners faced was obtained by asking an open-ended question, where the respondents answered in their own words which were then coded by the researcher into one of six categories, including one where the respondent did not reply to the question. This is an example of a qualitative component within an otherwise quantitative piece of analysis. This coding itself requires analysis, in the sense that you as the researcher have to decide on the categories into which the responses are going to be coded. Since the survey was to establish how widespread the experiences of political conflict were following some previous research by Baum and Forester, Hoch could have decided at the design stage that he would use categories which were suggested by the previous research as a basis for the categorisation of the types, or he might have decided to use some theory about responses, or finally he might have decided that he would start with the answers given by the respondents and use these as the basis of dividing up the responses.

Descriptive analysis

The aim here was to make some descriptive claims about the nature of the 'threatening political conflict' that planners in the USA faced during the course of their work, and what action they took when faced with this conflict. The analysis sought first to estimate the frequency of these different types of political conflict, displaying the data for this variable in a table called a 'frequency distribution'. **Variables** are the representations of the reality of social life that quantitative researchers are claiming to measure. There can be debates about how well such variables actually measure the reality in question (construct validity). We will see an example of this below.

Just over half (56%) of respondents reported a threatening political conflict during their career. Table 8.1 (based on Hoch, 1988) shows the frequency distribution of types of conflict faced by planners. This table shows the number of respondents who gave a particular answer and the percentage of total respondents in each category. The frequency distribution shows that the most frequent type of conflict arose over development that was in conflict with planning principles, or policies. The second most frequent involved a difference of view between the planner and local politicians (elected officials as they are called in the USA) or with the planner's supervisor. The paper illustrates these different categories of conflict by giving descriptions of some of the cases of political conflict reported in the survey by quoting verbatim what the planners had written on the questionnaire or summarised situations involving the planners, including sexual harassment. Obviously these are selected from the large number recorded on the questionnaires and provide 'quotable' quotes which can spice up what might be seen as a rather dry analysis.

Table 8.1 Types of Conflict Experienced

Type of Conflict	Number of Respondents	Percentage of Respondents
Planning vs. Politics	59	40
Political Loyalty	26	17
Ethical Disputes	21	14
Political "Squeeze"	20	14
Social Justice	11	8
No Response	12	8
Total	149	

Source: Hoch, (1988)

Another piece of analysis showed that one in three planners faced such conflicts more than once and 15% did yearly or more often. He makes an empirical generalisation on the basis of this evidence that 'while threatening political conflicts are fairly widespread among planners, they are not a frequent occurrence in most planners' careers.' (1988: 27) What did planners do in the face of conflict? Here the analysis is concerned with whether the planner had taken some action to avoid the conflict and whether that action had been successful in the view of the planner. Table 8.2 is a simple cross-tabulation – or a piece of bivariate analysis – in which these two variables are considered at the same time. The percentages in this table show the percentage of all those who had experienced potential conflict divided between the different cells of the table. The total of the percentages adds up to 100% and the N at the bottom of the table refers to the size of the sample from which these percentages have been calculated. This analysis shows four categories of response and outcome: planners were either 'successful', 'overwhelmed', 'insulated' and 'unprepared'. In this table we know that these categories were built on previous research, coming from a previous interview survey of Chicago planners carried out by Hoch and a colleague.

Table 8.2 Efforts to Prevent Political Conflict by Successful Avoidance

Effort to Prevent Conflict?	Avoidance Successful?	
	Yes	**No**
Yes	Successful	Overwhelmed
	20%	40%
No	Insulated	Unprepared
	24%	16%
	N=267	

Source: Hoch, (1988)

The descriptive claim here is that 'although three out of five planners either tried to avoid the possibility of conflict or sought to anticipate and resolve potential disputes before they became threatening, only a third were successful' (1988: 29). The problem with descriptive claims and empirical generalisations of this sort does not lie with data analysis, but with the inadequacy of the sample frame (are planners in the APA representative of all planners in the USA?) and the possible bias caused by the very large number of people who failed to respond to the questionnaire (see Figure 8.1).

Are those who have faced threatening political conflict in their careers, for example, more likely to have responded than those who had not? One reason for this might be that on receiving such a questionnaire, those who had not faced such conflict might have thought that there would be no interest in their replies since they had nothing useful to add to the survey. If this were the case the responses would be biased and the extent of the conflict would be over-stated.

An explanatory research question

In this case I look at some analysis conducted by Atkinson and Kintrea (2001). As we saw in Chapter 3, policy for the improvement of the lives of the poor and deprived in the cities of Britain in the early 2000s was based on the theory that 'the neighbourhood profoundly affects such outcomes as education, employment, and health' (Atkinson and Kintrea, 2001: 2277).

Atkinson and Kintrea wanted to test the theory that where you live (your neighbourhood) has an effect on such outcomes 'over and above', or controlling for, non-spatial factors such as gender and class. They were therefore involved in an evaluation of the policy, not in the sense that they were evaluating the impact of the policy, but in the sense that they were seeking evidence to either support or criticise the theory that where you live does have an independent impact on social outcomes, and which in turn would support (or not) a policy focus on the neighbourhood.

Causal analysis

Atkinson and Kintrea took advantage of a natural experiment by selecting areas which had different concentrations of poor people or different levels of social mix: 'deprived' areas (high concentrations) and 'mixed areas' (lower concentrations). Some, but not all, of the mechanisms that affect the outcomes for people are said to be caused by concentrations of people of a particular type in an area. For example, this might affect the reputation of the area and add to the difficulties that people living there might experience in obtaining employment once people find out where they live.

In recognition that educational, employment and health outcomes for people might also be affected by the larger place within which their neighbourhood is located (the city), they selected a deprived and a mixed area in two cities with different records of economic change in recent years (Edinburgh and Glasgow). They selected a sample of addresses in each of these 4 neighbourhoods, and conducted interviews with residents to establish, amongst other things, employment and health outcomes for residents. We should note at this point that they did not achieve a response rate of 100% of the addresses they sampled, the response rate was 53%. This means that there is a high chance that non-respondents (47% of addresses) were different from respondents, and that the sample did not represent the characteristics of the population in the neighbourhoods, and so one would be rather restricted in making an empirical generalisation from this data – what one could say about the characteristics of the population in these neighbourhoods (or in other similar neighbourhoods in Britain). And if the sample is unrepresentative, the sample would be 'biased' which makes the interpretation of any apparent associations in the data problematic.

Focussing here on the hypothesis that the social mix of the neighbourhood you live in (cause) affects your employment outcomes (effects), the starting point for an analysis would be the comparison of variables measuring employment outcomes for the groups living in the deprived and the mixed areas. The causal factor of interest in a piece of research is labelled the **independent variable** and the effect of interest is labelled the **dependent variable**. The objective of the analysis would be to assess the association between the two variables.

The analysis was done by means of a 'cross tabulation' of variables as shown in Table 8.3. The dependent variable, the 'effect', was the employment rate of residents, that is, as measured by the percentage of residents aged 16–65 in employment.

Table 8.3 Cross-tabulation of Employment by Tenure

	Edinburgh				Glasgow			
	Dalside		Lockhart		Westfields		Craiglee	
Tenure	Percentage	N	Percentage	N	Percentage	N	Percentage	N
Owner-occupied**	58.1	31	84.6	117	61.0	41	72.4	105
Local authority	28.6	98	33.3	3	22.1	95	22.2	36
Housing association**	54.5	33	45.5	11	11.1	19	0.0	3
Private renting**	100.0	3	63.2	38	0.0	2	0.0	3
Total	40.6	165	75.8	169	31.0	157	56.3	147

Base: All respondents aged 16–65 years.

** Indicates significant at the 5 percent level.

Source: Atkinson and Kintrea, (2001)

How do we interpret this table? First, there are two confounding factors or **'control'** variables here. The first control variable is represented by the division in the columns in the table between Edinburgh and Glasgow, the two representing more and less prosperous city contexts, rather than these cities being of any intrinsic interest in this situation. We might hypothesise that people in the two cities would be likely to have different employment prospects, so this difference is 'controlled for' in the analysis in the table. We would expect to find a higher level of employment in general in Edinburgh than Glasgow.

The independent variable, the supposed 'cause' in this analysis is the concentration of poverty (social mix) in the area. This is reflected in the sub-division in the table between two areas within each city, one of them a deprived area and the other a mixed area, the deprived areas being shaded. So in Edinburgh, the deprived area is labelled 'Dalside' and the mixed area is 'Lockhart' and in Glasgow they are 'Westfields' and 'Craiglee' respectively. In this analysis there are thus possible influences at different spatial scales on employment prospects for residents. This situation is sometimes described as multi-level analysis.

There are four columns in the table. At the top of each column is to be seen 'Percentage' and 'N'. The percentage here refers to the percentage of people of a given tenure. N is the size of the sample of respondents for each tenure. Thus, for Dalside, 58.1% of owner occupiers were in employment based on a sample size of 31 respondents in Dalside who were owner-occupiers.

Ignoring for the moment, the tenure of respondents, the test of the hypothesis about the impact of the concentration of the poor in an area on the employment outcomes would be measured by comparing the employment rate of two groups of people, one living in an area with a high concentration of the poor, and the other group living a neighbourhood with lower concentration. We can see that in both Edinburgh and in Glasgow, the deprived areas have a lower percentage of those in employment than those in the comparative mixed area. For example, employment for residents 16–65 in Westfields is 31% whilst it is 56.3% in Craiglee. So, at first sight, we have evidence of an association between the level of deprivation and the chances that a resident would be in employment.

But of course, the areas were selected in the first place on the basis of the levels of deprivation in the areas, and one of the indicators of deprivation is unemployment or people who are outside the labour market hence we would expect these differences to exist. Atkinson and Kintrea (2001: 2292) were concerned, however, 'whether there is an additional neighbourhood contribution to joblessness.' What we want to know, then, is whether people with similar characteristics but living in different areas have the same chances of obtaining employment. This is why they looked at tenure. This was their second control variable. They saw tenure as a 'proxy' for poverty: those in council renting were taken to be poor. Thus an analysis taking tenure into account 'controls for' some of the differences between people, and aims to ensure that in making comparisons between areas, we are 'comparing like with like'. A 'proxy' variable is one which in the view of the researcher does not measure directly the reality they are interested in measuring which in this case is 'poverty' but which for various practical reasons (like the difficulty of measuring income in a structured interview) represents a 'reasonable' approximation.

What does this table tell us, then, about the impact of living in areas with higher or lower concentrations of poverty on the chances of being in employment? On the face of it, the table suggests that the impact may depend on the tenure category that one is in. If we look at the prosperous city context first, it seems that owner-occupiers (taken to be more prosperous residents) in the deprived area are less likely to be in employment (58.1%) than owner-occupiers in the mixed area (84.6%) which is consistent with the hypothesis. For those in local authority rented housing, (those taken to be poor), there does not seem to be much of a difference between the two areas with 28.6% in the deprived area and 33.3% in the mixed area in employment, though the differences are consistent with the hypothesis. For the last two categories of tenure – housing association and private renting – the cause seems to have the opposite effect to the one hypothesised, in that employment rates seem to be somewhat higher for those living in the deprived area.

If we look at the less prosperous city, Glasgow, there is a rather similar pattern to that found in the more prosperous city, Edinburgh, for owner-occupiers, those in local authority rented housing, and those in housing association tenure. 72.4% of owner occupiers are in employment in the mixed area compared with 61.0% in the deprived area. For those in local authority housing, there is a very similar percentages of 22.1% and 22.2% for those in employment in both areas. For those in the housing association tenure, we find again that a higher percentage of those living in the deprived area (11.1%) are in employment compared with the mixed area (0.0%). This, of course, is contrary to the hypothesis that living in a deprived area reduces one's chances of employment. For those in private renting none are in employment in either the deprived or the mixed area, though the number of respondents in the sample are very small, with just two in the deprived area and three in the mixed area.

Chance or random sampling error in statistical analysis is always a possibility when the data being analysed is based on a sample of the population (see Box 8.1). This would mean in this example that the differences calculated between the deprived and mixed areas might be due to the nature of the specific sample that was selected for study, and would not be found in the wider population from which the sample was selected. Just by chance (because it is a random sample) you have selected an unrepresentative sample. One way to estimate the chance of this happening is to calculate the statistical significance of the differences. The tenures of owner-occupiers, housing association renting and private renting in Table 8.3 are all asterisked (**). The local authority tenure is not so marked. The differences with the double asterisk (**) are said to be 'significant at the 5 percent level'. The small differences between the levels of employment for those in the deprived and mixed area in local authority tenure are not statistically significant. Differences for this tenure are highly likely to be due to what is called 'sampling error'.

BOX 8.1

STATISTICAL SIGNIFICANCE OF TABLE 8.3 FROM ATKINSON AND KINTREA (2001)

How should we interpret statistical significance in this table? The tenures of Owner-occupied, Housing Association and Private renting are all asterisked **. This is described as meaning that the results are 'significant at the 5 percent level'. We have seen that when we look at the percentages in the table that there are differences between the deprived areas and the mixed areas for these three categories (though not for the local authority rented tenure). It is quite conventional to report the statistical significance of results. The 5 percent level is also conventionally accepted as being the lowest level of significance which is to be counted for research purposes as 'truly significant'.

One limitation of the paper is that it is not clear how this significance has been calculated. It seems likely that the authors used the chi-square test, a test which can be used where the data is 'categorical' as is often the case with structured interviewing. Here the answer to a question can be coded as one of a few categories. For example, what is the tenure of your accommodation? This has the categories: owner-occupied; local authority; housing association; private renting.

> Statistical significance in this context means that if there is no difference in employment rates between the two areas, the chance that we would get a difference of the reported size due to a random or chance effect is low. For every 100 (hypothetical) random samples drawn from residents in these areas, a difference of the reported size would be found in only five samples. Hence in taking this as the level of risk, one is gambling that the results one has from this particular sample is unlikely to be due to random sampling error. Differences in the percentages for the local authority tenure are small, and are not statistically significant. These differences could be due to sampling error.

What sort of causal claim can we make on the basis of this evidence? Figure 8.2 gives some possible reasons why a piece of analysis for a study might reveal an association between variables. It seems that we can eliminate chance or sampling error as an explanation for the association between the level of deprivation and employment, controlling for three of the tenures, but an important point to bear in mind here is that with a response rate of 53% the achieved sample is not a random sample of the population and may well be biased. This could, therefore, be one of the reasons why there is an association.

Some of the possible confounding factors have been controlled in this analysis. Atkinson and Kintrea (2001), however, point to a problem with interpreting the greater success of owner-occupiers in the mixed area in obtaining employment as evidence for the hypothesis. They suggest that there can be questions about the validity of tenure as a proxy measure of poverty. The character of owner-occupation itself may vary between the two areas, with home-ownership in the deprived areas being more marginal and consisting in part of those who bought their local authority housing under the 'right to buy'. So the analysis may not succeed in comparing like with like between the areas, even taking tenure into account. And there do seem to be differences between the areas in terms of the proportion of different household types. For example, there are more lone parent households in the deprived estate. These are usually female-headed households with low economic activity rates.

If tenure is a poor proxy variable for income levels then we cannot conclude much about the impact of the social mix of a neighbourhood in the cases studied. Part of the difference between areas reflects differences in the people living in the neighbourhoods. But if it is a reasonable proxy, then there do seem to be neighbourhood effects, once we control for 'income' in this way, though for people in some tenures (or income groups) social mix is associated with better employment prospects, but for others with worse outcomes. And, of course, there could be other factors influencing the neighbourhoods which are not taken into account or controlled in the research.

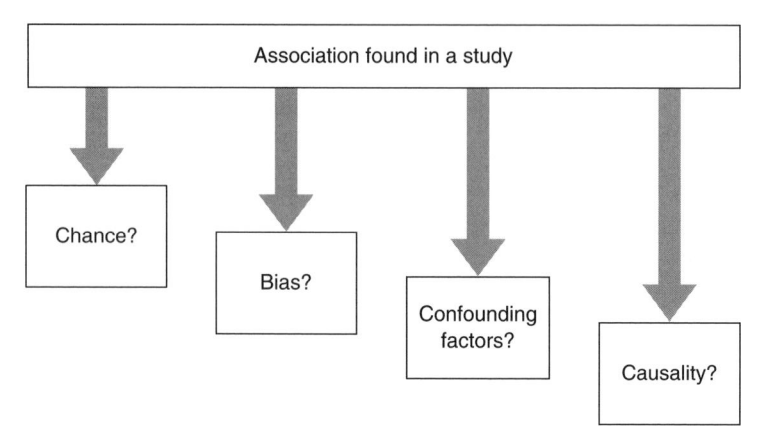

Figure 8.2   Some Possible Reason for Finding an Association in a Study

Finally, one of the criteria mentioned in Chapter 6 is whether the supposed cause came before the effect. One of the problems typically associated with the use of a survey to ask questions about the current behaviour or attitudes of people is that we know little or nothing about time order of variables. This is called 'cross-sectional' research as opposed to 'longitudinal' research which follows individuals or households over time. With longitudinal research it would be possible to track both the employment history of individuals and see how this related in time to changes in their place of residence. In this research we do not know whether the current employment (or lack of it) of residents came before or after residence in the neighbourhood. Concentration of people with certain characteristics in particular neighbourhoods is the outcome of processes by which people are able to gain access to housing in different areas, which itself might channel people who are unemployed into some neighbourhoods rather than others. Rich people have more choice about where they live because they can afford to pay for housing in a wider range of neighbourhoods than the poor.

What we are left with here is a bit of a puzzle. The results are not clear cut. The data are consistent with the possibility of neighbourhood effects, though some of the effects are contrary to effects suggested by the initial hypothesis. What is needed (as always!) is further research to explore this puzzle.

Qualitative analysis

Qualitative data can be found in many different types of research, whether one is trying to describe some aspect of the world or explain or understand why something happens in the way it does. As we saw in the previous section of the chapter, where structured interviewing or a postal questionnaire has been used to generate data, normally the types of answer to the questions are known broadly in advance, and answers can be pre-coded. However, there can be situations where open-ended questions are posed to which the answers are not clear, where the respondent is asked to write in their responses (questionnaire) or the interviewer records the answers given by the respondent. Here the data needs to be interpreted and coded. Researchers interested in analysing documents or interested in narratives or discourses will also be faced with making sense of words.

Here I look at a number of different ways in which researchers have made sense of the text they have captured and how they have presented it.

Qualitative data from interviews

Haughton et al. (2010) undertook an ambitious project which aimed to 'discover whether spatial planning and devolution are combining to produce a different and more geographically variable approach to future development' (Haughton et al 2010: 6) in the UK and Ireland. Behind this aim there is a descriptive research question 'What is the current approach to future development in these places?' This is a rather open-ended research question, appropriate for a new subject on which there is not much previous research. There is also a perhaps hidden comparative question: 'In what ways does that approach differ from approaches in the past?'

Data generation was via interviews with 147 people across the UK and Ireland, the interviewees being key players or informants, people who – because of their position, and because of their participation in the rather complex processes involved – are assumed to be authoritative sources on what happened and why it happened. Most of the interviews were semi-structured interviews with one or two people, and were taped and subsequently transcribed, though a few were summarised as notes. In addition they recorded the discussion in two roundtable events in Wales and in Cork and a final summary seminar event to which they invited key figures from across the areas they had studied.

Descriptive analysis

The descriptive analysis concerns the question of whether there was evidence of 'a different and more geographically variable approach to future development'. Their claim is that 'there was some diversity of experience emerging but perhaps not as much as we expected' (Haughton et al., 2010: 231). One aspect that stands out from their descriptive analysis is the different types of space for managing future development which were emerging. Some places in the UK and Ireland had developed some essentially rather ill-defined zones or zones with 'fuzzy' boundaries for the purpose whilst other places had not done so, continuing with the clearly defined administrative boundaries of the previous system.

With 147 interviews plus two roundtable events and a final summary seminar they would have a significant amount of textual data to manage and analyse. Methods like those advocated by Ritchie et al. (2003) discussed below would have been useful for this purpose. The authors acknowledge that in a project based on such a large number of interviews conducted in different places over an extended period, and dealing with a topic as complex as changes in the way that planning is conducted, that there are judgements about change which are 'subjective to an extent based on our collective assessment of many different viewpoints' and that 'they only provide summaries of broad trends' (2010: 232). They also recognise that people may dispute and argue over their conclusions, a consequence which they view positively. This illustrates the difficulty with qualitative research, raised at the beginning of this chapter, for those wishing to check the process of analysis and the way by which this collective assessment of the data has been arrived at.

Causal analysis

The authors propose two broad hypotheses about the factors which might explain any change: devolution and changing thinking about planning ('spatial planning' rather than 'land use planning'). The causal analysis developed here is very different from the variable analysis discussed above, and there is a recognition of the many factors involved in any situation. In Ireland, for example, they explain that the rapid economic growth from the late 1980s until the recession in 2008 produced considerable demand for development of land. The experience of rapid land development, it is claimed, resulted in a changing mood in the public and a changing political consensus towards development. They characterise this as a change from 'grabbing growth' to 'managing growth'. Part of the transformation to 'managing growth' was the creation of a system of regions within Ireland. To the implicit question 'why were regions developed?', the explanation the authors give is that regions within a country were required by the European Commission in order to make successful bids for European development funding, funding being a very attractive proposition at the time. Neither devolution nor changing views of planning would thus seem to be involved in this instance. An alternative explanation of the development of regions in Ireland, consistent with the changing views towards development in the country, might be that the regions were created in response to regional demands for some local control over development within the region. But these regions are, they claim, 'largely bureaucratic creations' (p. 58) and the evidence they have comes from some of their interviews that 'picked up on this'. They quote one interviewee who said:

> So there isn't a strong regional identity… people don't have the sense of being in such and such a region… it is purely pragmatic ….and opportunistic… A region can be anything it wants to be in this country. (Interview IR17, academic [former local planner] 2006) (2010: 59).

In this case they have quoted selectively from a particular interview, and use this as evidence to support their explanation of changes that had taken place. (The dots in the quotation indicate that some text has been left out from the transcript of the interview.) They explain why they chose particular quotations:

> When using quotes directly in the text, we generally choose them for their distinctive voice and ability to express things in ways that usefully capture either a particular widely held view, or a dissident view. Most quotes represent a viewpoint shared with others or that can be triangulated in some other way. Where this is not the case and we are trying to capture a more unique or idiosyncratic opinion, we try to make that clear in how we contextualise the quote (2010: 250).

It is not uncommon in research to find different accounts of events from interviews, and where this is the case, if one is aiming to get at the 'truth' there needs to be some way of adjudicating between accounts. For Haughton et al.

(2010) the account they give, in so far as it is supported by quotations from the interviews, thus seems to be based either on 'widely held views' about events (corroboration) or on a view that can be 'triangulated'. Triangulation here means that there is some other source of evidence which agrees with the claim being made by the interviewee. This could still leave the researchers with the decision of either choosing between the two competing accounts or acknowledging the differences of view. Where there was disagreement between the account given by an interviewee and other interviewees and, in addition, with another source of evidence (perhaps documents), then that view is ignored.

Making sense of the social world

Other researchers conduct semi-structured or unstructured interviews, record and transcribe them not with a view to giving a causal account of events but to find out from what people say in interviews, how they make sense of the world, what the key ideas, beliefs and interpretations are of the experiences they had in the social situations in which they found themselves. The assumption is that what people do – i.e., what they say when interviewed – gives a good indication of what is in their minds or what was in their minds at the time to which the interviewer is referring. Sometimes the aim is to describe the world view of the actors, but it can also be to use this understanding to account for how they responded in a given situation. Typically the analysis which is conducted starts from the transcripts of the interviews. These can be very rich in detail but rather disorganised, especially perhaps with unstructured interviews where interviewees have considerable freedom to discuss issues as they see fit. Managing the data as the first stage of thematic analysis involves in the first instance becoming familiar with the 'raw' data (reading through transcripts) and deciding on the initial themes or ideas under which the data will be organised. 'These may be of a substantive nature – such as attitudes, behaviours, motivations or views – or of a more methodological ilk, such as the general atmosphere of the interview or the ease or difficulty of exploring particular subjects' (Ritchie et al., 2003: 221). These themes can then be grouped into what Ritchie et al. call a conceptual framework or index and sorted and grouped under a smaller number of groups of related themes, drawing on but not restricted to the topics introduced by the interviewer. At this stage the concepts may be described as a loose collection of 'sensitising concepts' (Hammersley and Atkinson, 1995).

The logic of this process of analysis starts from the 'raw' data and attempts to see what it reveals, with an open-minded perspective on what is there. But given the arguments in Chapter 2 about the way that researchers are actively involved in selecting the topic and aspects of the topic to research, the raw data is already in part pre-conceptualised by the research agenda and the researcher's questions. Even with an open discussion there is always an agenda. There has to be a starting point. Burgess et al. (1988) illustrate this, asking the people in their group interviews about open space to discuss one week 'places I like' and the following week 'places I dislike'. The week after that they discussed memories of childhood places.

The next stage of the analytical process is to index or label the text to show which theme is being dealt with in a particular piece of text. Themes are likely to be intertwined in particular parts of the text and this may later help to reveal how ideas are inter-related in people's minds. Once chunks of text have been labelled, then they can be brought together by theme. Ritchie et al. (2003) also recommend constructing thematic charts which allow the themes developed to be cross-referenced in a matrix to the interviewee. The aim here is not to give detailed instructions on how to conduct thematic analysis but to consider how researchers use evidence from this analysis in their written accounts of the research to describe or explain events.

Burgess et al. (1988) had a research question which concerned the 'beliefs, values, attitudes and behaviours of urban residents' in relation to open space in urban areas in the context of their daily lives. The interest was in contact with nature and the natural world (see Chapter 2). This question I suggested involved both an interest in describing the behaviour of urban residents, but making sense of it (explaining it), too, in terms of beliefs, values and attitudes of the people involved. Burgess et al. (1988) organised their presentation of the data in their paper under four broad themes or, as they expressed it, 'the major dimensions of popular values for the urban green': The pleasures of contact with nature and the natural world; social and cultural values for open space; the dark side of open spaces; the everyday realities. Under the heading of 'The pleasures of contact with nature and the natural world', the authors write:

> One of the most striking themes to emerge in all four groups was the profound sense of personal satisfaction that individuals gained from experiencing the sensuous pleasures of being outside in open spaces: enjoying the changing seasons, feeling the sun, the wind and the rain, being able to walk, run or just sit down and enjoy the view. The living environments of open areas afford opportunities for escape, contemplation and an active involvement with nature. In the Eltham group, Richard describes the restorative value of Shrewsbury Park for him:

> 'When I'm depressed I like to sit, not walk. And there is one little bench on top of the hill at Shrewsbury Park that looks right out over the Thames valley….. and you can sit there and just look at the horizon and feel quite happy. And then I can walk into the wood down below and watch the squirrels which relaxes me. A little bit of wildlife around as well. It's marvellous.' (E3 1659–65) (1988: 493)

The quotation here from a single individual (his name has been changed to ensure confidentiality) is being used as evidence of a particular theme in the researchers' more general conceptual framework for analysing why some people might want to get out into open space, and how they might behave in open space. One motivation might be to escape from society for a period. They use this period of escape to contemplate the world, and to become actively involved with nature. The effect on the people concerned is 'restorative'. They give other quotations which aim to show that this desire to be alone, to escape and be in the presence of nature is more general amongst the people in their groups, and they make a descriptive claim – an empirical generalisation – here, too: 'People from all walks of life enjoy direct, sensuous encounters with nature, not just a sensitive or discriminating few who have the personal resources or knowledge to seek them out' (1988: 460). The authors think that in doing this, their interpretation may challenge 'elitist assumptions about aesthetic sensitivities for nature' (1988: 460–61). In this piece of analysis, as in much qualitative analysis, we do not have access to all the evidence (the transcripts and how they were indexed or coded) and we have to take it on trust that the interviews did indeed reveal, for those involved, this sensitivity to and enjoyment of nature. Of course, we may remain to be convinced about the degree to which the cases are representative of a wider population. Burgess and colleagues, conscious of this, conducted a survey of residents of different environments in the Borough, where people were shown four colour photographs of open space and were invited to comment about the features displayed. They summarise the number of comments about nature and natural features of open space in a table to support their claim.

Qualitative data analysis in an ethnographic study

As we saw in Chapter 7, ethnography typically involves a mix of methods of data generation, according to Forester (1993) interviews, observation and possibly participation in social situations of various types 'in the field'. Documents too, including the notes (or field notes) produced by the researcher whilst observing situations (or after them) are also obtained or produced. The raw data produced by these methods is likely to be in the form of words so qualitative analysis of the types we have already seen can be used by researchers.

The study by Henricksen and Tjora (2013), described in Chapter 6 used both observation and in-depth interviews. Conducted over a number of years, the research illustrates the iterative nature of qualitative analysis in which preliminary analysis suggests further questions to ask and cases to examine, broadly consistent with the grounded theory approach of Glaser and Straus (1967). The authors describe their analytical strategy as 'inductive', and were interested in exploring 'how community in the urban neighbourhood does (or doesn't) occur?' Unlike some versions of grounded theory, where analysis is meant to ignore existing theories and develop theory from the ground up (from the raw data as it were), they drew on existing theories and concepts. They examined the sorts of social interactions that take place within the physical arena of a neighbourhood. They started with the theory that it is through these interactions that community is created, maintained or changed. Their interest developed into a concern for how 'gatherings' of people developed into focused interactions or 'encounters' (drawing on concepts from Goffman, 1963). 'Our interviews and observations confirm that similar life situations or staying in the same physical space ('gatherings') are not enough to 'produce' social ties in the neighbourhood, although interaction occurs' (2013: 10). What is required are contextual matters or what they called 'interaction pretexts': 'a common reference or concern that legitimises an encounter, small-talk or a conversation, on the basis of passing-by or gathering in a shared physical space' (2013: 9). Examples are children playing, or pet ownership, or common seasonal activities which bring people outside into the public space and legitimises talk and interaction. Beyond interaction pretexts, the type of urban neighbourhood that develops, they argue, depends also on the degree of commitment that residents have towards shared activities in the neighbourhood.

These processes explain what was happening in the neighbourhood they observed in Trondheim and led them to develop a typology of neighbourhood types (see Table 8.4) which fits the types of neighbourhood to be found in Trondheim but also presents the possibility of its application to other neighbourhoods in different cities.

Table 8.4 A Typology of Neighbourhood Communities

	Low level of activity	High level of activity
High degree of interaction pretext	Passing-by community	Tight community
Low degree of interaction pretext	Weak community	Split community

Source: Henricksen and Tjora (2013)

Discourse analysis

'Much qualitative research treats language as a mechanism for understanding the social world, so that interviewees' replies are treated as a means of understanding the topics about which they are asked questions. For researchers working within traditions like conversation and discourse analysis, language is a topic in its own right' (Bryman 2008: 18–19). Discourse analysis is used to cover a wide range of types of analysis, with different theoretical assumptions, but, following Rapley (2007), the interest in much of the planning literature is in how language is used in specific contexts and what 'version of the world' is produced. Hence documents are analysed for the version of the world that they present. The works of Foucault are important in influencing the types of analysis which are undertaken, but not all types of documentary analysis are based on discourse analysis in this sense. The analysis by Harris and Hooper (2004) of Welsh Assembly policy documents to establish their 'spatial content', for example, following the introduction of the term 'spatial planning' in debates about planning in the UK, involved a form of descriptive content analysis where the text was indexed or coded to separate out 'spatial references' from other types of reference. Discourse analysis moreover is not just restricted to the analysis of documents, semi-structured and unstructured interviews can be analysed in this way too.

Atkinson's (1999) focus is on the various, and often conflicting meanings given to the notion of 'community participation' in official documents which deal with regeneration strategies. His contention is that 'there is no single authentic mode of assigning meaning to terms such as partnership and empowerment, that their meaning is constructed (i.e., produced and reproduced) in a context of power and domination which privileges official discourse(s) over others.' (Atkinson 1999: 59) Language is a central element of discourse and both have 'ideological overtones'. There can be political and ideological conflict over specific uses of language, but language is the medium through which ideology is produced and transformed. Atkinson is interested in how dominant discourses set the terms of the debate about a policy issue: 'structure what is officially sanctioned as thinkable and which bestow upon particular individuals/organisations the right to determine the appropriate (i.e., legitimate) scope of operations, form(s) of organisation, operating procedures, etc.' (1999: 61). Policy documents are thus interpreted as arguments about how we should define urban problems and what we should do to solve these problems. They thus attempt to create realities, rather than to reflect them, and to affect the practices of organisations, such as how community participation is practiced. He analyses a policy document by the Department of the Environment, Transport and the Regions (DETR (1997) *Involving Communities in Urban and Rural Regeneration: A Guide for Practitioners*), which is a manual for those who were involved in making bids for regeneration funds under the Single Regeneration Budget and City Challenge, bids which had to produce evidence that there had been community participation in making the bid for funds.

BOX 8.2

EXAMPLE OF DISCOURSE ANALYSIS

[Indented sections of text are from DETR (1997) *Involving Communities in Urban and Rural Regeneration: A Guide for Practitioners DETR*. Atkinson's analysis of the text is not indented]:

> The manual is written for all those involved in planning and organising regeneration programmes. Current regeneration programmes are led by partnerships that typically comprise representatives of:

local authorities	community organisations
TECs	voluntary organisations
other statutory bodies	the private sector
	(DoE, 1995: 2; DETR, 1997: 2).

Such a list appears to be all-inclusive. However, immediately prior to this it is stated that the manual aims to provide advice on:

> Who should *we* be seeking to involve in working up ideas for projects in our area?
>
> How do *we* identify them?
>
> How do *we* find out what improvements are wanted by those living on the estate/in this area/village?

(Continued)

> *(Continued)*
>
> What level of involvement from the community should *we* be seeking in managing the project?
>
> How do *we* set about generating interest and involvement? (DoE, 1995: 2, emphasis added; DETR, 1997: 2).
>
> In one sense, the above seems to represent an open approach to the issues, particularly given the frequent use of question marks. At this point it is useful to turn briefly to the narrow sense of discourse as language in order to understand how the 'we' is constructed and deployed. What is particularly interesting here is the frequent use of the pronoun 'we'. As Johnson (1994) notes, 'we' can be used in an inclusive sense, to create a specific community of interest, albeit one with a particular power hierarchy. However, 'we' can also be simultaneously used in an exclusive sense, to exclude and create boundaries. In the manual, 'we' clearly refers to a collectivity – to regeneration partnerships in general and the manner in which they can involve the community. The inference which may be drawn from this is that the partnership has already been constituted (it is the 'we') before the community has been involved.
>
> *Source:* Atkinson (1999: 65)

For the analysis Atkinson argues that 'We need to establish why the manual was produced; why *guidance* is offered; the audience that is being addressed; who should be involved and how they should be involved.' (1999: 64). His analysis of the text aims to show that the terms on which community involvement should take place and the sorts of demands and legitimate expectations that could be expressed may be limited by the official discourse. Box 8.2 shows an example of extracts he quotes from the manual with his own analysis of the text, which in this case focuses on the use of the word 'we' in the document. Atkinson goes on to argue that this suggests that the 'we' has been constructed in a hierarchical sense, the partnership will be composed of the strategic partners and that community will only subsequently be involved in the pre-existing structured hierarchy. Whether the official guidance has the effect intended on the readers of the document is a separate matter, however.

I discussed the Urban Task Force report (Urban Task Force, 1999) in Chapter 3 as an example of the sort of argument, a sort of problem-solution analysis of discourse (see Hoey, 1983 quoted in Gomm, 2004), that is used in planning policy debates to advocate particular policies where various claims to knowledge are mobilised to convince the reader of the relevance of the policy proposed to deal with the problem. Some discourse analysis has been influenced by 'critical discourse analysis' following Fairclough (1995) in which critique involves having a critical rather than descriptive goal for research, exposing the ideological nature of what seem to be 'commonsense' discourses and exposing the link between discourse and social structures. Lees (2003) conducts a critique of the discourse of 'urban renaissance' which was to be found in this document ['UTF'] and the Urban White Paper ['UWP'] which followed it (DETR, 2000). As Lees (2003: 62) puts it: 'text and language are approached as forms of discourse that help to create and reproduce social meaning. My focus is on the use of language and strategies of argument – that is rhetoric'. She 'loosely' follows Fairclough's

> three dimensional framework of analysis – text analysis, discursive practice and social practice. For textual analysis the vocabulary, grammar and text structure of the UTF report and the UWP will be scrutinised. In terms of discursive practice, I consider the context in which their policy statements are made and how they are linked to other debates and literatures. And in terms of social practice, finally, I am concerned with conceptualising the more general ideological context with which the discourses have taken place (2003: 62–3).

Her main argument is that the discussion about 'urban renaissance' ignores the fact that the groups that the Urban Task Force wants to attract to the city are middle class ones, and in practice the government is advocating gentrification in the guise of urban renaissance. She effectively claims that while there might be a problem with the advocacy of gentrification in political terms, who could be against such a neutral term as 'urban renaissance'? (Despite social construction she still believes in a 'real' social world in which planning policies will have effects – negative ones for the working classes).

Discourse analysis was also used in a study by Clifford (2006) of British press coverage of planning issues based on a survey of local, regional, and national newspapers plus coverage in *Planning*. His argument was that planning is portrayed in the press in a largely critical and negative way, as illustrated by the title of his article, and that this portrayal affects the way in which the public understands the planning system.

Summary/Key lessons

Analysis is the stage of research when you aim to turn your data into evidence that you will use to support and substantiate the claims that you will make as a result of your research. The argument of this book has been that the whole of the research design process should be directed to the purpose of making these claims but the interest here is in thinking in advance about the stage after the data has been generated and when the dissertation is to be written up.

From this perspective, the type of analysis that you will need to undertake will follow from earlier decisions about:

1. The purpose of the research question posed. This will affect the purpose of your analysis: to make descriptive or explanatory claims. The support of these claims requires different sorts of evidence.

2. The form of the research question: more open-ended, exploratory questions are likely to be answered using qualitative methods of analysis. The data will be the starting point for your analysis, and the data will need to be interpreted and coded as part of the analytical process.

3. The number of cases selected for study. With a large number of cases in a sample, it is sensible to use quantitative methods where decisions are made in advance of analysis on which variables to include in the project and how to measure and code them.

4. The methods of data generation chosen (e.g. groups interview vs. questionnaire). This will affect the form of the data generated, that is, whether it is qualitative or quantitative data.

Exercise: Assessing qualitative and quantitative analysis in the literature

This chapter has given you a 'taste' of how analysis can be approached if you have quantitative data or you have qualitative data. We have looked at a number of illustrations of analysis dealing with both descriptive and explanatory research questions selected from published articles in the planning literature. For your work, it is useful to see how researchers have approached the issue of analysis in the relevant research papers you have identified in your literature review. This exercise asks you to do that, and answer the following questions:

> 1. What methods of analysis have been adopted by the authors? Qualitative? Quantitative?
> 2. Are these methods of analysis ones that you might use in your own work?
> 3. Are there any limitations in these methods of analysis that you might be able to rectify in your own research? (Note: This could be a useful part of your academic argument for further research).

Further Reading

A consideration of analysis in the context of research design is a rather neglected topic. An exception, where analysis is considered in relation to experimental, longitudinal, cross-sectional, and case study designs is given in de Vaus, D. (2001) *Research Design in Social Research.* London: Sage.

A helpful discussion of guidelines and principles for the selection of techniques for both quantitative and qualitative analysis is to be found in Robson (2002) *Real World Research*, 2nd Edition. Oxford: Blackwell.

There are many books which deal with the practicalities of data analysis which you might use once you are that stage of the process, but scanning through them can be helpful at the research design stage too, to look for the way they approach analysis.

For qualitative analysis, students have found the following useful:

Ritchie, J. and Lewis, J. (2003) *The Practice of Qualitative Research.* London: Sage.

Miles, M.B., Huberman, A.M., Saldana, J. (2014) *Qualitative Data Analysis: a Methods Source Book*, 3rd Edition. Thousand Oaks, CA: Sage.

For a book which uses a non-technical approach to quantitative analysis, see:

Bryman, A. and Cramer, D. (2009) *Quantitative Data Analysis with SPSS 14, 15, 16.* London: Routledge.

The analysis of talk, discourse and documents is covered in:

Rapley, T. (2007) *Doing Conversation, Discourse and Document Analysis.* London: Sage.

A clear presentation of the consequence of non-response for the representativeness of the sample obtained, the factors which affect the seriousness of the problem, and some of the responses which might be made to the problem is to be found in:

Gomm, R. (2004) *Social Research Methodology.* Basingstoke: Palgrave Macmillan.

References

Atkinson, R. (1999) 'Discourses of Partnership and Empowerment in Contemporary British Urban Regeneration', *Urban Studies* 36 (1): 59–72.

Atkinson, R. and Kintrea, K. (2001) 'Disentangling Area effects: Evidence from Deprived and Non-Deprived Neighbourhoods', *Urban Studies* 38 (12): 2277–98.

Bryman, A. (2008) *Social Research Methods*. Oxford: Oxford University Press.

Burgess, J., Harrison, C.M. and Limb, M. (1988) 'People, Parks and the Urban Green: a Study of Popular Meanings and Values for Open Spaces in the City', *Urban Studies* 25: 455–73.

Clifford, B. (2006) 'Only a Town Planner Would Run a Toxic Pipe line Through a Recreational Area: Planners and Planning in the British Press', *Town Planning Review* 77 (4): 423–35.

DETR [Department of the Environment, Transport and the Regions] (1997) *Involving Communities in Urban and Rural Regeneration: A Guide for Practitioners*. Rotherham: DETR.

DETR [Department of the Environment, Transport and the Regions] (2000) *Our Towns and Cities: The Future: Delivering an Urban Renaissance*. London: HMSO.

Fairclough, N. (2010) *Critical Discourse Analysis*. Harlow: Longman

Forester, J. (1993) 'Learning From Practice Stories: the Priority of Practical Judgement', in F. Fischer and J. Forester (eds) *The Argumentative Turn in Policy Analysis and Planning*. Durham, NC: Duke University Press. pp. 186–209.

Glaser, B.G. and Strauss, A.L. (1967) *The Discovery of Grounded Theory*. Chicago: Aldine.

Gomm, R. (2004) *Social Research Methodology*. Basingstoke: Palgrave Macmillan.

Hammersley, M. and Atkinson, P. (1995) *Ethnography: Principles in Practice*. London: Routledge.

Harris, N. and Hooper, A. (2004) 'Rediscovering the "Spatial" in Public Policy and Planning: An Examination of the Spatial Content of Sectoral Policy Documents', *Planning Theory and Practice* 5 (2): 147–69.

Haughton, G., Allmendinger, P., Counsell, D. and Vigar, G. (2010) *The New Spatial Planning*. London: Routledge.

Henricksen, I.M. and Tjora, A. (2013) 'Interaction Pretext: Experiences of Community in the Urban Neighbourhood', *Urban Studies* 50 (10): 1–14.

Hoch, C. (1988) 'Conflict at Large: A National Survey of Planners and Political Conflict', *Journal of Planning Education and Research* 8: 25–34.

Hoey, M. (1983) *On the Surface of Discourse*. London: George Allen and Unwin.

Lees, L. (2003) 'Vision of "Urban Renaissance": the Urban Task Force Report and the Urban White Paper' in R. Imrie and M. Raco (eds) *Urban Renaissance?* Bristol: The Policy Press. pp. 61–81.

Rapley, T. (2007) *Doing Conversation, Discourse and Document Analysis.* London: Sage.

Ritchie, J., Spencer L. and O'Connor, W. (2003) Carrying Out Qualitative Analysis', in J. Ritchie and J. Lewis (eds) *The Practice of Qualitative Research.* London: Sage. pp. 219–62.

Urban Task Force (1999) *Towards an Urban Renaissance. Final Report of the Urban Task Force, chaired by Lord Rogers of Riverside.* London: Spon.

9

ETHICS OF RESEARCH

Key questions

What ethical considerations exist in research design?

What are the ethical arguments which arise in seeking to frame research closely to the needs of practice? How close should the relationship between academic researchers and practice be?

What issues will you need to consider in seeking ethical approval for your project?

Key concepts

Value relevance, value neutrality, instrumental rationality, value clarification, critical research, action research, phronetic research

Overview

The final condition for a well-designed piece of planning research is the need for an appropriate approach to ethical issues in your project. It was not very long ago that very little or no real attention was paid to the issue of research ethics in planning, but today the position has changed substantially. Students are routinely asked to consider the ethical implications of their proposed research and to complete ethical review forms. 'Questions concerning ethics in planning research confront me routinely nowadays when students request my signature on the "ethics review"

forms now required by our university for studies involving "human subjects".'
(Goonewardena, 2009: 57)

Ethics in research is about the basis, the values, on which decisions are made about the courses of action to adopt in any piece of research. They are moral decisions about the right and wrong things to do in any situation. Some of these decisions can be made at the stage when the research is being designed and planned, taking account of how the research might develop and what courses of action might be necessary or possible to deal with these issues. Clearly ethical criteria should underpin all research design decisions discussed in this book. Other decisions might have to be made once the research is underway. As a researcher, you will be interested in seeking the truth about the issues you investigate, though of course you will recognise from previous chapters that there will be differences of view about whether you have achieved this objective.

For the purposes of this chapter it is convenient to distinguish two aspects of research design: the framing of research and the practice of research, including issues which arise in the generation of data. I discuss these in turn.

The framing of research

We saw in Chapter 2 that one widely held view of science (often associated with positivism) suggested that the way that science proceeds is by the careful observation of the facts. Here the values of the researcher play no part in the process. However, according to post-positivism, this position is no longer tenable. At the early stages of the research process (see May, 2001) 'the interests leading to the research' (stage 1) – the topic which you as a researcher choose to investigate – is influenced by issues which interest you (unless your research is dictated by a tutor or supervisor or sponsor, though this is less likely for student dissertations). Similarly, we saw that it is impossible to research all aspects of a topic or problem. In the case of land ownership in cities the more precise question that you may pose is also selective, and this selection or framing of your research may reflect your political interests: what you see as the problem, why you think that problem exists and what you think could be done to improve matters. The aims, objectives and design of the research (stage 2) will reflect this orientation.

We also saw (Chapter 4) that some researchers justify their research by reference to values. Atkinson and Kintrea (2001) aimed to justify their research on the concentration of deprived households in certain parts of cities on the grounds that the government of the day thought that this issue was an important one and so it is officially valued as a topic of investigation, and the issue therefore has democratic legitimacy. Moreover, they argue that the fate of some people in these types of area is to fail to get a job because of where they live and that some inhabitants of these areas will die a premature death. Once again, since we will be expected to agree that both of these things are undesirable outcomes, we might be led to accept that better knowledge about these types of areas will be desirable (and might help policy to deal with them more effectively).

These considerations undermine the idea that research is value-free in any absolute sense. A key concern for some in research ethics is therefore the values which shape the choice of topic for research and the way that the research is framed, a process which tends to favour the perspectives of the powerful in society. Many social researchers have become concerned with their 'position' in the research process, and have written about this in their accounts of the research, covering questions, for example, about why they were motivated to choose the particular issue they investigated, their personal experience of the issue, and how their own experience and background has influenced their research interests and research practice – for an example in planning see Porter (2009). One enduring concern for urban planning researchers has been the orientation of research to the world of planning practice and the policy issues of concern to practitioners. This produces three models: practice oriented, disciplinary and critical.

How close should the relationship between academic researchers and practice be?

Practice-oriented model

There is a debate about how close the connection between research conducted by planning academics and planning practice should be. Some argue for what Hammersley (1995) calls the 'engineering or policy research model'. In some of this research activity, university researchers might be in competition with private sector planning consultants, or they might work in collaboration with such consultants on projects. Some research could simply involve routine investigations into topics which are required by practitioners but which practitioners themselves do not have the time or expertise to conduct themselves. Hence, researchers may carry out standard surveys of housing needs to provide evidence to underpin policies which support the need for affordable housing in an area. But usually a more collaborative model is assumed where advocates envisage a very close connection between research and practice and both sides benefit from the contacts (see, for example, Hambleton, 2007). Research provides descriptions and explanations of specific planning problems, as defined and framed by practitioners, and this information allows practitioners to develop innovative approaches to solving problems, whilst allowing researchers to understand the issues with which practitioners are grappling.

Researchers under this model could also conduct evaluations of practice, 'when planners and their clients want to know if plans, policies and actions would work or have worked.' (Healey, 1991: 448). In other words, they want to know if the aims and objectives they set for the policy have been or will be met. For example, one governmental aim for planning (quoted in Gilg 2005: 58) was the following: 'Our aim is to improve the quality of life for everyone in our towns and cities and to renew our most deprived communities so that no one is seriously disadvantaged by the place they live.' Another aim from the UK Biodiversity Framework (2012) which is to be achieved through 'planning, design and practice' is to 'Halt the loss of biodiversity and continue to reverse previous losses through targeted actions for species and habitats.' Hence an important question is whether planning policy and practice has met these aims, and if not, why not, and what might be done about it in the future.

Action research is a particular type of practice-oriented research linking together both the stage where policy is developed and the stage at which it is evaluated in a cyclic process where the consequences of actions are evaluated, and the lessons learned from the success or failure of past actions are incorporated into the next round of action (Stringer, 1999). Of course, there are often multiple aims in planning, and numerous criteria for assessing the actual or potential impacts of planning. Researchers may be asked to look at the broad environmental or bio-physical impacts of planning through strategic environmental assessment (SEA) of plans and policies as they are developed for an area, with the lessons from these appraisals being fed back into the policy process, and the rise of sustainable development as the purpose of planning systems has led to the assessment of a broad range of environmental, social and economic impacts of planning through 'sustainability appraisals' of various kinds.

Occasionally, university researchers may be involved in the production of plans for an area. Balducci (2007) describes one such project in Milan where a strategic plan was developed by academic staff of the university department to improve the 'habitability' or quality of life in the city region.

For those academic researchers who advocate a close relationship with planning practice, the moral or ethical argument is that researchers ought to help practitioners make practice more effective. Too much planning research produced by staff and students in planning schools, it might be claimed, fails to meet the needs of practitioners, and research should be 'relevant' to their needs and should provide evidence to underpin policy and practice. The starting point of research and the selection of problems to study reflects the interests and values of practitioners, and the design of the research is framed by the 'practical' problems that practitioners face. There are arguments that a very significant element of all social research these days is policy research (Mode 2 research) (Gibbons, 1994).

Accountability in this model is essentially to the needs of practice, and research is disseminated to practitioners and policymakers. This may be a model which is possible for you as a student where, for example, you are working part-time and studying part-time or where for a period within a full-time course you work on a 'real world' project with practitioners.

What gives some researchers doubts about tying their work so closely to the policy agenda and practical needs of the planning profession is that such work may conflict with their own beliefs about what would be a desirable outcome of policy. Taylor (2009) gives the example of a research project which had the objective of finding land for housing in areas of green belt or of great landscape value or of considerable ecological value. Here the researchers may feel that if this research leads to development of housing in these areas, the result will not be in the long-term interest of the environment or the public. Here there is an ethical dilemma. Should researchers give up the project because of their belief? Or should they undertake the project but do so in a way which minimises the impact on the landscape and environment? There is also the possibility that, because the research has been conducted by a researcher, the policy-makers may 'hide behind' the research to justify the policy publicly. Where the research work does not just provide evidence as an input to the policy work of practitioners but involves preparing a development plan, as in the case reported by Balducci (2007) in Italy, the academic researchers are deciding that they can legitimately establish the values that should guide planning in a particular place. In Milan the desire for 'independent' advice from the university about planning stems at least in part from the past corruption of the political system, 'While the world of professional planning practice was closely linked to the implicated political system, universities were seen as independent bodies whose scientific knowledge could contribute to the strengthening and legitimising of planning policies (Healey, 2007).' (Balducci, 2007: 533). The ethical question here is 'would our involvement as researchers produce a better outcome than that produced by professional planners?'

The disciplinary model

There are some who adopt what Hammersley (1995) distinguishes as the 'disciplinary model'. Research in planning in this view may make some ultimate contribution to policy and practice, though the application may not be very immediate or specific. The researchers provide a way of thinking about a problem or issue which may be helpful to practitioners and policy makers. This view has been labelled as 'research on planning practice' by Healey (1991) but is also known more generally as the 'enlightenment model' of the relationship between research and practice. Researchers like Kunzmann (2007) argue that while it is important to keep links with practice in order to understand changing political agendas and power structures and to explore new planning processes and approaches, researchers should keep their distance from practice. He argues that this stance avoids the problem of coming under political pressure to provide scientific justifications for what are essentially political decisions, and it allows researchers to adopt their own framing of the research issues, and thus to maintain a critical perspective on practice (see also Thomas, 2005).

For many researchers with this orientation, the approach they adopt towards values in research is consistent with the notion of 'value neutrality' associated with Weber but often used as a synonym for 'value-free' in debates about values. For Weber (1949), value neutrality did not mean the complete exclusion of all values from theory and research. Indeed, he was at pains to point out that the search for the truth was itself a value (see Hammersley, 1995) and, further, values must play a central role in defining the subject of theorising, and the particular aspect of the subject selected for study. You as a researcher might be interested in social issues, in the factors affecting the lives of the poor or excluded people in cities, and this will lead you to select this topic for investigation. This Weber called **value relevance**. In terms of the stages of research identified by May set out in Chapter 2, this covers the first stage of the research process: the interests leading to the research but also the aims, objectives and design of the project. But beyond, according to Weber, the selection of a topic to research and the more detailed design of the research, the fundamental value that should guide the subsequent stages of the research – the generation of data, the interpretation of data – was the pursuit of the truth, whatever the results of investigation in relation to what you were expecting to find, or hoping to find. This ideal involves the researcher in attempting to separate 'the facts' of research from the values which motivated the researcher to choose the topic in the first place. The difficulty or indeed impossibility for anyone to make this conceptual separation has been the subject of some debate.

This view of the role of the researcher is not inconsistent with views about the appropriate role of the planner in what came to be known as the rational planning process, developed within the science of policy analysis, notably in the US. Here values were acknowledged but, following this view of science, had to be kept separate from the collection of the facts. As Healey (1997: 24) explains 'values were seen as originating in the political process… The planner as policy analyst was a specialist in helping clients articulate their goals, and translating these into alternative strategies to maximise or at least "satisfice" the achievement of these goals, through careful analysis and systematic evaluation'. So, in this approach, commonly labelled **instrumental rationality**, researchers in planning helped politicians define the problems to be solved (though they of course did not express their own views on this), and undertook research or drew on research findings to advise which policies stood the best chance of solving those problems. The logic is something like this: 'If this is the problem, then, our research suggests that you might try this approach.'

Research could also be used to evaluate the effectiveness of current planning policies, in delivering the objectives that had been set for policy. This role for research was labelled **value clarification** by Weber, and was the second way in which he thought research could legitimately play a role in what were essentially political issues.

The publication of research, and the accountability of researchers, is to the academic community and is reflected in publication aimed at their academic peers, or in the case of students to their examiners. This is the typical model underpinning the orientation of student dissertations.

The critical model

A more explicitly critical approach to practice is found in the works of writers like Innes, Forester and Flyvbjerg, the former two being influenced by the critical theory of Habermas. The notion of critical research in planning is a difficult one to define and this is not the place for an extended treatment of this question. The critical research model is committed to progressive social change. Flyvbjerg claims that a lot of academic research fails to pass the 'so what?' test. The failure of social science is its irrelevance to policy and practice, so that social science does not matter to anyone. This is of course one of the arguments made for the engineering model of research in that it guarantees that the findings of studies will be relevant to practice because the research is designed with the needs of policy in mind. Flyvbjerg's prescription for planning research which matters involves three components. First, researchers should deal with 'real world problems', 'problems that matter to groups in the local, national and global communities in which we live should be addressed' (Flyvbjerg, 2004: 284). Second, researchers should engage with values. This has its resonance in opposition to the traditional value-free or value-neutral stance on social science research, and would seem to involve not just analysis of how a given set of goals could be achieved, but debates about the values which should guide policy and practice. What is ethically appropriate? Third, he advocates a role for academics in the policy debate: 'the results of research should be communicated effectively and dialogically to fellow citizens and their feedback should be carefully listened to' (2004: 284).

One common element in the writings of critical researchers is that it is critical of current social arrangements, that power relations are a key feature of social life and that science itself is distorted by power in society so that mainstream research by studying the world as it is implicitly accepts the status quo, which is one in which there are inequalities in society. For this reason, researchers are interested in issues to do with, for example, the way in which planning deals (or fails to deal appropriately) with gender, race and disability.

Innes (1990: 33) asks 'How can we assure that what we take as knowledge is just? That is, how can we assure that biases and assumptions do not reinforce power relationships and that knowledge is not a tool of oppression, but rather emancipation?' Forester (1989) and Hoch (1996) are interested in researching planning practice in order to change the behaviour of planners so that planning practice becomes more open and democratic, rather than one which reinforces existing power relations. Other researchers want to frame research in terms of the first-hand experiences of people whose voices and point of view on planning (and many other issues too) are rarely heard but who are, as Healey (2007: 242) says, 'knowledgeable and skilled about conditions that matter to them.' Participatory or community-based participatory research methods might be advocated as an ethical way of conducting research and tapping into this local knowledge (Corburn, 2005). Attili (2009) in a study of a house for homeless people quotes Denzin (2003: 258) approvingly 'participants have a co-equal say in how research should be conducted, what should be studied, which methods should be used, which findings are valid and acceptable, how the findings have been implemented, and how the consequences of such actions are to be assessed'.

There is certain ambiguity in the writing of some critical planning researchers. How far should they push the critical, value-driven approach and how far should they follow the value-neutral approach of the disciplinary model (Flyvbjerg, 2001, 2004; Lo Piccolo and Thomas, 2009). Flyvbjerg (2001), for example, argues that most schools of planning thought (including the communicative paradigm of Forester and Healey) that influence the nature of planning research should be rejected. 'The taken-for-granted 'truths' about the rational and progressive promise of planning should be replaced by an analysis of these truths and of planning, in terms of power' (Flyvbjerg, 2004: 284). He encourages planning researchers to engage with values, to question value rationality and to ask the following questions for what he calls 'phronetic planning research': Where are we going with planning? Who gains and loses, and by which mechanisms of power? Is this development desirable? What, if anything, should we do about it? This looks like a radical approach to the role of values in social and political inquiry with phronetic planning researchers both making value judgements about the impacts of planning and offering recommendations on what should be done. His Aalborg case study, however, seems to illustrate not a questioning of the values underlying the approach to planning in Aalborg and its impacts, but a rather conventional example of a researcher engaging in policy evaluation, accepting the rather uncontroversial city council view that traffic management in Aalborg should aim at 'environmental objectives', and evaluating the extent to which the policy, as implemented, was successful in achieving these objectives. My conclusion is that, judged by the account of phronetic research in his case study, this would seem to be research as 'value clarification', albeit that he did engage in debate in the public arena rather than in the lecture room or the pages of scholarly journals (though, having said that, it is not unusual for researchers to be interviewed about their research on the local or national media).

Both critical model and the engineering model value, a close engagement with practice and/or with 'fellow citizens'. In some cases they may be treated as co-researchers rather than participants in the research, and people to whom such research is accountable for the truth. Whatever its ethical attractions, this model may not be one that many of you, as students, will find to be a practical way of conducting research.

The generation and analysis of data

As discussed above, these days it is very common for universities to have ethics committees and for ethical approval to be sought for the conduct of any research which involves human participants, not just for research in medical faculties.

Often a university will require a clear project proposal which discusses and addresses the ethical issues concerned, so that the proposal can be reviewed and approved in order to ensure adherence to ethical guidelines. You will normally have a supervisor or tutor who will play an important role in the process of approval of your project. There may be a distinction between the level at which study is undertaken. If you are an undergraduate student, your supervisor may be able to approve the project if it represents a 'low risk', that is the risk of harm to participants is low. Postgraduate and doctoral students may be asked to complete full ethical approval questionnaires, which will then be submitted to an appropriate university body for approval.

During the conduct of research when data is being generated from human participants the following range of considerations are usually to be considered (see ESRC Framework for Research Ethics 2012):

- Participants must be fully informed about the purpose, methods and intended use of the research
- The confidentiality of information supplied must be respected.
- The anonymity of participants must be respected.
- Harm to participants must be avoided (physical and psychological harm, discomfort or stress).
- The independence of research must be clear
- Those who participate in the research must do so voluntarily.

Homan (1991) argues that the literature and practice of ethics in social research is more concerned with the recognition of consensual standards within the research community and the judgement of any piece of proposed or actual research by these standards rather than a philosophical debate about the values which should govern research.

The 'official' line is not without its critics. Greener (2011) raises some questions about the ESRC Framework. He sees codes of ethics as having a valuable purpose in providing guidance to researchers when thinking through the sorts of situation they might find themselves in during the conduct of their research. But he argues that the principles may not apply to all situations or groups involved. Particular care, perhaps, needs to be taken with vulnerable groups whose right to withdraw participation must be protected. And, as with any set of rules, there can be conflict between them. Sometimes, to get at the truth, which is a fundamental goal of research, covert research might be justified because if you were open, the behaviour of the people you wanted to study would change, a point also made by Gomm (2004). Getting ethical approval at the beginning of a project may incline researchers to neglect ethical considerations subsequently, or to do what is 'ethical' according to the guidelines but not what is right. Both are wrong: ethics should be considered throughout the process and you should do what you reason is the right thing to do rather than what is 'ethical'. Critics, like Attili (2009), influenced by the critical tradition in planning, make a similar point.

Whilst codes of ethics in social research focus on potential harm to participants in any research, the potential of harm or risk for researchers themselves should also be considered. This can involve physical risk though most planning research may take place in danger-free situations. But there can be emotional and psychological harm to the researcher (Lee-Treweek and Linkogle, 2000).

Summary/Key lessons

1. Ethical decisions, I have suggested, are moral decisions about what would be the right and what would be the wrong thing to do in any situation. This is a key criterion by which all decisions in research design should be judged. This is not, therefore, a separate stage of the research design process though you may well be asked to seek ethical approval for your proposed project after making research design decisions and producing a proposal, and before you can start the data generation stage.

2. As we saw in Chapter 2, the framing of research and the way that research questions are posed may have political implications for the sort of recommendations that might emerge from a project, and this framing might have been adopted for explicitly political purposes. There has been much discussion of the ethics of planning, and of the link which should exist between the worlds of the academic community and that of professional practice in planning, a link which is more often characterised as constituting something of a 'gap' between the two. However, in recent years, all social researchers including planning researchers have been asked

to contribute more directly to the world of policy and practice. A practical justification for the conduct of research is quite common in published papers as we saw in Chapter 4.

3. The close relationship with practice, as suggested by the engineering model in its various guises, is unlikely for most students of planning, though some of you may be part-time students working in practice and studying at the same time. Other full-time students may spend a short time out in practice on a placement in which they may be asked to produce a report on practice, and might be able to use this opportunity to identify practice-based topics for a dissertation.

4. The critical model, like the engineering model, values a close engagement with practice, but also with 'fellow citizens'; something that may not be feasible for most students unless you have opportunities as part of your course to work with local groups on issues that concern them.

5. Most of you are thus likely to adopt something like the disciplinary model, where the topic of research is selected for its value relevance, that is, for its real world significance, but where policy implications are seen as a contribution to an academic debate about policy rather than something that can be immediately applied.

6. Staff and students are now being asked to consider research ethics at the design stage of research more explicitly so that one might hope to find an increased attention to ethical issues in the future. But there is also the possibility that the existence of ethical guidelines and ethical questionnaires may result in what has been called a 'tick box' mentality regarding ethical thinking about research.

7. In giving attention to the needs of participants you should not neglect consideration of your own safety.

Exercise: The ESRC Framework for Research Ethics

You are asked to download the ESRC Framework for Research Ethics and consider the principles set out there and how you are going to meet these requirements in your project. It is likely that your institutional regulations will be closely based on the ESRC model. Typically your tutor will be asked to confirm that these principles have been considered and that the research for your dissertation will involve procedures that meet these requirements. However, the precise requirements will differ from institution to institution. You should discuss these issues with your tutor, and also examine whether the research you propose to do might also pose some threat to your physical or emotional well-being.

Further Reading

The key reference on the ethics of planning research is: Lo Piccolo, F. and Thomas, H. (2009) *Ethics and Planning Research*. Farnham: Ashgate.

This contains a number of chapters in which planning researchers reflect on ethical issues in the practice of planning research.

Lee-Treweek, G. and Linkogle, S. (eds) (2000) *Danger in the Field: Risk and Ethics in Social Research*. London: Routledge.

Hammersley (2000) *Taking Sides in Social Research*. Abingdon: Routledge.

References

Atkinson, R. and Kintrea, K. (2001) 'Disentangling Area Effects: Evidence From Deprived and Non-Deprived Neighbourhoods', *Urban Studies* 38 (12): 2277–98.

Attili, G. (2009) 'Ethical Awareness in Advocacy Planning Research' in F. Lo Piccolo and H. Thomas (eds) (2009) *Ethics and Planning Research*. Farnham: Ashgate. pp. 207–18.

Balducci, A. (2007) 'A View From Italy', in A. Balducci and L. Bertolini (eds) 'Reflecting on Practice or Reflecting with Practice?', *Planning Theory & Practice* 8 (4): 532–55.

Corburn, J. (2005) *Street Science: Community Knowledge and Environmental Health Justice*. Cambridge, MA: MIT Press.

Denzin N.K. (2003) *Performance Ethnography: Critical Pedagogy and the Politics of Culture*. Thousand Oaks, CA: Sage.

ESRC (2012) *Framework for Research Ethics (FRE)*. Swindon: Economic and Social Research Council.

Flyvbjerg, B. (2001) *Making Social Science Matter*. Cambridge: Cambridge University Press.

Flyvbjerg, B. (2004) 'Phronetic Planning Research: Theoretical and Methodological Reflections', *Planning Theory & Practice* 5 (3): 283–306.

Forester, J. (1989) *Planning in the Face of Power*. London: University of California Press.

Gibbons, M. (1994) *The New Production of Knowledge*. London: Sage.

Gilg, A.W. (2005) *Planning in Britain*. London: Sage.

Gomm, R. (2004) *Social Research Methodology*. Basingstoke: Palgrave Macmillan.

Goonewardena, K. (2009) 'Planning Research, Ethical Conduct and Radical Politics' in F. Lo Piccolo and H. Thomas (eds) *Ethics and Planning Research*. Farnham: Ashgate. pp. 57–70.

Greener, I. (2011) *Designing Social Research*. London: Sage.

Hambleton, R. (2007) 'The Triangle of Engaged Scholarship', *Planning Theory & Practice* 8 (4): 549–53.

Hammersley, M. (1995) *The Politics of Social Research*. London: Sage.

Healey, P. (1991) 'Researching Planning Practice', *Town Planning Review* 62 (4): 447–59.

Healey, P. (1997) *Collaborative Planning*. London: Macmillan.

Healey, P. (2007) *Urban Complexity and Spatial Strategies*. London: Routledge.

Hoch, C. (1996) 'A Pragmatic Inquiry about Planning and Power', in J. Seymour, L. Mandelbaum and R. Burchell (eds) *Explorations in Planning Theory*. New Brunswick, NJ: Research Center for Urban Policy Research. pp. 30–44.

Homan, R. (1991) *The Ethics of Social Research*. London: Longman.

Innes, J.S. (1990) *Knowledge and Public Policy: The Search for Meaningful Indicators*. New Brunswick, NJ: Transaction Books.

Joint Nature Conservation Council and Defra (on behalf of the Four Countries' Biodiversity Group) (2012). *UK Post-2010 Biodiversity Framework July 2012*. Peterborough: JNCC.

Kunzmann, K. (2007) 'More Courage to Stem the Tide: Academia and Professional Planning Practice in Germany', in A. Balducci and L. Bertolini (eds) 'Reflecting on Practice or Reflecting with Practice?', *Planning Theory & Practice*, 8 (4): pp. 545–54.

Lee-Treweek, G. and Linkogle, S. (eds) (2000) *Danger in the Field: Risk and Ethics in Social Research*. London: Routledge.

Lo Piccolo, F. and Thomas, H. (2009) *Ethics and Planning Research*. Farnham: Ashgate.

May, T. (2001) *Social Research*. Buckingham: Open University Press.

Porter, L. (2009) 'On Having Imperial Eyes', in F. Lo Piccolo and H. Thomas (eds) *Ethics and Planning Research*. Farnham: Ashgate. pp. 219–32.

Stringer, E.T. (1999) *Action Research*, 3d Edition. Thousand Oaks, CA: Sage.

Taylor, N. (2009) 'Consequentialism and the Ethics of Planning Research' in F. Lo Piccolo and H. Thomas, H. (eds) *Ethics and Planning Research*. Farnham: Ashgate. pp. 13–28.

Thomas, H. (2005) 'Pressures, Purpose and Collegiality in UK Planning Education', *Planning Theory and Practice* 6 (2): 238–47.

Weber, M. (1949) *The Methodology of Social Sciences*. New York: Free Press.

10

CROSS-NATIONAL COMPARATIVE RESEARCH IN URBAN PLANNING

Key questions

What is cross-national comparative research? What is its purpose?

What research purposes and questions do researchers investigate?

What justifications are there for such questions?

What is an appropriate logic for answering the question?

What methods of data generation are available?

How is data analysed?

What ethical issues are involved?

Key concepts

Cross-national comparative research, policy transfer, the rule of maximum similarity, the rule of maximum discreteness of focus

Overview

In recent years there have been many opportunities for students from the UK to begin to identify some differences in the way planning is practiced elsewhere in Europe. Mechanisms include courses on international comparative planning, and short field trips abroad, but also exchanges with planning schools abroad, where students may spend a period of perhaps a semester or more in a foreign country, and participation in cross-national workshops and seminars where groups of students from different countries make presentations on issues of common concern. Most of these activities require some reflection on what has been learned and some students will be sufficiently inspired by this experience to write a dissertation with a comparative dimension. In parallel with students from the UK travelling abroad there has been an increase in students from abroad coming to the UK to study, and some of these may also write a dissertation. This chapter looks at some of the research design issues involved, issues which have been discussed in earlier chapters in this book, but drawing on the decisions and research practice of established comparative workers.

What is cross-national comparative research in planning?

Masser and Williams (1986) distinguish between studies of planning in specific foreign countries and comparative planning research. The essential difference they draw between these two types of study is that comparative planning involves the cross-national comparison of planning activities in two or more countries.

Masser (1986) argues that there is general agreement that there is no distinct field of cross-national comparative planning studies. The subject matter of cross-national comparative planning therefore differs from planning as a whole only in its cross-national dimension. There could be cross-national studies of planning for any subject that a researcher studying planning within their own country might study: housing, retailing, economic development, urban region governance, urban regeneration and so on. What is distinctive is that each country may have a different set of institutions responsible for planning or influencing planning, thus the context for studying planning in different countries is different. Cross national planning research, then, is 'the study of planning problems and practice in different countries in relation to the institutional context' (Masser, 1984, quoted in Masser, 1986: 12). This is consistent with the definition of Bendix (1963: 532) (quoted in de Vaus, 2008) that comparative studies 'represent an attempt to develop concepts and generalizations at a level between what is true of all societies and what is true of one society at one point in time and space'.

What is the purpose of cross-national comparative planning? In a recent book which brought together cross-national comparative studies of a variety of planning subjects for Britain and France, Breuillard and Fraser (2007) quote Faludi and Hamnett's (1975) three generic purposes: the advancement of theory in planning; the improvement of planning practice; harmonisation of planning systems. In relation to the development of theory, the contribution of comparative cross-national approach, given the definition by Masser, is to develop theory which falls somewhere between the belief that 'every country and culture is different' and 'all countries are essentially the same' or, following de Vaus (2008: 251) to: 'identify the extent to which social phenomena are shaped by universal system factors and the extent to which they are shaped by unique factors intrinsic to the specific time, place and culture in which they occur.'

There has been something of a debate in planning about the balance between these sets of forces. There has been a recent acknowledgement of the multiplicity of perspectives on social life more generally, and thus on the idea of planning itself (Sanyal, 2005) and on the definition of planning problems (Sandercock, 1998). An extreme relativist interpretation of this view might be to assume that actors involved in managing development in different places live in 'different worlds'. But, on the other hand, there has also been a tradition in planning theory (both rational planning and communicative planning) of making the (ontological) assumption that planning is 'an unproblematic global activity' (Huxley and Yiftachel, 2000: 336), with no significant differences between countries and places due to local and national factors. A mid-way view sees the possibility of dialogue between cultures though recognising local contextual factors as important influences on how planning operates (Watson, 2002).

The last two purposes mentioned by Breuillard and Fraser (2007) for comparative research point to the frequent evaluative dimension to comparative studies: the desire to see if the way that planning works abroad represents an improvement on the way that it is practiced at home. This leads into a discussion about the scope for transferring policy ideas from one country to another and the obstacles there might be to such a process. Research could in principle help to identify 'good practice' in another country and this could then be implemented in Britain more widely. But there is some scepticism about whether there are 'lessons to be learned' (Cullingworth, 1993). The 'political terrain' will be different in another country. The general research point here can be posed in terms of the concept of external validity (see Chapter 6). Can we generalise from the cases we have studied? There is no guarantee that a causal mechanism which seems to work in one setting (country x) will work equally well, or in the same way in a different setting (country y).

Not everyone in any case, I expect, would see the harmonisation of planning systems as a desirable objective but the borrowing of 'good practice' from abroad would tend to lead to some convergence in planning in different countries. There is something of a debate on this at the moment in the context of discussions about the impact of the European Union on planning systems in Europe. The literature referred to in this chapter is largely to cross-national studies involving countries in Europe. Some studies are cross-national in the sense that they compare aspects of the national planning systems in two nations (Booth et al. 2007; Farthing 2008). Much recent work, however, has involved a comparison of cases *within* different nations in Europe, rather than a comparison of nations *as* cases. For example, Herrschel and Newman (2002) were interested in the nature and workings of city regions in a sample of cities in Germany and England.

Research purposes and research questions

There is a range of descriptive and explanatory purposes in comparative research, and 'what' and 'why' questions are as appropriate to comparative research as they are to research within a country. Individual pieces of research often attempt to answer both.

Descriptive questions

Couch et al. (2003) have aims which are both descriptive and explanatory in relation to their research into urban regeneration in European cities. Their descriptive aim is to provide 'a comprehensive and informed presentation of urban regeneration problems and policies in a number of European cities' and the editors 'examine the similarities and differences in the processes of urban regeneration between different situations (p. 4).

Much comparative research describes itself as exploratory. This may be because the writer claims that there is not much evidence about policy in different countries. But another reason, and a strong theme in the literature from the 1980s (Masser and Williams, 1986) and again more recently in the 2000s (Knieling and Othengrafen, 2009) is that the 'institutional context' means paying attention to the importance of understanding differences in planning 'culture' between countries whilst emphasising the difficulties of doing so. Booth (1996: vii) points out the difficulties he had in the early 1980s in understanding French planning: 'I attempted to grapple with the complexities of French planning, so that in turn I could brief my students. And I had a hard time of it. Such French sources as I could find, and the few English sources which then existed, all seemed to be based on assumptions that I did not seem to share. Intrigued, I dug deeper.' Sharpe (1975: 26–7) makes a more general 'ontological' point that 'countries are really very different', and he pointed to the 'immense difficulties in making comparisons of public policies in different countries and of the machinery and processes through which policies are given effect'.

This view, highlighting the importance of culture, would suggest that to understand planning in a different country from our own we need to understand how planning is interpreted and understood by those who work in the system and interact with it. For example, Booth (1996: 2), interested in how development is controlled in Britain and France, writes 'Britain and France have radically different understandings of the nature of the state, of the nature and purpose of administration, and by extension of the way that [planning] control should be practiced'. The concept of 'town and country planning' as used in Britain follows, then, from a particular view of planning rooted in a set of institutions and a history which shapes how planners in Britain (and planning academics like Booth mentioned above) see planning. This concept is different from the concepts of 'urbanisme' or 'aménagement du territoire' which are used in the context of French planning.

One might conclude from this perspective that it is a sufficiently challenging task to study the system of planning in another country without introducing a comparative element. Here the aim of research would be essentially descriptive. Cropper (1986) indicates that an ethnographic account might be the aim in these studies with the purpose being to present as authentically as possible, the experience of planning, and of those in planning in the place in question. This would provide an understanding of planning in that place of how and why actors operate in the way they do in that locality. But there is a practical dimension to this: how well-versed a researcher is in the language of the country in which the study is to be conducted, language being a key mechanism through which social reality is represented (see the discussion in Chapter 8 on discourse).

Following the logic of this argument, in order to understand how 'planning' operates in another country requires that a considerable length of time to be devoted by comparative researchers on their research learning the culture of planning, compared with studies restricted to their own country. Established research staff may have this luxury but students may not have the same opportunities. It is not unknown even for a doctoral student, with three years full time research, to start a project with the intention of completing a cross-national study but to later drop one of the countries involved.

These difficulties led Sharpe (1975) to formulate a rule of thumb to be adopted in any proposed comparative study: the rule of 'maximum discreteness of focus'. This rule means that projects which aim to compare, say, recent changes to the planning system in two countries (The Netherlands and UK) should be avoided and something more sharply focussed such as the example given by Williams (1986), 'motorway planning and approval procedures' would be more appropriate. Williams even cautions against subjects like 'urban renewal' where the scope of the study could be widened dangerously (in terms of completing a study) in many directions. Both Davies (1980) and Eversley (1978) also point to this conclusion. I followed it in my study of urban fringe residential development in the cities of Bristol (UK) and Poitiers (France) (Farthing, 2001).

Explanatory questions

Explanations in comparative studies as answers to 'why' questions seek answers which combine common factors across countries but also nation-specific factors or institutional or administrative factors. Couch et al. (2003) are aware of the complexity of the institutional context in different countries and cities in Europe, and the wide range of organisations that might be involved in generating new economic activity in urban regeneration. This is one reason why they use local experts to conduct the research in some of the cities, because these local experts will understand the institutional context 'from the inside' as it were, thus reducing the need for the UK research team to discover this for themselves. The explanatory aims of Couch et al. (2003: 4) in relation to urban regeneration policy and practice in Europe are to: 'examine the similarities and differences in the processes of urban regeneration between different situations, drawing out conclusions around key aspects of the process. Thus factors such as location, regional economic conditions, previous land-use patterns and building forms, together with the nature of local land markets, administrative structures, tools and mechanisms of intervention, are all shown to be important in shaping local differences in urban regeneration and its outcomes.'

Of course, if you are writing a dissertation you are not normally going to be able to adopt this approach, and you won't be permitted to get an outside expert to write your dissertation for you!

A justification of the question

In Chapter 4 we saw that planning academics usually justify their published research on two grounds: practical and academic. In relation to the first, one of the generic purposes and justifications of cross-national study outlined above is that this might lead to learning some lessons about good practice.

An academic justification could be that an interesting question has not been answered, that there is a gap in the literature, or that there have been attempts to answer it but these answers have not been satisfactory. A review of the literature either confirms the argument that there is a gap in the coverage of the question or the argument that the literature unearthed by the review has certain limitations that mean that further research is warranted.

When it comes to cross-national studies, the same argument applies. It is important to establish what claims and conclusions previous researchers have made. But there may be difficulties here. Booth (1996) referred to the paucity of sources in English and of accessible French sources on French planning. The output of work on planning has grown substantially since then. For various reasons, much is published in English language journals. There is a substantial literature in other languages referring to research on planning in specific countries, but in order to read this literature you need some language skills.

Comparative research can also be stimulated by published research into planning in Britain. For example, if there is a study of the preparation of local development plans in Britain, this could be used as the basis of a comparison with the production of a local plan in another country. The study by Wilson (1983) of local plans in France, although restricted to observation of working groups preparing local plans in four départements in France, with no equivalent research in Britain, was effectively a cross-national comparative study. It was a study of local plans in France from someone whose perspective on local plans was shaped by her understanding of the system in Britain with explicit comparisons being drawn between the nature of participation in the process between the two countries.

An appropriate logic for answering the question

Cases and sampling

A question which arises in designing research with both descriptive and explanatory aims is 'what is the population?' that is, the widest set of potential cases which you are going to represent by the research you conduct on your selected cases. For practical reasons, any small scale research for a dissertation is likely to have to use the non-probabilistic method of convenience sampling, as described in Chapter 5, that is, a case or cases which are readily available in countries to which you happen to have access, or where you have contacts. This sampling practice is also followed by more experienced academics like Healey, who in the account of her study of spatial strategy-making in three urban regions in Europe argues that 'The selection of cases for in-depth qualitative research is always more a practical question than the product of systematic choice criteria' (2007: 291), and who states, 'The three cases chosen … are very diverse and should not be considered in any sense as a "sample" or as exemplars of "good practice". They are merely examples of efforts at spatial strategy-making for cities or urban areas' (2007: 32). The consequence of this approach is that you will have to acknowledge that the cases you study may not be 'representative' of the countries in which they are located or of any wider population of interest, and empirical generalisations of the sort associated with probability sampling are not appropriate.

As we saw in Chapter 6 making a causal claim is to make a universal claim, about what will happen when the causal conditions are met. But in social research the context counts (Flyvbjerg, 2001), and at best theory might apply to certain historical periods, and they may also apply only to certain places where contextual conditions are similar. The broader population to which the theory might apply is thus limited in time and space. There has been an influential causal theory which has been of interest to British comparative planning researchers interested in planning in Europe. This theory claims that European integration has led to a change in the agenda of spatial planning in cities – from urban managerialism to urban entrepreneurialism – in order to attract businesses and employment. And as part of this shift there has been accompanying institutional change – from overarching metropolitan authorities (government) to public-private sector partnerships (governance). The first part of the theory suggests that European integration, that is the creation of a single European market during the period from the 1970s to the 2000s has had the effect of changing the objectives of policy in cities (and city regions) from a concern with delivering services to the local population to one focused on attracting jobs and businesses. At the same time, this change of objective has been accompanied by institutional change so that private sector partners have become more prominent in policy formulation and implementation. This theory might be 'ethnocentric', in the sense that it assumes that what has happened in Britain over the last 40 years or so has happened or is happening everywhere in Europe. But it is a testable theory and the population to which it refers is all cities or city regions within the EU. Where a small sample of cases may be a problem if the objective of the research is a descriptive one, where there may be an interest in empirical generalisation, in this situation, since this theory is meant to apply to all these cases, research into trends in any one city region within Europe examining the objectives of policy and the institutional context could in principle falsify this theory (see Chapter 6 on the falsification of theories).

When comparing countries, Sharpe (1975: 28) proposed the 'rule of maximum similarity' to ensure that, as far as possible, in any comparative study, and in so far as one can tell from existing evidence, one should compare like with like. 'In this way we can minimise the number of variables to be compared'. If the idea is to compare the nature and working of city regions, and one has the hypothesis that the nature and working of city regions are influenced by, (a) the general constitutional provision for regions within a country, and (b) the nature of urban settlement in the region, then the countries of Germany and England are useful to select for comparative research because they differ in these variables of interest but 'other factors' which might influence the nature and working of urban regions, like the general level of economic development of the country, the democratic nature of the country, and the influence of the European Union on policy and practice are all controlled by this selection (Herrschel and Newman, 2002). This, of course, also restricts the population to which the results of the research can be generalised. A further example of a restrictive definition of the population of interest in cross-national study in Europe is the research by Couch et al. (2003) introduced above. They were interested in how the processes of urban regeneration differed between 'obsolescent urban areas' in Europe, and why they differed. The population of cases to which their theory might be generalised was, however, limited to those that met certain criteria. First, the population was limited to cases within countries which in the European context could be considered to have 'a broadly similar experience of economic development, urbanisation and economic restructuring' (2003: 14) (UK, the Netherlands, Belgium, Germany, France and Italy). All were described as 'prosperous industrialised countries'. Within those countries they were only interested in: conurbations large enough to be regional centres but not capital cities; conurbations that had experienced large scale restructuring; conurbations that had some distinctive characteristics of locality that could be easily identified and whose impacts could be examined. The sample of eight cities they selected however was a convenience sample, where 'localities of which we had some prior knowledge and where we had local academic contacts being favoured over others.' (2003: 14–15). Their approach to explanation of how the processes of urban regeneration differed was inductive, derived from the evidence.

Methods of data generation

Interviews and questionnaires

Comparative researchers are interested in studying specific cases of planning activity: episodes of spatial strategy-making for urban regions (Healey, 2007), urban regeneration problems and policies (Couch et al. 2003), 'framing of strategic urban projects' (Salet and Gualini, 2007). Following the practice recommended by Masser (1986), many researchers call their studies, 'case studies' and identify this with a mix of essentially qualitative methods. Because of the conceptual difficulty of understanding the culture of planning in different countries and the practical difficulty of access to current, let alone past, cases of planning activity, such as cases of spatial strategy-making, people are important data sources who have country-specific knowledge and who can report on what happened, and why it happened. Though in principle, a structured approach to asking questions either through face-to-face interviews or through a questionnaire might be possible, comparative researchers acknowledging the complexity of the phenomena they are investigating often rely on asking questions of key informants such as practitioners who have been involved in the cases concerned, but also local experts, who often turn out to be academic staff at a local university. Sometimes the academics are also working with or as practitioners. Roughly half of the 'discussions' Healey (2007) conducted in her three cases were with academics or academics/practitioners. As with all interviews about the 'facts' of a case, about the chain of events, we are not directly observing the behaviour, but we are relying on the accounts of events filtered through the eyes and memory of the person concerned. Hence, as always, there are issues about the reliability of the data generated in this way. Healey (2007) may also have been interested in these accounts, not because they reveal what 'really' happened in these episodes of spatial strategy making, but as evidence of the way that the people involved themselves understood what was happening. Interviewing of key informants would thus seem to be a very useful method of data generation if such people can be identified in advance and it seems possible to set up interviews with them.

Ethnography and observation

We have already seen that there are practical issues to do with access to settings and the time available for the research when an ethnographic approach to generating data on planning activities is contemplated. For her research which was concerned with state–local relations in planning in France, Wilson (1983) managed to negotiate access to formal *groupe de travail* meetings where local plans were being prepared in four *départements*, meetings which were not open to the public. Being fluent in French, she observed the working of the *groupes de travail* which brought together actors from the locality and from the central state in a 'natural setting' in the field. It is assumed that her presence did not make a significant difference to the way the meetings proceeded. Such observations are selective in terms of timing in that the preparation of the local plan takes some (considerable) time to complete, and she could only observe behaviour at certain stages of the process, during times when she could be in France. They are also selective in terms of behaviour that takes place outside the meeting. She was of the opinion that significant discussions and agreements were reached at informal meetings which were beyond her observation.

For comparative study, access problems for students studying planning abroad are likely to be more salient than for studies at home. These difficulties could be reduced by the staff contacts with facilitators in the country concerned, who could open up access to the settings of interest, but the limited time available to conduct such research and the difficulties of understanding the language of planning in a different country remain obstacles to many student researchers.

Textual documents

Documents of various kinds play an important role in comparative research, as in all research in planning. In many countries, the law and constitution plays a significant role in defining the nature and scope of planning, unlike in Britain. They also play a role in setting out rules about the procedures which must be followed for a process to be valid and safe from threat of legal action by those who disapprove of an outcome. Some understanding of these issues is important in comparative study of planning. More sources are appearing in English, so the need to be able to read texts in a foreign language is perhaps reducing.

Any studies of planning in the country of interest written in English will be an obvious document to refer to. It is very obvious, for example, that the narrative that Healey (2007) recounts about episodes of spatial strategy making in Amsterdam relies heavily on two documentary sources. The first is official plans. The second are articles and papers by Dutch academics, who often publish in English. Of course, this impression of Healey's reliance on documentary sources is partly reinforced by her decision not to make direct references in the text to her 'conversational discussions' because she says that 'a book is not quite the same as an academic research thesis' where the 'authors have to make their methodology explicit' (2007: 293). Moreover, she decided that she had to write up not just the most recent episodes of spatial strategy making, but delve into the past because she came to realise that the past significantly shaped the present and 'that the vocabulary, emphasis and metaphors of present policy debates are difficult to understand without recognising their resonance with past discourses and values' (2007: 293). This, too, would have to rely on documents.

In other research, local academics or practitioners are not necessarily interviewed but invited to write an account of the case that they know about using some common set of headings or a 'template' as Couch et al. (2003) describe. These documents have then to be interpreted by the lead researchers.

Official statistics

There are few difficulties these days in obtaining official statistics about different European countries through EUROSTAT, but there remain considerable difficulties in using official statistics to compare countries or sub-national regions and conurbations within Europe in the way that researchers might like (Couch et al. 2011: 7). Such statistics vary 'in terms of availability, definition of terms, periodicity and methods of data collection, level of aggregation, and questions of interpretation'. Carrière et al. (2007), in a study that looked at the issue of small towns in rural areas in England and France, pointed to the different definitions of the 'rural' in England and France linked to their social, economic and political histories and the distinctive national contexts for the appreciation of rural issues. These contexts have shaped the approach to the issue of small towns in rural areas and have had consequences for the statistical definitions employed in each country so that 'systematic comparisons of the performance of small towns, and the nature of the problems they face in the two countries are difficult to present' (2007: 120). Such comments highlight the way that official statistics can represent concrete evidence of the ways that governments in different countries see the world, or the version of reality that they represent.

Analysis

Analysis of the data generated by their research is how researchers answer their research questions and thus make the descriptive or explanatory claims they do about the situations and cases they have studied. All of the examples of comparative research quoted here have used methods of data generation which have produced qualitative data.

Many recent studies in comparative research in planning have both descriptive and explanatory aims, reflecting their research questions. One long-standing criticism of comparative studies is that they may never progress beyond the descriptive stage and fail to come up with explanations for the similarities and differences which their descriptions suggest (Masser, 1986). This suggests another, somewhat greater, difficulty in comparative research than in research within one's own country.

Chapter 6 dealt with the analysis of data when the interest is in explanation, and whether researchers are primarily interested in causal analysis or in understanding how the actors involved interpreted the situation they faced, what their motives were and how they responded to the situation. Difficulties for those interested in inductively developing explanations about the causes of similarities and differences between cases from the descriptions of the cases studied, flow from a number of aspects of the research design. In some cases, the number of case studies produced in comparative studies are large. Sometimes this may be encouraged by a desire to get some sort of representative sample of cases across Europe, or to include cases across the north-south and east-west divisions of Europe. Another reason may be because a large sample (a 'large N' approach influenced by ideas from statistical analysis) is seen as providing what some describe as a more 'robust' base for generalisations about planning in Europe. Salet et al. (2002), for example, had 19 case study metropolitan regions in their study (admittedly 19 is not a large sample in statistical terms) of the role of strategic spatial perspectives in coordinating public and private action within the metropolitan region. On top of this there are detailed descriptions for each case of the particularity of the places concerned. The cases were studied simultaneously by different researchers so that there was no opportunity to develop the analysis through using a grounded theory approach (see Chapter 8) in which early results from the cases studied could inform later stages of data generation and analysis. Such limitations of research design obviously could be avoided in future and we can learn from more successful examples.

By dealing with a smaller sample of cases (eight) and setting out in advance a conceptual framework for data generation, the study by Couch et al. (2003) had an easier time inductively identifying the factors involved in shaping the differences between approaches to urban regeneration and the success of such efforts. In thinking about causation, they quoted Masser's approach: 'It is necessary to proceed step by step to develop in the first place an adequate explanation of each case in its own right, before going on to evaluate the findings for several cases and then proceeding to develop a common explanation relating to the phenomenon' (Masser, 1986: 15; quoted in Couch et al., 2003) In doing so, they looked for an association or link between a factor and the nature of urban regeneration. The logic of comparison here is described as the method of difference (de Vaus, 2008). The aim is to identify the one factor which is always present, when urban regeneration is 'successful', and absent when it is 'not successful'. This involves judgement about the success or otherwise of the cases examined and relies on there being just one factor that varies in the same way as 'successful' regeneration. As discussed above, the explanations they developed and the theoretical generalisation from these cases were restricted to cities of particular types. Farthing (2008) looked at two countries with city region governance models and asked why the models took different forms in the two countries (France and England).

There are some examples of research which is interested in understanding planning cultures in different places. I am not aware of any cross-national research by one researcher comparing the 'world views' or 'assumptive worlds' of planners in two different countries published in English. There are some accounts of planning cultures in different countries in the published collection by Sanyal (2005) and in Knieling and Othengrafen (2009). Some of these articles are not explicitly comparative, though often the point of the description is to highlight differences from what might be done elsewhere. Tynkkynen (2009) reports on the culture of planning in St Petersburg, Russia based on 14 thematic interviews, describing the way that planners explain the reasons for what they do. This study, however, concludes with a comparison of the thinking of planners with what is considered appropriate from the point of view of 'Western' planning theory. Although described as 'discourse analysis', the analysis conducted would seem to be more concerned with reading the minds of planners, akin to the thematic analysis of interview data described in Chapter 8. Healey (2007) in her study of episodes of spatial strategy-making in cities in three European countries is also interested in discourse, but in a way that is less concerned with what is in the minds of individual planners. Here, discourses are seen as a meaningful part (or ontological component) of the social world, existing outside the ideas and thinking of individuals but nevertheless having an underlying role in structuring practices or behaviour of individuals. (On discursive policy inquiry, see Fischer, 2003: 41–7).

Ethics

There are no distinctive ethical issues associated with comparative research, and the same ethical guidelines will apply to these studies as others. However, there may be particular issues with the guidelines that states that 'participants must be fully informed about the purpose, methods and intended use of the research'. If there are language problems on either side, it may be difficult to ensure that this can be satisfactorily be achieved.

> **Summary/Key lessons**
>
> 1. Cross-national comparative research in planning is research which attempts to describe and compare the way planning is conducted in different countries. I have suggested that any aspect of planning can be the subject of this comparison, but following Sharpe's rule of thumb 'maximum discreteness of focus', the scope of the key concepts in the research question dealing with the particular type of development to be studied needs to be defined perhaps even more narrowly than I have already suggested for a non-comparative study.
>
> 2. Differences and similarities between the way that planning is conducted naturally lead to 'why' questions. Why are policies and practices different? Part of the answer is that 'institutional contexts' are different, though you should also be

aware of other wider factors which might be common to a number of countries (the influence of the European Union, for example). Whilst in your own country you might understand the 'institutional context', the way that people think about planning and its practice, when the study involves a foreign country then these things may not be obvious, and may require quite a lot of work to get 'inside the culture', and it will require some competence in the language of the country concerned to talk to people or to read documents. You need to be realistic about your skills and the time you have available.

3. The issues to do with research design are no different in principle from researching planning in any one country, questions which have been addressed in the chapters of this book. But in practice, there may be constraints on what can be achieved. Sampling of, and access to cases of planning to study is likely to be more difficult in a foreign country than at home, so that convenience sampling may be more typical. And in general you will need to accept, and acknowledge in your dissertation, a more pragmatic approach to research design.

4. Given these practical challenges of comparative research, it would seem that in contemplating a cross-national comparative study you should think carefully about the support that might be available to you, and whether this will be sufficient to support your work. Is your tutor or supervisor someone who is familiar with the countries to be studied? Are there specific courses or modules aimed at increasing your understanding of comparative planning? Are there courses in foreign languages open to you? Is there a network of contacts in a foreign country established either by some link between your department and one overseas (Herson and Couch, 1986) or by researchers in your own department actively researching abroad (Wilson, 1986)? Such links can be called upon to facilitate access to cases of planning activity abroad and give access to appropriate data sources (people and places).

Further reading

An early but still very useful text on cross-national comparative planning is: Masser, I. and Williams, R. (1986) (eds) *Learning from Other Countries*. Norwich: Geo Books.

A short chapter covering both the nature and purpose of cross national designs and an evaluation of case study-based and survey-based forms of research is to be found in de Vaus, D. (2008) 'Comparative and Cross-National designs' in P. Alasuutari, L. Bickman and J. Brannen (eds) *Social Research Methods*. London: Sage. pp. 249–64.

There is also a useful chapter setting out the potential and problems of cross-national research in May, T. (2000) *Social Research*, 3rd Edition. Buckingham: Open University Press.

References

Bendix, R. (1963) 'Concepts and Generalisations in Comparative Sociological Studies', *American Sociological Review* 28: 532–9.

Booth, P. (1996) *Controlling Development*. London: UCL Press.

Booth, P., Breuillard, M., Fraser, C. and Paris, D. (eds) (2007) *Spatial Planning Systems of Britain and France*. London: Routledge.

Breuillard, M. and Fraser, C. (2007) 'The Purpose and Process of Comparing French and British Planning', in P. Booth, M. Breuillard, C. Fraser and D. Paris (eds) *Spatial Planning Systems of Britain and France*. London: Routledge. pp. 1–13.

Carrière, J.-P., Farthing, S.M. and Fournier, M. (2007) 'Policy for Small Towns in Rural Areas' in P. Booth, M. Breuillard, C, Fraser and D. Paris (eds) *Spatial Planning Systems of Britain and France*. London: Routledge. pp. 119–34.

Couch, C., Fraser, C. and Percy, S. (eds) (2003) *Urban Regeneration in Europe*. Oxford: Blackwell.

Couch, C., Sykes, O. and Borstinghaus, W. (2011) 'Thirty Years of Urban Regeneration in Britain, Germany and France: The Importance of Context Dependence', *Progress in Planning* 75: 1–52.

Cropper, S. (1986) 'Do You Know What I Mean? Problems in the Methodology of Cross-cultural Comparison' in I. Masser and R. Williams (eds) *Learning From Other Countries*. Norwich: Geo Books. pp. 23–39.

Cullingworth, J.B. (1993) *The Political Culture of Planning: American Land Use Planning in Comparative Perspective*. New York: Routledge.

Davies, H.W.E. (1980) *International Transfer and the Inner City: Report of the Trinational Inner Cities Project* (Occasional Papers 5). Reading: School of Planning Studies, University of Reading.

de Vaus, D. (2008) 'Comparative and Cross-National Designs' in P. Alasuutari, L. Bickman and J. Brannen (eds) *Social Research Methods*. London: Sage. pp. 249–64.

Eversley, D.E.C. (1978) *Report on Anglo-German Conference on Public Participation*. London: Royal Town Planning Institute.

Faludi, A. and Hamnett, S. (1975) *The Study of Comparative Planning*, (CES Conference Papers no 13). London: CES.

Farthing, S.M. (2001) 'Local Land Use Plans and the Implementation of New Urban Development', *European Planning Studies* 9 (2): 223–42.

Farthing, S.M. (2008) 'National Planning Systems and the Emergence of City Region Planning in England and France' in R. Atkinson and C. Rossignolo (eds) *The Re-creation of the European City*. Amsterdam: Techne Press. pp. 177–98.

Fischer, F. (2003) *Reframing Public Policy: Discursive Politics and Deliberative Practices*. Oxford: Oxford University Press.
Flyvbjerg, B. (2001) *Making Social Science Matter*. Cambridge: Cambridge University Press.
Healey, P. (2007) *Urban Complexity and Spatial Strategies*. London: Routledge.
Herrschel, T. and Newman, P. (2002) *Governance of Europe's City Regions*. London: Routledge.
Herson, J. and Couch, C. (1986) 'The Ruhr-Mersey Project and a Research-Led Teaching Programme' in I. Masser and R. Williams (eds) *Learning from Other Countries*. Norwich: Geo Books. pp. 195–9.
Huxley, M. and Yiftachel, O. (2000) 'New Paradigm or Old Myopia? Unsettling the Communicative Turn in Planning Theory', *Journal of Planning Education and Research* 19 (4): 333–42.
Knieling, J. and Othengrafen, F. (eds) (2009) *Planning Cultures in Europe*. Farnham: Ashgate.
Masser, I. (1984) 'Comparative Planning Studies: a Review', *Town Planning Review* 55: 137–60.
Masser, I. (1986) 'Some Methodological Considerations' in I. Masser and R. Williams (eds) *Learning From Other Countries*. Norwich: Geo Books. pp. 15–26.
Masser, I. and Williams, R. (1986) (eds) *Learning From Other Countries*. Norwich: Geo Books.
Salet, W., Thornley, A. and Kreukels, A. (eds) (2002) *Metropolitan Governance and Spatial Planning: Comparative Case Studies of European City-Regions*. London: Routledge.
Salet, W. and Gualini, E. (eds) (2007) *Framing Strategic Urban Projects: Learning From Current Experiences in European Urban Regions*. London: Routledge.
Sandercock, L. (1998) *Towards Cosmopolis: Planning for Multicultural Cities*. Chichester: John Wiley.
Sanyal, B. (2005) *Comparative Planning Culture*. London: Routledge.
Sharpe, L.J. (1975) 'Comparative Planning Policy – Some Cautionary Comments' in M.J. Breakell (ed.) *Problems of Comparative Planning, Working paper 21*. Oxford: Oxford Polytechnic, Department of Town Planning.
Tynkkynen, V.-P. (2009) 'Planning Rationalities Among Practitioners in St Petersburg, Russia – Soviet Traditions and Western Influences' in J. Knieling and F. Othengrafen, (eds) *Planning Cultures in Europe*. Farnham: Ashgate. pp. 151–68.
Watson, V. (2002) 'Conflicting Rationalities: Implications for Planning Theory and Ethics', *Planning Theory and Practice* 4 (4): 395–407.

Williams, R. (1986) 'Translating Theory into Practice' in I. Masser and R. Williams (eds) *Learning From Other Countries*. Norwich: Geo Books. pp. 23–39.

Wilson, I.B. (1983) 'The Preparation of Local Plans in France', *Town Planning Review* 54 (2): 155–73.

Wilson, I.B. (1986) 'An Integrated Package: Researching and Teaching French Planning' in I. Masser and R. Williams (eds) *Learning From Other Countries*. Norwich: Geo Books. pp. 187–93.

11

CONCLUSION

Introduction

I have written this book in the belief that an important way in which students can improve the quality of their dissertations, and in which tutors can help them to do this, is by spending more time than is often devoted to it, on thinking *in advance* about research design. That is, contemplating the key decisions which have to be made in the conduct of research. Effort spent in thinking through these issues will make the conduct of the research much more straightforward, and will help with writing up the dissertation. It will help to avoid the situation, for example, in which you might find yourself somewhere near the deadline for submission of the dissertation with a lot of data but no clear idea of what sorts of claims you can reasonably make with the data you have.

In this short concluding chapter, I aim to highlight some of the key themes covered in detail in earlier chapters.

Hidden assumptions in research

Thinking about research design also means thinking about what is meant by 'research'. All students will have some idea about research, and equally many may have become aware of a range of approaches to the conduct of research that are found in the planning literature. I believe that it is helpful to have some understanding of the often hidden, or unstated, assumptions that lie behind the decisions that are made in designing research. These assumptions cover what the social world is like, what it is composed of, what we can know about it, and how to go about investigating it. We can't do research to answer these questions. The answers will form the starting point for thinking about any research.

What research question should I pose?

Urban planning students often write dissertations on topics which they care about, and where they hope they can find solutions to current planning problems. Being concerned about an issue is a good starting point, but in order to make progress, all research needs to be guided by a research question, one that is in principle answerable by the generation of appropriate data. You need to think about how you can translate your interest in a policy issue into a descriptive or an explanatory research question (or both). This will help in clarifying exactly what it is you want to discover.

What justification is there for the research question to be studied?

Apart from any practical justifications for investigating a question, students are expected to make some academic case for their research, perhaps in a research proposal, but certainly in their dissertation. A literature review should develop an argument about previous research that aims to show that no one has answered this research question satisfactorily, and further research is therefore justified.

What is the logic of the approach I will use to answer my research question?

It is important to distinguish between the types of answer different questions require. Descriptive research questions aim to provide descriptions, perhaps of the urban world, perhaps of potentially problematic aspects of that world, or perhaps of the operation of planning systems. Here, your concern may be with the 'representativeness' of the cases you investigate, that is, the degree to which your description can be generalised from the sample studied to a wider population of cases. With explanatory research questions, the claim you will make is why something happened or what the consequences have been of something having happened. For example, what have been the consequences of introducing a planning policy? Has it been successful in achieving its aims? Whether accounting for an event or making predictions about the consequences of an event, having some explicit, prior hypothesis can be useful in guiding research. In terms of the accounts which might be given, I have made a simple distinction which I think will be helpful between 'explanation', which is concerned with making causal claims about events, and 'understanding', which focuses accounts on what was in people's minds and the reasons they had for acting in the way they did.

What methods will I use to generate the data?

It is quite common in the planning literature to see the choice facing a researcher as one between the adoption of either quantitative or qualitative methods. On the whole in this book, I have avoided this dichotomy, which I believe is unhelpful in discussing the choice of methods. The choice of method to generate data needs to allow you to answer your research question, but, in doing so, you should also take account of the potential data sources through which your data will be generated, the practical constraints on what you can do in the limited time available, and methodological arguments about the way that research should be conducted. There are only a limited number of methods of research but how you use them, and how you interpret what the results of these methods tell you, can vary.

How will I analyse the data?

Analysis frequently is a neglected part of the whole research design process. The purpose of analysis is to turn the data you have generated into 'evidence' that you can use to support and substantiate your claims, whether these are descriptive or explanatory claims. The nature of the data determines whether it can be analysed by qualitative or quantitative means. Important though analysis is, it will never on its own make up for any inadequacies in the data that has been produced.

Have I thought about the ethics of what I am proposing? Will the project get ethical approval?

It is very likely these days that you will have to get ethical approval for the research you propose to conduct, and for this reason, thinking about research design is a valuable preparation for this exercise. Attention to research design means that a consideration of research ethics is not something 'tacked onto' the end of the process but is part of the process of design. The most common concern of the codes of ethical conduct is the risk of harm to participants in the research. But the debate about research ethics in urban planning is wider than this and covers the audience for the research as well as the associated values which shape the research process. Is the audience: the world of planning practice; the academic community; or the local community?

Conclusion

I hope that this book is useful in producing a 'well-designed' piece of research. I want to end by stressing that research design, as I have described it here, is a cyclical process because earlier decisions may need to be revisited as work proceeds. Once you have developed an answerable research question, for example, it might be useful to write it down and put it somewhere where you can view it whilst working on research design. Your research question needs to be reconsidered from time to time during the design stage in the light of further reading and in the light of practical considerations, such as the time and money you have at your disposal, which will limit the scope of what you can investigate.

INDEX

Aalborg, 108, 113, 186
academic papers, 61–2
access to sources of information, 135, 207
    see also 'gatekeepers'
accountability, 182
action research, 181
Allmendinger, P., 17
Alvesson, M., 139
American Planning Association (APA), 152, 155
analysis of research data, 8, 149–74, 204–6, 213
    descriptive, 154–6, 164
    interaction with data generation, 150
    multi-level, 158
    for qualitative data, 151, 163–73
    for quantitative data, 151–63, 174
    thematic, 166–7
area effects, 26, 62–3, 67–8, 100–3, 109, 136; see also neighbourhood effects
association between variables, 101–2, 107, 161–2
assumptions made by researchers, 3–6, 14, 17, 22–4, 33, 126
    hidden, 23–4, 211–12
assumptions made by planners, 105, 194
'assumptive worlds' (Young and Mills), 105
Atkinson, Paul 88, 113, 155
Atkinson, Rob 139–40, 170–2
Atkinson, Rowland, 25–6, 32, 53, 62–3, 67, 100–3, 109, 128, 130, 141, 151, 156–61, 179–80
Attili, G., 185–8
attitudinal questions, 130

Balducci, A., 181–2
Barcelona, 42
Becher, T., 38–9

Bell, J., 68
Bendix, R., 193
Berke, P.R., 137–8
biases in the research process, 127, 157, 161, 185
Biodiversity Framework, UK, 181
Blaikie, N., 2, 23–5, 45, 79, 85, 116
Blaxter, L., 142
Blowers, A., 132
Booth, P., 195–8
Bradford Hill, A., 101
Breuillard, M., 194
Brindley, T., 91
Brotherton, I., 142–4
Bryman, A., 170
budgeting for research, 126
Bunnell, G., 7
Burgess, J., 29–32, 48–9, 63–8, 76, 80, 87–91, 105, 130–1, 167

CACI Acorn Types, 89
Campbell, D., 103
Campbell, H., 78
Campbell, T., 102
Cardiff, 141
Carmin, J., 16, 39
Carrière, J.-P., 203
case studies, 116, 201, 204
cases for study, selection of, 198–9, 205
causal analysis of social life, 86, 99–100, 117, 156–66
causal relationships, 98–107, 110–11, 117
    criteria for assessing the existence of, 101–2
    identification of, 99–100
    in the social world, 24–5, 33
Census of Population, 140–1
Chadwick, G., 14
Chalmers, A., 15, 22

chance in statistical analysis, role of, 160–1
chief planning officers, 7
Clifford, B., 173
cluster sampling, 86–7
codes of conduct, 187–8, 214
communicative theory of planning, 32
community involvement, 70–1, 171–2
comparative research on planning, 9, 113, 192–7, 201–3, 206–7
computers
  use for data analysis, 151
  use in planning, 133–4
confidence levels, 86
confounding factors, 103, 158
Conroy, M.M., 137–8
'constant conjunction' model of causation, 98
control variables, 158–9
convenience sampling, 90–1, 199–201, 207
conversation analysis, 170
Cook, T.D., 103
core concepts in research, 77–8, 92
costs of undertaking research, 131
Couch, C., 195, 197, 200–1, 205
covert research, 132–3, 188
'critical case' analysis, 108
critical discourse analysis, 173
critical research in planning, 184–6, 189
Cropper, S., 196
cross-national studies of planning, 9, 192–200, 206–7
cross-sectoral research, 162
cross tabulation of variables, 157
cultures of planning, 195–6, 201, 205

data generation, 8, 79–82, 123–6, 133, 138, 143–4, 151, 163, 168, 174, 201–4, 213
  choice between methods of, 125, 144
  interaction with analysis stage of research, 150
  time available for, 125–6
data sources, 79–82, 92, 123–5, 134–7, 142
  gaining access to, 107, 135
  people in planning offices used as, 134
  potential, 125
database searches, 46
Davies, H.W.E., 197
deductive approach to research, 7, 97, 116–17
definition of phenomena being researched, 78

Denzin, N.K., 185–6
Department of the Environment, Transport and the Regions (DETR), 171–2
dependent variables, 102, 157
descriptive analysis, 154–6, 164, 212
de Vaus, D., 5, 78, 194
development plans, 137, 181–2
development pressure, 143
deviant cases, 112–13
Devon, 69–70
difference, method of, 205
'disciplinary' model of research, 183–4, 189
discourse, 56, 105–6, 137, 139, 206
  in planning, 19
discourse analysis, 170–3
  'critical', 173
  example of, 171–2
discussion groups, 29–32
documents, 136–40
  created through the research process, 139
  definition of, 136
  reasons for researchers' use of, 137–40
  textual, 136–7, 202–3
dominant discourse, 170
Dorset, 54–5, 83

'ecological validity' of research, 28, 126
Economic and Social Research (ESRC) Council Framework for Research Ethics, 187
Ela Palmer Heritage, 46, 53–4
electoral register, 85–6
Ellen, I., 100
'embedded' policy ideas, 56
embourgoisement thesis, 108
empirical generalisation, 83, 92, 150, 152, 155, 168, 199–200
empirical research, 15, 52–3, 104
'engineering' model of research, 180, 185–6, 189
'enlightenment' model of the relationship between research and power, 183
entrepreneurialism, 199
epistemic communities, 21
epistemological realism, 33
epistemology, 14–15, 23–4, 76
'escape from the city', 39–40
ethical approval for research, 9, 179–80, 187–8, 213

ethics
　of planning, 188
　of research, 8–9, 178–89, 206, 213
ethnographic methods of research, 130–5, 196
　qualitative data from, 168–9
　retrospective application of, 139
　students' use of, 135
　usefulness of, 133–5
European Union, 165, 195, 199–200, 206–7
EUROSTAT, 203
evaluation research on planning policies and practice, 45, 181, 184, 194
Eversley, D.E.C., 197
evidence-based policy, 3, 141
experimental methods of research, 102, 106, 108, 126
　in a social context, 99, 103
expert knowledge, distrust of, 21–2
exploratory research, 195
'external valiity' of research, 103, 110
extreme cases, 112

Fainstein, S.S., 19
falsification of theories, 22, 104, 108, 200
Faludi, A., 194
Farthing, S.M. (*author*), 14, 70, 102, 109, 133, 195, 197, 205
Fay, B., 107
field notes, 168
Fielding, N., 127, 133
filter questions, 129
Fischer, F., 3, 19–21, 32–3
Fischler, T., 113
flexibility in research, 5
Flyvbjerg, B., 99, 104, 108, 112–13, 116, 184–6
focus groups, 131
Forester, J., 106, 112–13, 126, 132, 152–3, 168, 184–6
Foucault, Michel, 137, 139, 170
'framing' of research projects, 8, 18, 56, 179–80, 183, 188
France, 137, 195–8, 202–5
Fraser, C., 194
frequency distributions, 154
further research, establishing the need for, 66, 68, 71, 212

'gatekeepers', 132, 135
generalisation of findings, 7, 68, 83–6, 99, 103, 106, 150, 212–13; *see also* empirical generalisation; theoretical generalisation
gentrification, 52–3, 173
Germany, 195, 200
Glaser, B.G., 113, 169
Goldstein, H.A., 16, 39
Goldthorpe, J., 108, 116
Gomm, R., 151, 188
good practice in planning, spreading of, 194–5, 198
Gorard, S., 65, 100, 103
government documents, 136–7
Greed, C., 131, 135, 138–9
Green Belt, 56–7
Greener, I., 132, 187–8
Greenwich, 29–31, 87–90
Greenwich Village (New York), 50
grounded theory, 113, 115, 150, 169
group-analytic theory and therapy, 31, 68
group interviews, 131
Guba, E.G., 84
Guy, C., 141

Haas, P.M., 21
Habermas, Jürgen, 184
Hakim, C., 2, 44
Hammersley, M., 28, 32, 79, 85, 88, 98, 113, 132, 166, 180, 183
Hamnett, S., 194
Harding, S., 25
Haringey, 28
harm to research participants and researchers, 188
harmonisation of planning systems, 195
Harris, N., 170
Haughton, G., 140, 163–6
Healey, P., 3, 21, 23–5, 56, 105, 138, 181–6, 199–203, 206
Henricksen, I.M., 113–15, 133, 135, 169
Herrschel, T., 195
Hobbs, P., 138
Hoch, C., 81, 83–5, 126, 139, 152–5, 185
Homan, R., 187
Hooper, A., 170
Hopton, J., 99
housing associations, 21
Housing Corporation, 21

Howard, Ebenezer, 56
Hunt, S., 99
hypotheses, 50, 52, 57, 65, 96–7, 100, 104, 108, 112–13, 117–18, 128, 157, 213

'idiographic' accounts of behaviour, 84
independent variables, 102, 157–8
induction, principle of, 101–4
inductive approach to research, 22, 97, 106, 110, 113, 116, 118, 169
Innes, J., 105–6, 113, 185
institutionalist approach to research, 23
instrumental rationality, 184
'interaction pretexts', 169
'internal valiity' of research, 102–3, 109–10
interpretivism, 19–20, 24, 76
interviews for research purposes, 127–33, 140
  breadth versus *depth* in, 130
  formal and *informal*, 133
  with individuals or with groups, 131
  with key informants, 201–2
  qualitative data from, 163–4
  structured, *semi-structured* and *unstructured*, 128–30
  types of, 128
  see also transcripts
Ireland, 164–5

Jacobs, Jane, 50
'judgement' sampling, 91, 108
justifications for research questions, 61–71
  academic and *practical*, 61–2, 71, 198, 212

key decisions about research, 4
key informants, 201–2
Kintrea, K., 25–6, 32, 53, 62–3, 67, 100–3, 109, 128, 130, 136, 141, 151, 156–61, 179–80
Kitchen, T., 132, 135
Knieling, J., 205
knowledge claims, 3, 33, 38–43, 51, 173
  typology of, 41–2
Krizek, K., 3
Kuhn, Thomas, 22
Kunzmann, K., 183

labelling of text, 167
land ownership, research into, 18–20, 179
language, uses of, 170

language abilities of researchers, 198, 203, 206–7
Laurie, I.C., 63
'least likely' cases, 108
Lees, L., 139, 173
life-chances, influences on, 26–7, 62–3
Lincoln, Y.S., 84
literature reviews, 6–7, 46–7, 62–72, 76, 78, 84, 134, 136, 198, 212
  'critical', 64–6
  quality of, 62
  structure of, 68–72
literature searches, 65–6
local planning authorities (LPAs)
  appeals against decisions of, 111, 141–2
  negotiating styles of, 110–11, 141, 143
local provision of services, 109
longitudinal research, 162
Luton, 108, 116

Macdonald, K., 136
Machiavelli, Niccolò, 99
magazines used as data sources, 136
mail questionnaires, 152
making sense of the social world, 166–8
Mason, J., 8, 79, 81, 105, 139
Masser, I., 193–4, 201, 205
maximum variation case sampling method, 109
May, T., 17, 21, 139, 142–3, 183
methodology of research, 4, 31–2
Milan, 181–2
Mills, L., 105
Mitchell, J.C., 116
modernism, 14
moral decisions, 188
Moseley, M.J., 70–1
'most likely' cases, 108
multi-level analysis, 158
'myth', Innes's concept of, 105

Nagel, E., 17
'naïve realism' (Hammersley), 32
national parks, 142
'natural experiments', 99, 103
'naturalism' in the research process, 28, 68, 106, 126
nature, enjoyment of, 167–8
neighbourhood effects, 161–3; *see also* area effects

Index

neighbourhood statistics, 141
neighbourhood types, 169
Netherlands, the, 56
New York, 50
Newman, P., 195
newspapers used as data sources, 136
Nietzsche, Friedrich, 99
non-probabilistic sampling, 84, 87–92
  types of, 87
non-response, 86, 155, 157, 161
normative nature of theory, 17

'objective' knowledge, 15, 17
observation as a method of data
  generation, 133
Office for National Statistics (ONS), 141
official statistics, 136, 140–4, 203–4
ontological assumptions, 17, 23, 25, 32
ontological realism, 33
ontology, 14, 23
open-ended research, 76–7, 96–7, 106, 124,
  129, 163, 167
open spaces, research into, 29–31, 44–50,
  63–7, 77–83, 86–90, 98, 105, 130–1,
  167–8
Othengrafen, F., 205
'output areas', 140
over-sampling, 86

'paradigm wars', 14
paradigms, 22
participant observation, 28, 133
participatory research, 185
philosophy of science, 15
photographs, use of, 136
phronetic planning research, 186
plagiarism, 47
planning applications and planning
  permission, 99, 110, 134, 137, 142–4
planning gain, 7
Planning Inspectorate, 110
planning policy, 38–43, 56–7, 96, 112,
  181–4
  arguments used in debates on, 39–43
planning theory, 14–15, 56, 194
policy analysis, 184
policy documents, 137–40, 170
policy implications of research findings, 19
policy issues, 6, 38–9, 45–6, 51, 56–7
political issues, 6, 8, 19, 152–6

Popper, Karl, 50, 104
populations as distinct from samples, 82,
  198–9, 212–13
positivism, 13–16, 20–4, 32, 143, 179
post-positivism, 5–6, 16, 179
postcode address file, 86
poverty, research on, 100, 104, 159
practical benefits derived from research, 6
practice-oriented model of research, 180–3,
  188–9
predictions and predictive claims, 41–2,
  56–7
Prescott, John, 43
pressures on researchers, 21–2, 183
probabilistic sampling, 84–7, 90
provisional decisions about research, 2, 4–5
provisional nature of research findings, 104
proxy variables, 159, 161
publication of research papers, 61–2
'purposive' sampling, 61, 91, 108–9

qualitative data
  from ethnographic studies, 168–9
  from interviews, 163–4
qualitative interviews, 130
qualitative and *quantitative* approaches to
  research, 4, 8, 84–7, 97, 112, 124, 130,
  136, 144, 151–2, 213
qualitative components in otherwise
  quantitative analysis, 153
'quasi-causal' accounts, 107
questionnaires, 80, 127, 152
quota sampling, 88–91
quotations, use of, 154

random sampling, 84–6, 90–2
random sampling error, 160
Rapley, T., 136, 139, 170
'rational planning' process, 184
reactivity of research subjects, 28, 126
Reade, E., 45
realism, different types of, 33
'realist' model of causation, 102
reality, nature of, 32
regeneration projects, 53–5, 197, 200
Rein, M., 18
reliability of research, 81–2, 127
renewable energy, 51–4
representativeness, 76, 82–4, 87, 92, 157,
  199, 212–13

research-based knowledge, 15–16
research design, 1–9, 23, 37–8, 56, 211
   'control' in, 25–8, 68, 128
   cycle of, 4–5, 214
   types of, 3–5
research proposals, 2, 8, 187
research questions, 3, 6–7, 37–57, 92, 124, 138, 150, 167, 174, 212–14
   created from initial ideas, 51–6
   descriptive or *explanatory*, 7, 38–40, 43–5, 49, 51, 56, 116–18, 152–3, 156, 195–7, 212–13
   generation of, 46–7
   hypotheses and theories underlying, 50
   importance of, 56
   justifications for, 61–71
   order of asking, 46, 57
   in published research, 47–50
   and research purposes, 195–7
   scoping, 76–9
'researchable' questions, 6, 37, 51–2, 55, 57, 75, 212, 214
response rates, 152
retroductive model of causation, 102
retrospective studies, 80, 139
Ritchie, J., 164–7
Robson, C., 130
rural issues, 203
Rydin, Y., 39, 98

St Petersburg, 205–6
Salet, W., 204
sample frames, 85–6
sample size, 86
sampling, 76, 79–92, 107, 109
methods of, 84–92
sampling error, 160
Sandercock, L., 14, 124
Sanyal, B., 205
'satisficing', 184
scepticism about research findings, 22
Schon, D., 15–16, 18
scientific disciplines, 39, 179; *see also* philosophy of science
'scientific' model of research, 5–6, 117
scoping, 76–9, 97
secondary sources and secondary analysis, 79, 140–2
selective nature of all research, 17–18, 33

'sensitising concepts' (Hammersley and Atkinson), 166
Sharpe, L.J., 196–7, 200, 206
Shaw, T., 138
snowball sampling, 88–9
social construction
   of identities, 23
   of knowledge, 19–20, 32
   of the world, 32
social housing, 21, 27, 40
social research
   aim of, 68
   characteristics of, 24, 28, 104–6, 180, 182
'so what?' test, 184–5
sponsored research, 21–2
SPSS package, 151
Stanley, J., 102
statistical significance, 86, 160–1
strategic environmental assessment (SEA), 181
stratified sampling, 86, 90
Strauss, A.L., 113, 169
Stretton, H., 18
subjective element in research, 17
supervisors of research, 187
survey data, analysis of, 150–63
sustainable development, 78, 181
systematic sampling, 85–6

Tait, M., 135
Taylor, N., 78, 182
technical disciplines, 39
textual documents, 136–7, 202–3
thematic analysis, 166–7
theoretical generalisation, 96, 100–4, 107, 150
theoretical sampling, 113–15
theory, nature of, 98–9, 112
'thick description', 112
time available for research, 125–6, 131, 135, 214
Tipton, C., 136
Tjora, A., 113–15, 133, 135, 169
Town and City Indicators Database, 143
transcripts of interviews, 166
triangulation, 166
Trondheim, 115, 133, 169
Trowler, P.R., 38–9

Turner, M., 100
Tynkkynen, V.-P., 205–6

understanding of the social world, 105–7, 117, 170
Underwood, J., 28–9, 31–2, 106, 126, 133, 135
'unobtrusive' methods of research, 28
Urban Task Force report (1999), 39–43, 52, 139, 172–3

validity of research, 81–2, 126–7, 143; see also 'ecological validity'; 'external validity'; 'internal validity'
value claims, 41–2
'value clarification' and 'value relevance', 64, 183–4
'value-freedom' and 'value-neutrality', 8, 15, 17–18, 180, 183–6
value of research findings, 32
values
  of research subjects, 130
  of researchers, 17–22, 39, 63, 179, 184

variables, 154
  dependent and independent, 102, 157–8
verbatim quotations, 154
Vigar, G., 137
'voice', giving of, 21
volunteer sampling, 91

Watson, V., 105
Weber, Max, 183–4
Welsh Assembly, 170
White, P., 50
Williams, R., 193, 197
Wilson, H., 70
Wilson, I.B., 198, 202
withdrawal from research by participants, 188
Wong, C., 141, 143
Wood, R., 110–12, 141–2
worldviews, 20, 105, 166, 205

Yin, R., 2
Young, K., 105